UNDER THE GUNS OF THE
KAISER'S ACES

BÖHME, MÜLLER, VON TUTSCHEK, WOLFF
THE COMPLETE RECORD OF THEIR VICTORIES AND VICTIMS

UNDER THE GUNS OF THE
KAISER'S ACES

BÖHME, MÜLLER, VON TUTSCHEK, WOLFF
THE COMPLETE RECORD OF THEIR VICTORIES AND VICTIMS

NORMAN FRANKS
AND HAL GIBLIN

GRUB STREET · LONDON

Published by Grub Street
The Basement,
10 Chivalry Road,
London SW11 1HT

British Library Cataloguing-in-Publication Data
Franks, Norman L. R. (Norman Leslie Robert), 1940-
Under the Guns of the Kaiser's Aces: Böhme, Müller, von Tutschek and Wolff:
The Complete Record of their Victories and Victims
1. Böhme, Erwin 2. Müller, Max von 3. Tutschek, Adolf Ritter von
4. Wolff, Kurt 5. World War, 1914-1918 – Aerial Operations, German
6. World War, 1914-1918 – Casualties – Statistics
I. Title II. Giblin, Hal
940.449430922
ISBN 1904010024

Printed and bound in Spain by Bookprint, S. L.

CONTENTS

ACKNOWLEDGEMENTS

Once again, the research distilled into these pages came to us from all around the world. The authors cannot overstate their gratitude to the following for their absolutely invaluable help and assistance:

Mark Abbott, Ormskirk;
All Staff, Commonwealth
    War Graves Commission,
    Maidenhead;
All Staff, Central and
    Reference Libraries,
    Liverpool;
Sian Anthony, Newport
    Reference Library;
Frank W Bailey, USA;
Paul Baillie, Cambs;
David Baldwin, Stafford;
Peter Barlow, Southport;
Mike Blackburn, St Helens;
Roger Bragger, Tamworth,
    Staffs;
Frank Cheesman, Margate;
Neil Clark, Southport;
John Creery, Vancouver, BC:
Joe Devereux, Cheltenham;
Peter Elliot, RAF Museum;
David Empson, Ipswich;
Andrew Farthing,
    Southport Reference
    Library;
David Hancock, Bexhill
    Library, East Sussex;
Mac Hawkins, Bridgwater,
    Somerset;
Vernon Henstridge,
    Wareham, Dorset and
    Boscombe, Hants;

Mrs R E Ivory, Carey Bay,
    NSW;
W/Cdr C G Jefford MBE,
    Oxon;
M W Jobling, Long Eaton
    Library;
Simon Jones, Liverpool
    Museums and
    Galleries;
Keeper and Staff, Public
    Records Office, Kew;
Brad King, IWM, London;
Stuart Leslie, N Yorks;
Dr Peter H Liddle,
    The Liddle Collection,
    University of Leeds;
Bob Lynes, Bristol;
Anthony J Martin,
    Southend-on-Sea
    Library;
Dr. -Ing Niedermeyer;
Mike O'Connor;
the late Neal O'Connor,
    E Sussex;
Elizabeth O'Kiely, West
    Vancouver, BC;
Mary and John J Parry,
    Ripon, Yorks;
Walter Pieters, Belgium;
Simon Pile, Huyton,
    Liverpool;
Keith Rennles, Surrey;

Alex Revell, Cornwall;
Mark Richmond, The
    University of Melbourne
    Archives;
Bob Rogers Jnr, Vietnam
    Veteran (USMC) and
    WW1 Historian, Stone
    Mountain, Georgia;
Neil Rose, Birkdale;
Harry Rudd, Hightown,
    Liverpool;
Graham Sacker,
    Cheltenham;
Mike Schoeman, Vlaeberg,
    South Africa;
Robert Smith, Cowling,
    Nr Keighley, Yorks;
Bill Tagg, Liverpool;
Jeff Taylor, Rubery,
    Birmingham;
Prof John Taylor,
    Kirkby Overblow
Brian J Turner,
    Leigh-on-Sea;
Greg VanWyngarden;
Mrs Winter, Crewe Library.

INTRODUCTION

As with the previous books in the *'Under the Guns...'* series, we have selected four more of the Kaiser's Pour le Mérite ('Blue Max') winners for an in-depth examination of their WWI combat careers. All four were unit leaders, one commanded a Jagdesgeschwader, the others commanded Jagdstaffels. All four were destined to die in combat actions with the Royal Flying Corps.

Once again we have tried to 'flesh out' with personal biographical detail, snapshot profiles of the Allied airmen these four formidable German aces engaged in deadly combat. Interestingly and gratifyingly, we have not received any significant challenges to our identification of victories and victims in the two earlier *'Under the Guns...'* books and live in hope that we can continue the run with this one. Certainly, if extensive and exhaustive effort in searching out records and the careful study of maps, timings and intelligence reports — contemporary and retrospective — counts for anything, then, hopefully, we may succeed!

Again we have attempted — so far as it is possible more than eighty years later — to find photographic likenesses of the protagonists in the many dramas played out in this book. Naturally, the authors will welcome any further information or photographic material which would help us to expand the chronicling of those fascinating times.

Norman Franks, Bexhill, East Sussex.
Hal Giblin, Hightown, Liverpool.

CHAPTER 1

OBERLEUTNANT ERWIN BÖHME

Erwin Böhme was older than most Jasta pilots. Born in Holzminden, on the Weser river in north-west Germany on 29 July 1879, he was 35 years old when WW1 began. His was a large family – Erwin being the second of five boys and a sister. A qualified engineer, he had studied at the technical college in Dortmund and had worked in both Germany and in Switzerland before taking up a six-year contract in German East Africa in 1908. He had, therefore, sampled life to a fuller extent than most of his contemporaries by

the time war came. Even before hostilities began he had returned to his native Germany. Upon mobilisation, he went back to his former Jäger Regiment having served with the Garde-Jäger Regiment during his national service in 1899. Soon afterwards and despite his age, he volunteered for flying duties.

Training at Leipzig-Lindenthal, he received his licence in December 1914. No doubt because of his maturity and exceptional ability, Unteroffizier Böhme was retained

Erwin Böhme (right) during his two-seater days. He is pictured in front of his 'Dragon-marked' Albatros CIII (766/16) whilst serving with Kasta 10 of Kogohl 2 on the Russian front in the August of 1916. With him is his observer, Leutnant Lademacher, who shared his first victory against the French ace Edwards Pulpe on 2 August 1916.
(Dr.- Ing, Niedermeyer)

for over a year as a flight instructor before finally being able to persuade his superiors to send him to a front-line unit. He was posted to Kagohl 2 on the Saarbrücken Front in late November 1915, a unit then commanded by Hauptmann Wilhelm Boelcke, brother of the peerless Oswald who was making a name for himself as a single-seater Fokker pilot on the Western Front.

Assigned to Kampstaffel 10 of Kagohl 2, he flew Albatros C1 aeroplanes and was promoted to the rank of Offizier-stellevertreter. Operating from Mörchingen (30 miles south-east of Metz) his unit patrolled the front lines and made bombing raids to Bar-le-Duc and Ligny. In February 1916, Kagohl 2 were also involved in the opening stages of the Verdun offensive. As a matter of passing interest, his observer in Kasta 10 was even older than Böhme – a 47-year-old man by the name of Sanders. In the spring of 1916, Böhme's unit was visited by Oswald Boelcke flying a visibly combat-damaged Fokker.

In March Böhme had an encounter with two French Farmans and a Nieuport Scout – his first recorded combats. They would be the first of several occurring over the next few weeks. In May 1916, Böhme received his commission. He was, by this time, flying the LFG Roland C-types as well as the Albatros. In June 1916, his unit was transferred to the Eastern Front, operating from a base at Kovel, Russia, around 270 kilometres south-east of Warsaw. One of his fellow pilots was none other than Manfred von Richthofen – still then, of course, a noviciate. On the Russian Front Böhme flew Albatros two-seaters, and had one (C766/16) decorated with a dragon motif running along the fuselage – his observer at this time was Leutnant Lademacher. Böhme met Oswald Boelcke yet again, this time on the distinguished flyer's visit to front-line units in the early summer of 1916. Impressed with Böhme's obvious abilities, Boelcke invited him to join a new fighting unit he was about to form for service on the Western Front. Flattered, Böhme readily agreed.

Still, for the moment, his business on the Eastern Front continued apace. Böhme was soon again in action and achieved some modest further success. On 11 and 13 July, he and Lademacher fought inconclusive combats with Russian machines – identified as *grossflugzeug* – large aeroplanes. At this stage the German designation for a large, or giant, aeroplane – *riesenflugzeug* – was not commonly used or defined, so it can be assumed these two aeroplanes were Russian Sikorsky types.

VICTORY NO. 1
2 August 1916 Nieuport XII 10th Fighter Detachment am

In a letter dated 3 August, Böhme wrote: '... *yesterday I shot down a Nieuport single seater over Rozyszczt, the actual Head-quarters of General Brussilov, on which we were dropping bombs.*' The Nieuport was patrolling over the Styr river, its Latvian-born pilot must first have spotted five German aircraft flying over Rozyszczt, some distance below. Soon afterwards, two of the German aircraft broke formation and headed for their lines. The Nieuport closed the distance and as soon as he was directly above the remaining German trio, dived upon them. A lengthy battle ensued – some say for up to an hour – but at the end of it, the Nieuport and its gallant, if foolhardy pilot, finally went down. The pilot had been hit twice – one bullet causing serious internal injuries. The aileron control on his Nieuport had also been shot away. When ground troops reached the crashed machine, Sous-lieutenant Pulpe was still alive. He asked for a drink of water and then died.

SOUS-LIEUTENANT
EDWARDS PULPE,
ESCADRILLE MS23

Born in Riga, Latvia, on 22 June 1880, he was living in France when war came in August 1914. He already had his Civil Pilot's Brevet (Number 1571 gained on 19 December 1913) and decided to offer his talents to the French Aviation Service. After the appropriate training, he qualified for his Military Pilot's Brevet (Number 602) and was posted to Escadrille MS23 on 1 May 1915 with the rank of Sergent. Awarded the Medaille Militaire on 29 October 1915,

'Voluntarily enlisted Sergent of Escadrille MS23, a pilot of exceptional courage and audacity, who has already shown this at times in bombardments and aerial combats. On 23 September 1915, a comrade had failed to execute a difficult mission, and he spontaneously offered to replace him and under particularly perilous conditions succeeded in accomplishing the mission successfully'. By the time of his fourth victory in March 1916, Pulpe had been promoted to the rank of Adjudant. Sent to Russia with a French Aviation Mission, Pulpe achieved his fifth victory on that front before being mortally wounded in his clash with Erwin Böhme on 2 August 1916.

Selected for Jasta 2 at Bertincourt, Böhme returned to France on 8 September 1916 to join the first of the new dedicated hunter/fighter units dreamt up and created by Boelcke himself. Until now, single-seat fighters had been assigned in small numbers to the two-seater Abteilung for escort and scouting duties. Now a specialist fighter force was being unleashed with deadly effect upon the Allied intelligence gathering, photo-reconnaissance and artillery spotting machines.

Boelcke had been given free rein to select his own pilots and among the tyro fighter pilots making up Jasta 2 were Manfred von Richthofen, Max Müller, Hans Imelmann, Rudolf Reimann and Otto Höhne. Once in France, and with the arrival of a number of fighter biplanes, Jasta 2's new pilots began to score kills.

VICTORY NO. 2
17 September 1916   Sopwith 1½ Strutter (No.A1913)   70 Squadron   0745

Not much is known of this action except than Jasta 2 attacked a formation of Sopwith two-seaters, and Böhme brought down A1913. The pilot was killed and Wood, the observer, was hit whilst still in the air and

rendered unconscious. He remained *non compos mentis* for two weeks and was never subsequently able to recall anything of the action or of the consequent crash. Böhme was flying an Albatros DI.

SECOND LIEUTENANT
OSWALD NIXON,
ESSEX REGIMENT AND 70 SQUADRON, ROYAL FLYING CORPS

Born on 3 May 1896, Oswald was the youngest of the five sons of Colonel F W Nixon, Royal Engineers and Edith Eliza Rose Malote Nixon of The Castle, Cape Town, South Africa and Commonside, Reigate, Surrey. He was educated at Dulwich Preparatory School (1907-09), at All Saints School, Bloxham (1909-10) and at Felsted School (1911-13) from where he entered Hampshire County Agricultural School, Basingstoke (1913-14). He interrupted his agricultural studies to enlist as a private soldier (Number 1900) in the Essex Regiment. Selected for officer training, he was gazetted Second Lieutenant into the 10th Battalion of his regiment on 5 October 1914 and promoted to Lieutenant two months later. By this time, all five of the Nixon boys were serving – Captain E M Nixon, Jacob's Horse, Indian Army; Lieutenant Commander G A Nixon, Royal Navy; Sergeant R L Nixon, 88th Regiment of Canadian Infantry and Second Lieutenant J I Nixon, 10/Royal Sussex Regiment. All but Oswald survived. Because his son was originally reported as missing, Colonel Nixon wrote to his observer's father in Headingley, Leeds, to enquire what knowledge young Wood had of their final minutes in the air. Mr Wood Senior was obliged to advise the Colonel that because his son, Ronald, had been, *'shot unconscious in the air and did not come round for two weeks'*, he could not help in any way. Oswald was originally commemorated on the Arras Memorial to the Missing but his remains were subsequently discovered and re-interred in Serre Road Number 2 Cemetery, Puisieux, France. Age 20.

SECOND LIEUTENANT
RONALD WOOD,
7/WEST YORKSHIRE REGIMENT AND 70 SQUADRON, ROYAL FLYING CORPS

The son of Mr and Mrs George Wood of 14 Welburn Avenue, Headingley, Leeds. Gazetted Second Lieutenant 7th Battalion, West Yorkshire Regiment before transferring to the RFC in early 1916. Badly wounded and rendered unconscious for two weeks after Böhme's attack, he was never able to recall the circumstances of their encounter with the German. Spent months in the Osnabruck POW Camp – mainly hospitalised – before being exchanged into Holland on 9 April 1918. Finally repatriated to the UK on 2 July 1918.

UNCONFIRMED VICTORY
23 September 1916   Martinsyde G.100 (No.7475)   27 Squadron   0955

Six Martinsyde Elephants led by Captain O T Boyd, were flying an Offensive Patrol over Cambrai, having taken off at 0830 hours. They were attacked over the town by five Albatros Scouts led by Boelcke and two were shot down in very quick order – one by Hans Reimann, the other by Manfred von Richthofen. As the fight continued, the Martinsyde piloted by Lieutenant L F Forbes rammed the machine flown by Hans Reimann. The stricken Albatros spun down, crashing near Noreuil and killing its occupant. Forbes in the Elephant was more fortunate, managing to get his crippled machine back over the lines to crash-land near Bertangles. In the general confusion, Böhme's victory was not confirmed as it fell just inside the foremost Allied lines near to Le Transloy.

LIEUTENANT
ERIC JAMES ROBERTS,
27 SQUADRON, ROYAL FLYING CORPS

The son of Mr and Mrs William Roberts of 'The Maples', Killara, Sydney, New South Wales, Australia, he was born on 21 May 1895. Educated at Sydney Grammar School, at Hawkesbury Agricultural College and at Sydney University. A volunteer with the Australian Light Horse from 1913 to 1916. A qualified automotive engineer, he married Miss Margaret Smith and set up home at 'Dunroon', Harrison Street, Bowral, New South Wales. Left Australia to travel to England (where one of his brothers, Dr Albert Roberts, was already serving in the Royal Army Medical Corps), leaving his wife Margaret pregnant and expecting their first child – a son, also to be called Eric James – who he was destined never to see. On arrival, volunteered for service with the RFC. Dr Roberts was the first in the family to learn of Eric's death in action on 23 September 1916. Because his remains were never recovered, he is commemorated on the Arras Memorial to the Missing, France. Age 21.

VICTORY NO. 3
10 October 1916 FE2b (No.4856) 18 Squadron 0950

There has, over the years, been some confusion over the identity of this Böhme victory largely because of the contemporary German difficulties in discerning between the various British 'pusher' type – or 'gitter-rumpfs' – lattice-tailed machines.

Three such machines were in combat this day. Böhme's claim was for a kill east of Longueval, on the British side of the lines, at 0950. While Pozières and Longueval are not too far from each other, a 32 Squadron DH2 that had taken off at 0600 (0700 German time) would not still be airborne nearly three hours later and therefore should be eliminated from the possibilities. A DH2 from 24 Squadron had been accounted for by Müller near to Pozières at 1010. An FE2b of 18 Squadron, on an OP and reportedly attacked by four German scouts, seems a safer bet. The pilot of the badly damaged FE2b, Lieutenant Charles Shaumer, put

down inside British lines west of Morval, and Morval *is* east of Longueval. Furthermore, the Jasta 2 records give the machine as an FE2b, 'inside Allied Lines'. The machine was wrecked and written off.

LIEUTENANT
CHARLES GERSCHELL SHAUMER,
MID, 24/LONDON REGIMENT TF AND 18 SQUADRON, ROYAL FLYING CORPS

From 20 Steadella Road, Herne Hill, London. Gazetted Second Lieutenant to the 24th (County of London) Battalion, The London Regiment, (The Queen's) on 7 August 1915. Accepted for pilot training and posted to Reading on 15 February 1916. Awarded his 'Wings' and sent to join 18 Squadron at the front on 24 July 1916. Shaumer was apparently unhurt in the crash that followed Böhme's attack. Promoted Lieutenant on 1 November 1916. Hospitalised on 16 December 1916 but returned to operational flying with 18 Squadron on the first day of the new year of 1917. Returned to the Home Establishment on 17 June 1917 and was subsequently appointed as Wing Bombing Instructor at HQ, 7th Wing. Continued to instruct in the UK for the rest of the war. Demobilised on 1 March 1919. Mentioned in Despatches *'for valuable services'*, *London Gazette* of 29 August 1919.

1AM
L HARDINGE,
18 SQUADRON, ROYAL FLYING CORPS

Like his pilot, Hardinge was unhurt in Böhme's attack upon, and the consequential wrecking of, their FE. Unfortunately, however, only five days later, flying as observer/gunner to Second Lieutenant A R Crisp in another 18 Squadron FE2b (6346), he was taken prisoner after their machine was forced to land behind German lines.

VICTORY NO. 4
20 October 1916 FE2b (No.4867) 11 Squadron 1030

Following a sortie by 11 Squadron taking photos over Douai for 3rd Army Intelligence, the patrol was intercepted by Jasta 2 as the FEs made their way home. In his post-war debriefing following repatriation from prison camp, William Black related his experiences on this day. His pilot was not flying their usual aircraft – which had developed engine trouble – but a replacement. Attacked over Douai at 10,000 feet, his pilot was killed in the air returning from a reconnaissance mission and Black himself was severely wounded. He was struck by bullets several times and had one leg fractured. On seeing his pilot slump over, Black tried to get into the pilot's cockpit in an attempt to gain control but then fainted. The FE appears to have come down completely uncontrolled and, inevitably, crashed. The wounded observer was thrown clear of the wreckage and taken prisoner by German troops. Böhme recorded his victory down north-west of Monchy, on the German side. The wreck was shelled by British artillery.

Boelcke, in the meantime, brought down a further FE – his 32nd victory – which fell just inside British lines but not before the unfortunate observer fell out of the cockpit to his death.

SECOND LIEUTENANT
NORMAN RAUSCH DE POMEROY,
11 SQUADRON, ROYAL FLYING CORPS

The only son of Edward William Norman and Julia Charlotte de Pomeroy of 'Pantile',

Aldington, near Hythe, Kent, he was born in London on 2 August 1891. He was educated privately at Scottow Vicarage, Norwich (1902-08). Passed the matriculation examination of the University of London in July 1909. Entered the City and Guilds Technical College, Finsbury, to take a two-year course in electrical engineering. Appointed a pupil with the British-Thomson Houston Company of Cannon Street, London, spending three years in their workshops in Rugby. Upon the completion of his apprenticeship in September 1914, he and a number of his friends in Rugby enlisted in the 1/5th Warwickshire (Howitzer) Battery, Royal Field Artillery, 4th South Midland (Howitzer) Brigade. Accompanied his unit to France and by 1 April 1915 was serving at Armentières in the Second Army area. Employed as a telegraphist in a forward observation post at Ploegsteert Wood and at Hébuterne. Later diagnosed as suffering from eczema and blood-poisoning, he was invalided home to Clandon Park, Guildford and Heywood Park Auxiliary, Cobham, hospitals until he recovered his health in December 1915. An application to join the flying service approved, he was directed to Brooklands, Surrey, on 28 December 1915, to be attached to Number 2 Reserve Squadron, 7th Wing, RFC. Gained his Royal Aero Club Certificate (Number 2346) on 28 January 1916. Having passed his initial instruction, he was gazetted Second Lieutenant to the RFC via the General List on 28 February 1916. His progress was halted when he had to have an operation on his knee and so it was not until 11 September 1916 that he was awarded his 'Wings', being placed first on a list of 180 candidates who had undergone the examination at Oxford. Posted to 11 Squadron, then at Le Hameau in France on 21 September 1916. His parents were informed by letters from his friends that he had taken off for the purpose of taking photographs and carrying out a reconnais-sance over the area Famboux-Douai-Cambrai-Bapaume. On its return journey, when the patrol was almost home, they encountered a superior enemy force. It

would be seven months before, in May 1917, it was definitely confirmed that he had been killed. He was buried with full honours by the Imperial German Air Service, the grave being discovered by an army chaplain in the wake of a British advance in November 1917. The grave, marked by a cross formed by propeller blades, was near Les Fosses Farm, just off the Arras-Cambrai road. The 'Wings' he had worn on his khaki jacket were attached to the cross as was an inscription: *'Here rests the English Airman N de Pomeroy. d. 20.10.16. Number 29847. RIP'*. The grave was subsequently lost but then found again to be re-located at Cagincourt Cemetery, France (Fr647) by the Imperial War Graves Commission (now the Commonwealth WGC). Age 25.

SECOND LIEUTENANT
WILLIAM BLACK,
DURHAM LIGHT INFANTRY AND 11 SQUADRON, ROYAL FLYING CORPS

The son of steamship owner William and Mrs Black of 1 Asqlaigh Villas, West Boldon, near Sunderland, young William was born on 15 December 1896. Educated at Rossall School (1910-13) where he was a member of the OTC. An apprentice clerk in a shipping company, he enlisted in his local regiment, the Durham Light Infantry, early in the war. Gazetted Second Lieutenant to his own regiment on 7 December 1914. Sent to join a battalion of his regiment at the front in May 1916, he fought in Flanders and on the Somme before being accepted into the RFC in September 1916. Was still very much a 'green' probationary observer when he and his pilot were shot down by Erwin Böhme days after he had arrived to join 11 Squadron at the front. Taken prisoner, he was first sent to the German hospital at Vitry. Hit by machine-gun bullets in the air and badly injured in the subsequent crash, he had wounds to the left elbow, to his legs, in his left side and right breast. His left hand was paralysed as a consequence of dead nerves. His severely fractured right leg was badly set, causing it to be 3cm shorter than his left.

After the German doctors patched him up, he was sent to a succession of camps including Stettin, Stralsund, Augustabad and, finally, Heidelberg. Exchanged via the Red Cross into Switzerland on 27 December 1917, he was finally repatriated to the UK on 14 June 1918. Pronounced permanently unfit for military service by a medical board on 28 October 1918. Returning to civilian life in Sunderland, he became a shipbroker. His older brother, Kenneth Wilkinson Black, inherited their father's ship-owning company, becoming a CBE, a JP and an Alderman of Sunderland. Despite the injuries and traumas he had suffered in the Great War, William volunteered to serve in the army on 20 September 1939, just over two weeks after the Second World War broke out. He was retired and living in Edinburgh with his wife when he died on 12 January 1982 at the age of 86.

VICTORY NO. 5
22 October 1916 Sopwith 1½ Strutter (No.7786) 45 Squadron 1150

45 Squadron mounted a morning Offensive Patrol intended to cover the Bapaume-Péronne area, taking off at 1015 hours. They soon ran into a fighting patrol of Jasta 2 led by Boelcke and three of the Sopwiths fell to their guns. Boelcke claimed one south-west of Grevillers Wood, and Böhme one down at Les Boeufs. The third fell to Leutnant Wilhelm Frankl of Jasta 4 who arrived on the scene a little after the fight started, his victims going down near Driencourt. It was Frankl's 14th victory.

Oswald Boelcke recorded the incident in his field book: *'1145 – Several of my men and I headed off two enemy biplanes coming from the east. Both fell. The one I attacked was shot apart.'* This was Boelcke's 37th victory. Later a message was dropped by the Imperial German Air Service over British lines confirming the deaths of all six airmen – one Captain, four Second Lieutenants and one Sergeant.

SECOND LIEUTENANT
OLIVER JOHN WADE,
9/ROYAL WEST KENT REGIMENT AND
45 SQUADRON, ROYAL FLYING CORPS

Born in Purley on 1 May 1896, he was the son of Mr and Clara Jane Wade of Hunstanton Lodge, Downe, Orpington, Kent. He volunteered for service in early 1915, enlisting into the 10/Royal West Kents. Sent for officer training to the Inns of Court OTC (Number 3/3142) on 29 March 1915. Gazetted Second Lieutenant to the 9th Battalion, Royal West Kent Regiment on 21 June 1915. Posted to the 2/4th Battalion of his regiment on 1 May 1916 and proceeded to Egypt. After only a month in the Middle East, his application for a transfer to the RFC was approved and

he embarked from Alexandria to return to the UK on 8 June 1916. Gained the Royal Aero Club Certificate (Number 3343) on 24 July 1916. Awarded his 'Wings' and appointed Flying Officer in September 1916 and, on 12 October 1916, accompanied 45 Squadron to France. Killed in action only ten days later. The following message was dropped by the Germans into the Allied lines: *'Lieutenant Oliver John Wads (sic) – born at Purley on 1 May 1896. Pilot Certificate Number 3343. He and his Observer are dead'*. Wade was obviously carrying his Royal Aero Club Certificate in his pocket. Although buried by the Germans, his grave was subsequently lost and hence he is commemorated on the Arras Memorial to the Missing, France. Age 20.

SECOND LIEUTENANT
WILLIAM JOHNSON THUELL,
45 SQUADRON, ROYAL FLYING CORPS

Born on 2 November 1895, he was one of the five children of Mr and Susan Ellen Thuell of 12 Market Street, Falmouth. He was educated at Falmouth Grammar School and, after leaving school, secured a

position at the Penzance branch of Lloyds Bank on 8 September 1913. Volunteered for the 28/London Regiment – Artist's Rifles – in October 1915. Gazetted Second Lieutenant to the Northumberland Fusiliers on 7 July 1916 before subsequently transferring to the RFC via the General List. Successfully completing his observer training, he accompanied 45 Squadron to France on 12 October 1916. His and his pilot's graves were lost in the subsequent fighting over the area and hence he is commemorated on the Arras Memorial to the Missing. Age 20.

Eight days later – by which time Boelcke had increased his score to 40 – tragedy and disaster came to Böhme and Jasta 2 in equal measure. In a fight with DH2s of 24 Squadron, the two aces collided. Böhme's wheels smashed into the upper wing of his Staffelführer's Albatros. As the other Jasta pilots watched in horror, their celebrated and revered leader fell to earth. So died one of the most famous German fighter pilots of the whole war. Not only was he the leading aviation tactician of the day but also the leading ace with, for those early days, an astonishing total of 40 victories. The war had two more years to run and yet only a handful of German pilots would attain higher personal scores.

Böhme was devastated, distraught even. It speaks volumes for his strength of character that he forced himself back into action and carried the fight to his country's enemies for a further thirteen months.

In a letter home Böhme described the fateful day. He and Boelcke had been playing chess at the airfield during that Saturday afternoon of 28 October. After being ordered into the sky to counter a British incursion, they enjoined the intruders in a combat over Flers:

'In our abrupt mutual efforts to dodge, with both Boelcke and my views hindered by our wings, we did not see each other for a moment. Here is where it happened. How

Erwin Böhme before the award of the Pour le Mérite.

can I describe my feelings from that moment on, when Boelcke suddenly appeared just a few metres to my right, how he dived, how I jerked upward, and how we nevertheless grazed each other, and both plummeted downward! It was only a slight touch, but at such breakneck speeds that also meant a strong impact. Fate is usually so horribly irrational in its choice. Only a portion of my undercarriage was torn away. He lost the outermost portion of his left wing. After falling a couple of hundred metres I regained control of my aircraft and could follow Boelcke. I saw his aircraft in a gradual glide, left wing drooping a bit, drifting towards our lines. .... he struck the ground near a gun battery.'

It had been a complete accident but the memory of his friend and leader falling was to haunt him for the rest of his life.

VICTORY NO. 6
9 November 1916 FE8 (No.6409) 40 Squadron 1510

A 40 Squadron afternoon patrol flew out at 1300 hours. Their beat was to take them well south of Douai but still they ran into Jasta 2's fighters. In the course of the fight, Herbert Evans in 6409 was hit in the spine and consequently forced to make a landing north-west of Cambrai. 40 Squadron also lost another FE8 on this day. Its pilot, Captain T Mappelbeck was taken prisoner after being hit, or so he afterwards said, by AA fire. These were the first two combat losses of this Squadron – also the first unit to receive the FE8 – but certainly not the last, as will be seen.

SECOND LIEUTENANT
HERBERT FARMER EVANS,
BERKSHIRE BATTERY, ROYAL HORSE ARTILLERY (TF) AND 40 SQUADRON, ROYAL FLYING CORPS

Born on 20 April 1897, he was the elder son of Henry and Mrs Evans of 149 Nantwich Road, Crewe, Cheshire. Educated at the County High School, Crewe, at Malvern College and at École de St Michel, St Brieuc, where he was studying mechanical engineering. When the war started, he was apprenticed to the Crewe Locomotive Works. Joined the Inns of Court OTC (Number 2/3688) on 20 May 1915. Following training he was gazetted Second Lieutenant to the Berkshire Battery, Royal Horse Artillery (TF) on 26 September 1915. Transferred to the RFC in June 1916, training at Reading and at the Central Flying School, Upavon. Passed his examinations with distinction and was awarded his 'Wings' on 8 September 1916, ferrying a new FE8 across the Channel to 40 Squadron in France ten days later. Said to have brought down an enemy machine in flames. His Squadron commander, the actor and first man to fly across the Irish Sea, Major Robert Loraine, DSO MC, wrote to his parents on the evening of the very day he was posted as 'missing in action', '....... *it is now 8 pm and I have no word of him. It is possible that he is a prisoner of war, in which case they will probably advise us sooner or later....*' . After his forced landing, Evans was unconscious for two days, regaining consciousness in a Douai hospital. With a bullet lodged in his spine, he was paralysed in both legs and suffering from continuous dribbling of urine. Eventually exchanged via the Red Cross in June 1918. Confined in a series of hospitals in the UK before being invalided out on 19 February 1919. A medical board held in November 1919 reported that the bullet was still lodged in his spine, that he had impaired control of his legs – especially the right – and walked only with the aid of two sticks. Yet another long term casualty of the Great War.

VICTORY NO. 7
22 November 1916　Morane Parasol (No.A248)　3 Squadron　1410

A high-winged monoplane, this Morane Parasol was on a photographic sortie west of Flers, having taken off at 1245 hours. At 1310 (British time) it was attacked over Longueval and both crew members were wounded in the air. The pilot managed to dive back into the British sector but front line observers on the German side were satisfied that it had been destroyed and so awarded an official victory to Böhme.

Morane. RFC Communiqué Number 14 – 10 October 1915: *Lieutenant Johnston* [Harold Richard Johnson, West Kent Yeomanry and RFC, who would be killed while flying on 19 January 1916] *and Corporal Roberts of 3 Squadron in a Morane armed with a rifle, when doing photography over Hulluch at 2.15pm were attacked by a hostile aeroplane*

LIEUTENANT
ELMER PETER ROBERTS,
MC, DFC, DCM, ROYAL SUSSEX REGIMENT AND 3 SQUADRON, ROYAL FLYING CORPS

Born on 6 March 1892 at Waldren, Sussex, he was living with his parents at Marle Green Farm, Horsham Road, Sussex when the war came. Enlisted into the RFC on 11 September 1914 (Number 1689) – four years with the colours, four years with the reserve – having already taken his 'ticket' at his own expense at the Pashley School, Shoreham on 29 August 1914 (Royal Aero Club Certificate Number 889). Promoted 1AM with 3 Squadron on 1 May 1915 and Corporal on 1 June. Whilst flying during an intense artillery bombardment on 25 September 1915 – the first day of the Battle of Loos – Roberts reported actually seeing a shell travelling through the air close to his

E P Roberts's unique combination medal group: left to right: MC, DFC, DCM, 1914 Star (with 'Underfire' Bar'), British War Medal, Allied Victory Medal, General Service Medal, GVR, with clasp, 'Kurdistan'.

which approached behind them unseen and fired 20 rounds from a machine-gun hitting Corporal Roberts in three places. The Morane then returned to our lines'. Awarded a DCM (Flying) as a Corporal – *London Gazette* 11 March 1916, *'For conspicuous good work as an Observer. In September, when certain photographs were urgently required and clouds were very low, he took the photographs under a heavy fire'*. Gazetted Second Lieutenant to one of the two Regular Battalions of the Royal Sussex Regiment on 23 October 1915. Immediate transfer back to the RFC followed and he was awarded his 'Wings' and appointed a Flying Officer on 21 May 1916. Posted again to 3 Squadron – now as an officer and a pilot. RFC Communiqué Number 56 – 1 October 1916: *'Lieutenant Roberts and Lieutenant Jones, 3 Squadron, when taking photographs, were attacked by 7 Rolands. The attack was driven off with the assistance of two FE's who joined the fight. One of the Rolands, apparently hit by fire from one of the FE's fell in a nose dive and crashed'*. Promoted to Lieutenant on 1 November 1916. Having fractured a leg in his clash with Erwin Böhme on 22 November 1916, he was sent home for treatment aboard the

hospital ship *Western Australia* on 30 November. Subsequently awarded the Military Cross, *London Gazette* 3 March 1917: *'For conspicuous gallantry in action, he three times dispersed an enemy working party with bombs and machine-gun fire from a height of a 1,000 feet. On another occasion, he shot down an enemy machine. He has shown great determination on many occasions in taking photos under most difficult and trying conditions'*. Roberts stayed on in the Royal Air Force after the war and went on to win a Distinguished Flying Cross in the Iraqi campaign of 1924, *London Gazette* of 28 May 1926, page 3458: *'In recognition of gallant and distinguished service in connection with the operations in Iraq during the period September to November 1924'*.

CAPTAIN
GRAHAM LAUDER WATSON,
7/WEST YORKSHIRE REGIMENT AND 3 SQUADRON, ROYAL FLYING CORPS

Born on 20 June 1891, he was the son of Mr and Mrs J F Watson of Leeds. An engineer, he worked for J Sankey & Sons of Bilston,

A smiling Böhme during a visit to Jasta 2 by the Red Baron's father. Left to right: Ltn Constantin Krefft stands with hand on hip next to Ernst von Althaus (Jasta 10), Manfred von Richthofen, Erwin Böhme and Major von Richthofen.

Staffs from 1909 to 1914. Confirmed with the rank of Captain in the 7th Battalion of the West Yorkshire Regiment (Leeds Rifles) on 1 October 1914. Appointed Flying Officer observer with seniority from 21 May 1916 in the *London Gazette* of 15 November 1916. Joined 3 Squadron as an observer on 2 September 1916. Wounded on 22 November 1916 in the action with Böhme, he was admitted to 8 General Hospital with injuries to his scalp and back before eventually being returned to the UK on the hospital ship *Goorkha*. His wounds were sufficiently serious to preclude the possibility of a return to operational flying. He joined 2 Cadet Wing as an instructor in early 1918 before being sent to work with the Ministry of Munitions on 15 August 1918. Suffered an attack of angina in September 1918 and was finally demobilised on 10 January 1919.

VICTORY NO. 8
26 December 1916 BE2c 5 Squadron 1515

Oddly enough, rather like Böhme's seventh victory, this BE also managed to avoid destruction and get home. In this early period of the war, BE2s on bombing missions often flew without an observer to increase their bomb-carrying capacity. On this very morning, two 5 Squadron BEs bombing Vaulx-Vraucourt had been shot down by Jasta 1 pilots. Now Böhme attempted a 'hat trick' for the Jastas but although his fire did wound the pilot, his intended victim still managed to skip across the lines low down west of Courcelette at 1415 British time. From the German side of the lines, however, it may well have looked that the machine was about to come to a sticky end.

SECOND LIEUTENANT
WILLIAM HENRY HUBBARD,
DFC & BAR, 5 SQUADRON, ROYAL FLYING CORPS

Born in Kingston, Ontario, on 19 May 1886, his family moved to Toronto in 1915. Gazetted Second Lieutenant to the Special Reserve on 1 January 1916. Gained the Royal Aero Club Certificate (Number 2871) on 9 May 1916. Fought with 7 and 5 Squadrons in 1916, gaining one victory and being wounded by Böhme on 26 December. After recovering from his wounds, he was posted to the Home Establishment as an instructor. In 1918 he was sent out as a Flight Commander with 73 Squadron (left), gaining eleven more victories and two Distinguished Flying Crosses by the war's end. DFC *London Gazette* 3 August 1918, page 9200: *'During recent operations he has repeatedly descended to low altitude to release his bombs and to open machine-gun fire on the troops and transport. He has shown the greatest gallantry, judgement and presence of mind. On several occasions he has attacked and driven down out of control enemy aeroplanes'*. The Bar to his DFC was announced in the *London Gazette* of 3 December 1918: *'This officer has shown great bravery and devotion to duty both in destroying enemy aircraft – ten of which he has accounted for – and in silencing anti-tank guns. On 27 September flying at altitudes between 200 and 1,500 feet, he engaged and silenced many anti-tank guns, thereby rendering valuable service. He at the same time completed a detailed and accurate reconnaissance of the area, locating the position of our troops'*. William Hubbard died in Canada in 1960 at the age of 74.

VICTORY NO. 9
7 January 1917 DH2 (No.7851) 32 Squadron 1230

The DH2 'pusher' scouts of 32 Squadron took off for an Offensive Patrol at 1100 hours. They lost one of their number in a fight with Albatros Scouts and Böhme's was the only DH2 claim of the day, shot down over Beugny on the German side of the lines.

SECOND LIEUTENANT
ETHELBERT GODWIN STOCKWELL WAGNER,
ROYAL WARWICKSHIRE REGIMENT AND 32 SQUADRON, ROYAL FLYING CORPS

Born in Taifrin, Federation of Malay States on 12 March 1893, he was the son of Mr and Mrs Wagner who, upon returning to England, lived at 110 Bristol Road, Birmingham. He was studying medicine at Birmingham University when he decided to enlist into the Royal Warwicks. Gazetted Second Lieutenant to the regular battalions of his own regiment on 29 August 1915. Applied for transfer to the RFC, gaining his Royal Aero Club Certificate (Number 3489) on 6 September 1916. Awarded his 'Wings' and appointed a Flying Officer one month later on 6 October 1916. Buried in the Achiet-le-Grand Cemetery Extension, France (Fr518). Age 24.

VICTORY NO. 10
4 February 1917 DH2 (No.A2536) 32 Squadron 1505

Böhme went on leave on 9 January, returning on 3 February. He was back in action the next day.

Having been on leave it was almost a month since his last combat, so it was something of a coincidence that this next confrontation was where Böhme had left off – against the 'pushers' of 32 Squadron. The pushers and Albatros Scouts clashed near to Achiet and on this occasion Böhme was up against a seasoned and very capable British air fighter. During the course of the fight, Captain W G S Curphey had already successfully sent one Albatros down out of control. However, as the fight continued, Curphey was himself wounded in the head.

Böhme's claim, confusingly, was for a *Sopwith* one-seater over Le Transloy – just inside British lines. The Germans at this time often confused types and maker's names even when an Allied machine fell inside their own lines. Present-day aero historians are often heard to complain about the thoughtlessness of the Great War aviators in their lack of consideration of we flustered and flummoxed latter-day chroniclers who want everything spelt out in black and white terms! However, it does give us something to do and as there were no other single-seater fighters lost this day – the others all being two-seaters – it is reasonable to assume that Curphey was Böhme's victim.

CAPTAIN
WILLIAM GEORGE SELLAR CURPHEY,
MC & BAR, ROYAL BERKSHIRE REGIMENT AND 32 SQUADRON, ROYAL FLYING CORPS

The son of civil servant William Salvador Curphey and Mrs Curphey of 87 Canfield Gardens, Hampstead, Middlesex, William was born in 1895. He was educated at Glasgow Academy, at University College School, Hampstead and at London University where he was a member of the OTC. Enlisted into the Royal Berkshire Regiment in the early weeks of the war and was gazetted Second Lieutenant to that regiment on 16 November 1914. Transferred to the RFC in 1916 and, after gaining his 'Wings' accompanied 32 Squadron to France on 28 May 1916. Awarded the Military Cross, *London Gazette* 14 November 1916: *'For conspicuous skill and gallantry. He brought down an enemy machine and two days later attacked and brought down another. He has recently attacked formations of hostile aircraft and driven* *them down'*. Appointed a Captain and Flight Commander on 9 January 1917. A Bar to his Cross followed, the announcement in the *London Gazette* of 12 March 1917: *'For conspicuous gallantry in action. He, with a patrol of four machines, attacked a hostile formation of ten machines. After a prolonged fight he drove one enemy machine down. Later, although wounded, he again led another attack on a hostile machine and succeeded in bringing it down. He has on many previous occasions done fine work'*. After escaping the close attentions of Erwin Böhme on 4 February 1917, he recovered from the slight wounds he had received and was soon in the air again. On 14 May 1917, Curphey and two of his colleagues successfully attacked three enemy balloons some six miles behind the lines. After turning for home, they were pounced upon by six hostiles. An Albatros on Curphey's tail was shot up – and down – by Lieutenant St Cyprian Churchill Tayler – the second of his eventual 10 victories before he, too, was killed in action, a victim of Leutnant Heinrich Kroll of Jasta 24, on 17 March 1918. Tayler's intervention was in vain, however, as Curphey was immediately afterwards hit by fire from Hauptmann Franz Walz, leader of Jasta Boelcke. Curphey was desperately unlucky, his machine, A2622, bursting into flames a mere 20 feet from the ground. He died the following day at Bouchain in a German field hospital. Had he lived, he was due to be appointed to his Majority within weeks, a promotion which would, effectively, bring his combat flying to an end. Buried in the Caberet-Rouge Cemetery, France (Fr924). Age 21.

VICTORY NO. 11
4 February 1917 BE2e (No.7105) 15 Squadron 1530

Shortly after achieving his tenth officially recognised victory, Böhme went after a two-seater on an artillery observation flight. The BE crew had taken off at 1350 hours to liaise with a gun battery in area L.27 (Map sheet 57D). Their last signal came at 1405 British time and front line observers saw the BE descending, seemingly under control. Both crew men, however, were dead, killed either in the air or in the crash that followed

Opposite: Erwin Böhme's 13th victory was over a Nieuport XVIIC1 from 40 Squadron. Its pilot, Lieutenant G Davis, managed a crash landing and sat out the war as a prisoner.

Böhme's onslaught. Böhme located his claim in the area north-west of Puisieux, just inside British lines. In all, Jasta 2 pilots accounted for three BEs engaged on artillery observation during the course of this afternoon.

SERGEANT
FREDERICK JAMES SHAW,
15 SQUADRON, ROYAL FLYING CORPS

Born on 17 April 1892, he was the son of Albert Edward and Alice Shaw of 6 Bow Street, Rugeley, Staffordshire. Enlisted into the Royal Flying Corps (Number 917) on 15 October 1913. Proceeded to France with the rank of 2AM with 5 Squadron on 14 August 1914, thus qualifying for the 1914 Star. Gained a Royal Aero Club Certificate (Number 3386) on 3 June 1915. RFC Communiqué Numbers 11 and 13 of 19 September and 3 October 1915 respectively, credit 1AM F J Shaw (with Lieutenant Powell driving) as accounting for a Rumpler G1 and an LVG. The Communiqué of 11 October 1915 (Number 15), however, describes how the crew of a German machine managed not only to escape the attentions of Powell and his gunner, Fred Shaw, but also wounded the latter in the leg and knocked three holes in their Vickers'

petrol tank. Served as a Sergeant gunner/observer with 16 Squadron from 4 October 1915 before joining 15 Squadron as a pilot. His remains were never found and hence he is commemorated on the Arras Memorial to the Missing, France. Age 25.

SECOND LIEUTENANT
GEORGE WILLIAM BATHURST BRADFORD,
15 SQUADRON, ROYAL FLYING CORPS

The son of W K and Mrs Lora Bradford of 32 Park Road, Kimberley, South Africa, George was born on 30 April 1895. Educated at St Andrew's College (1909-10). He was in business in South Africa when the war came, immediately enlisting into the South African Infantry (Number 3901). Served in the South African rebellion and in the German East African campaign before coming over to England at his own expense and given a 'New Army' commission on 13 March 1916. An application to join the flying service was granted in the summer.

Co-author Hal Giblin pictured alongside G W B Bradford's newly carved name on the Addenda panel of the Flying Services Memorial, Arras, France. Better late than never!

Opposite: Erwin Böhme was finally brought down in a combat with an AWFK8 'Big Ack' of 10 Squadron RFC on 29 November 1917, crewed by Lieutenants J A Pattern and P W Leycester.

His observer training completed on 1 December 1916, he proceeded to France and 15 Squadron a few weeks later.

NB: During the course of researching the details concerning George Bradford, the authors discovered that not only had he no known grave but that he was entirely un-commemorated – his name did not appear anywhere in the records of the Common-wealth War Graves Commission. Following representations to the official body and after furnishing the required irrefutable proof of his active service and of his death in action, the authors were proud to receive confirmation from CWGC that the name of Second Lieutenant George William Bathurst Bradford has been added to the Flying Services Memorial, Arras, France. Age 21.

VICTORY NO. 12
10 February 1917 DH2 32 Squadron 1220

This early afternoon action was yet another where the German references to a 'gitterrumpf' confuses the issue for historians. The 'lattice-tail' on this occasion was said to have been a two-seat FE2b, but the fact is that no FEs were reported lost or damaged this date, so once again we are left with the probability that it was a DH2 pusher. Böhme's claim was for a victory west of Gommecourt, his victim going down inside British lines. In our previous book, we examined the known circumstances of 32 Squadron's fight with Jasta 2 and concluded that Werner Voss had shot up and wounded the patrol leader, Captain L P Aizelwood. Nothing has since occurred to alter our view and we must also conclude that Böhme engaged and shot up the DH2 flown by Second Lieutenant A V H Gompertz.

A four-strong 32 Squadron group had taken off on a Line Patrol at 1015, the DH2s piloted by Aizelwood, Mare-Montembault, Cross and Gompertz. An hour later (ie; 1215 German time) the British patrol saw, above them, nine German aircraft attempting to cross the lines. Disadvantaged, the DH2s nevertheless climbed to the attack. The Germans saw them coming and dived, aggressively, to engage. Captain Aizelwood drove one down, which had streamers on its struts. He went down after it and it was shortly after this that he was wounded by Voss. In the course of the fierce scrap, Gompertz's machine was damaged and his engine shot through, forcing him to break off the fight and make for the lines. He force-landed near Souastre, which is just west of Gommecourt. Voss, of course, was also with Jasta 2 at this time, he and Böhme both making claims for RFC aircraft down inside Allied lines.

The Flying Services Memorial, Arras, France.

SECOND LIEUTENANT
ARTHUR VINCENT HOWARD GOMPERTZ,
32 SQUADRON, ROYAL FLYING CORPS

Born on 21 August 1895 at 19 Lansdowne Road, Bedford, shortly before his family returned to Yercaud, Madras, India, where they had business interests. Sent home to complete his education, he attended Bedford Modern School (1906-09) before going on to Bedford Grammar (1910-13) where he proved especially proficient in latin, Greek, French, English and Maths. Returning again to India after leaving school, he was given a commission in the Indian Army Reserve of Officers on 9 April 1915 but was forced to resign due to ill-health on 22 September 1915. Came again to England in March 1916, living at 70 Westbourne Terrace, Hyde Park,

Second Lieutenant Arthur Vincent Howard Gompertz, 32 Sqaudron RFC, with friends, left to right: 2Lt M J J G Mare-Montembault, Gompertz, Capt J M Robb (a future Air Chief Marshal) and Lt E L Heyworth. *(Via B Gray)*

London, his status registered as 'visitor'. Sought and was given a commission in the RFC with effect from 5 August 1916. Had he not secured his commission when he did, he would have been obliged to return to India, as his visitor status would have expired. Survived the attack by Erwin Böhme and survived the remainder of the war. Returned to India at the war's end, being transferred to the reserve in December 1922 before finally resigning his commission on 17 December 1923.

The next day, 11 February, Böhme was wounded. He wrote home on the 13th: *'The bed from which I am writing is in a field hospital because of a malevolent Englishman who, the day before yesterday and who by all rights should no longer be alive, treacherously shot me in the left arm. It was a two-seater Sopwith which I had already put out of action and who was headed downwards. For that reason, I spared him in a show of sportsmanlike grace – that's what I get for my noblesse!'*

The wound kept him from operational flying for some time, during which absence two more of Boelcke's original contingent of Jasta pilots fell. Indeed, as Böhme wrote at the beginning of April 1917, only he and Manfred von Richthofen were left from the 'founder members' of the Boelcke squadron (Richthofen, by this time, was in command of Jasta 11). Some consolation came his way on 12 March 1917, when he was decorated with the Knight's Cross with Swords of the Royal Hohenzollern House Order.

Böhme was next sent to Valenciennes as an instructor. The School (Jagdstaffelschule Nr.1 at Farmars) was commanded at the time by Hauptmann Martin Zander. Weeks later, at the end of April, Manfred von Richthofen was due to go on leave and paid Böhme the great compliment of asking him to take temporary command of Jasta 11 in his absence. Higher authority, however, intervened and would not allow him to leave his instructing post for the time being. In fact, he was not allowed to leave until the following July.

In early July, Böhme was given command of Jasta 29, taking over the post from Kurt Wolff who had returned to command Jasta 11 – now a component part, along with Jastas 4, 6 and 10, of Manfred von Richthofen's JGI (Circus).

Böhme's new command, Jasta 29, was located at Bersée, to the north-west of Douai (6th Army). It was in this sector that Böhme achieved his thirteenth victory. On 18 July 1917, Jasta 29 re-located to Handsaeme on the 4th Army Front.

VICTORY NO. 13
14 July 1917 Nieuport XVII (No.A6783) 40 Squadron 0720

40 Squadron had recently exchanged its old FE8 pushers for French-made Nieuport Scouts. On this occasion an Offensive Patrol which had taken off at 0525, found itself in the vicinity of Douai a couple of hours later. The five scout pilots, Second Lieutenants G L Lloyd, H B Redler, G Davis, W MacLanachan and Lieutenant H A Kennedy, were delighted with their Nieuports and confident that they would give a good account of themselves should they confront trouble in the shape of the Imperial German Air Service.

East of the town they ran into a force of German fighters, six below them and four higher up. The enemy scouts, they noticed, were predominantly green in colour. Bill MacLanachan fired just six rounds at one enemy machine before his gun jammed and, suddenly defenceless, he was forced to make a run for it. In the meantime Redler attacked another German aircraft with tracer and saw it begin to fall out of control. Almost as quickly as it started, the fight petered out but not until Redler was chased all the way back to his own lines. As the brief flurry of action died away, the remnants of the RFC patrol attempted to re-assemble their formation only to find that Godfrey Davis was missing.

Böhme later wrote that one Nieuport had attacked him at 5,000 metres but he had finally overpowered it almost over the Jasta's base. He went on to say that he had 'winged' two others far over on the British side of the lines. Perhaps, therefore, it was actually Böhme who, as well as accounting for Davis, attacked both MacLanachan and Redler, pursuing them back to their lines. Redler it was, of course, who subsequently shot down

von Tutschek whilst flying with 24 Squadron in 1918, as we shall read later in this book.

SECOND LIEUTENANT
GODFREY DAVIS,
7/LONDON BRIGADE, ROYAL FIELD ARTILLERY AND 40 SQUADRON, ROYAL FLYING CORPS

Served as a bombardier in the trenches with the Honourable Artillery Company before being gazetted Second Lieutenant to the 7th London Brigade, Royal Field Artillery

Nieuport XVII (A6783), 40 Squadron, shot down by Böhme on 14 July 1917 when flying with Jasta 29. Its pilot, Lt G Davis, was made POW. (Greg VanWyngarden)

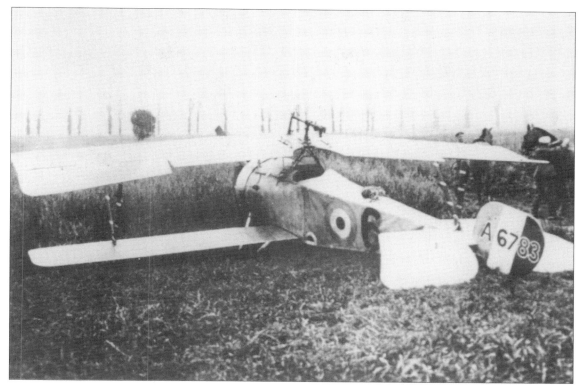

(Territorial Force) on 28 January 1916. Transferred to the School of Aviation on 25 September 1916. After successfully completing his flying training, he was awarded his 'Wings' and formally seconded to the RFC on 23 February 1917. Sent out to France and 40 Squadron on 13 June 1917. Taken prisoner of war in the clash with Böhme a month later on 14 July 1917, he was incarcerated mostly at Karlsruhe and at Holzminden. Repatriated, at last, on 14 December 1918, he left the service with the rank of Captain, going on to the Unemployed List on 7 July 1919. Lived, post-war, at 'The Firs', Bangor, Newport, Monmouthshire.

Jasta 29 moved to Thourout on 1 August, still under the aegis of the 4th Army. However, before Böhme could add to his score, he was wounded again on 10 August. This time he was hit by a bullet in his right hand. He was in the process of attacking an artillery spotting aeroplane when a single-seater scout came up from below and opened fire – one of the bullets ploughing a furrow through the back of his hand. It was not a serious wound but was painful and would leave a scar.

His attackers were almost certainly one of two French pilots from Spa 3, Lieutenant Gustave Lagache or Adjudant René Fonck. Lagache engaged a German scout which was, in turn, attacking a two-seater east of Dixmude at 1515 hours. Fonck, too, shot at an enemy machine which was attacking a two-seater, a little later at 1715 near Ypres. As Böhme recorded the action as 'happening in the evening hours', Fonck's attack at 1715 would seem the most likely.

Despite his wound and being temporarily grounded by the medics, Böhme remained in command of his unit and it was whilst he was *hors de combat,* that he received a telephone call to tell him he was to return to his old Jasta 2 – as Staffelführer – with effect from 18 August 1917. Jasta 2 was based at Ghistelles, also on the 4th Army Front. On 27 August, Jasta 2 would become part of Jagdgruppe Nord (Jastas 2, 17, 20, 28 and Kest 8) under Hauptmann Otto Hartmann, and move yet again, this time to Varssenaere on the same front.

VICTORY NO. 14
19 September 1917   RE8 (No.B5012)   9 Squadron   1047

Böhme's first victory following his return to Jasta 2 was at the expense of a 'Harry Tate'. The RE8 had left its base at 0945 hours to liaise with the 145th 8" Howitzer Battery. The gunners, however, were to lose their 'eye in the sky' in an unequal contest in the vicinity of Langemarck at about 1045 – the reconnaissance machine soon falling out of control. The pilot made an attempt to regain his lines and, in fact, was partially successful in that the RE8 did hit the ground inside British territory. German observers noted the RE8's precipitant descent culminating at Boesinghe, north of Ypres. There can be little doubt that this was the actual RE shot down by Böhme despite the times recorded by both sides being identical (German and Allied times were one hour apart at this stage). Only two other RE8s were lost this date, one a little earlier in the day and west of Ypres, the other later in the afternoon and further down the lines nearer to Arras. This was the Staffelführer's first flight since returning to Jasta 2 – he had obviously not lost his touch despite the time which had elapsed since his previous action.

SECOND LIEUTENANT
HENRY LITTLE DEVLIN,
5(TF)/ARGYLE AND SUTHERLAND HIGHLANDERS AND 9 SQUADRON, ROYAL FLYING CORPS

The son of Henry and Anne Davidson Risk Devlin of Victoria Place, Kelly Street, Greenock, he was born 1 August 1890. Educated at Greenock Higher Grade School and at Glasgow Technical College, where he studied chemistry. When the war started he held a position with the Demerara Sugar Company, Georgetown, Demerara, British

Guyana. Returning to Scotland, and because he had previously served in the Territorial Force (Corporal), he was offered a commission in the 5th (TF) Battalion, Argyle and Sutherland Highlanders (Princess Louise's) which was gazetted on 27 October 1915. Henry's father, also Henry, served as a Lieutenant in the 5/Argyle's. Henry Junior's brother, James, fought as an observer in the Royal Air Force during 1918 and, like his father, survived the war. Henry Junior became an instructor in gymnastics and bayonet fighting at Ripon before transferring to the RFC in September 1916. Whilst training at Montrose, his machine side-slipped and was completely destroyed. Showing remarkable coolness, he went up again the following day and completed two hours flying. Shortly after being awarded his 'Wings', he was sent out to join 9 Squadron at the front on 13 April 1917. Buried in Mendinghem British Cemetery, Belgium (Bel 18). Age 27.

SECOND LIEUTENANT
FREDERICK ADAM WRIGHT,
DUKE OF CORNWALL'S LIGHT INFANTRY AND 9 SQUADRON, ROYAL FLYING CORPS

Born in 1893, he was the son of Mr and Mrs Wright of 49 Co-operative Street, Derby. Buried in Mendinghem Cemetery, Belgium (Bel 18). Age 24.

VICTORY NO. 15
21 September 1917 RE8 (No.A3617) 53 Squadron 0852

Böhme's next victory was another RE8 brought down, according to him, at Comines on the German side. The 53 Squadron machine had taken off at 0635 hours to fly an artillery observation mission and was seen to be attacked by six German fighters at around 0655 near Warneton. The locations precisely agree, although once again we have a timing problem. There is no other British loss that fits both the time and vicinity scenario and so once again we must assume a recording error has occurred. The Germans sometimes confused RE8s with AWFK8s or even BF2b Fighters and although there were indeed losses of these other types on this day, none of them come near to fitting the known circumstances.

As the RE8 came down, British observers were convinced that the crew had the machine under control – sadly they were mistaken.

CAPTAIN
ROBERT NICHOLAS FENWICK MILLS,
MID, ARMY SERVICE CORPS AND 53 SQUADRON, ROYAL FLYING CORPS

Born on 30 December 1889, he was the second son of Robert Fenwick Mills of Tapton Grove, Chesterfield, Derbyshire. He was educated at Rugby (1903-07) where he captained the running VIII and played for

the cricket First XI. After leaving Rugby he took up an apprenticeship as a mining engineer with Markham and Company of Chesterfield. Several years later, as a qualified mining engineer he obtained a post with the Clay Cross Coal and Iron Company. Volunteering for service in the Territorial Force in 1912, he was offered a commission in the Army Service Corps (Notts Brigade TF). Mobilised as soon as the war started, he was amongst the first to land on Gallipoli, serving on that accursed peninsular until the final evacuation. Received a Mention in Despatches (*London Gazette* 12 July 1916) for his service in Gallipoli. Served in Egypt as a Transport Officer for over a year, before

next successfully seeking a transfer to the RFC. Returned home for pilot training and was awarded his 'Wings' in June 1917. In the same month he married Marjory Frances, the second daughter of Sir Francis Blake. He arrived in France only days before his death in action. News of his death in combat with Erwin Böhme was dropped onto his home airfield by a German aircraft on 12 October 1917. Robert Mills is buried in Pont-du-Hem Cemetery, France (Fr705). Age 28.

LIEUTENANT
WILLIAM ANGUS BROWNE,
8/ROYAL INNISKILLING FUSILIERS AND 53 SQUADRON, ROYAL FLYING CORPS

The son of William and Eleanor Browne of Kirkcubbin, County Down, William was born in 1893. Educated at Belfast University, he was working in a London bank when the war came. Enlisted as a private soldier (Number 4419) into the 20th (3rd Public Schools) Battalion, Royal Fusiliers on 7 September 1914. Subsequently gazetted Second Lieutenant to the 8/Royal Inniskilling Fusiliers on 18 November 1914. Following a period of service in the trenches he successfully sought a transfer to the RFC. On 18 October 1917, William's married sister, Harriet Davie, living at 'Hazelmere', Richmond Avenue, Bognor, received notice that the German Air Service had dropped a message from one of their aircraft confirming her brother's death on 21 September 1917. He too is buried in the Pont-du-Hem Cemetery, France (Fr705). Age 24.

The CWGC headstone of Lieutenant William Angus Browne, 53 Squadron RFC, who lies buried alongside his pilot. His family added the sentiment: 'Gladly He Lived and Gladly Died'.

VICTORY NO. 16
5 October 1917 BF2b (No.B1133) 20 Squadron 0815

On 1 October 1917, Jasta 2 again moved base, this time to Rumbeke, near Roulers. Five days later Böhme was leading a morning patrol which engaged, near Moorslede, a formation of Brisfits that had taken off on an

OP at 0740. The ensuing sky battle between the opposing airmen drifted to an area north of Dadizeele. In his post-war de-briefing following his release from captivity in January 1919, Captain Walrond-Skinner reported that at 0800 hours his engine had failed – caused by AA shrapnel hits to the fuel tank or possibly a con-rod. Unfavourable winds – the prevailing wind was almost invariably west to east – would, he thought, have probably prevented him from reaching his lines, when, suddenly, and to add to his mounting woes, he found himself being chased by seven or eight enemy fighters. He was hit in the face – a bullet nicked his nose – before he was forced to crash-land. Walrond-Skinner's observer, Private Frank Johns, received injuries to his midriff in the subsequent crash. The Bristol Fighter was seen going down north of Roulers.

CAPTAIN
DONALD DACRE WALROND-SKINNER,
1/MONMOUTHSHIRE REGIMENT (TF) AND 20 SQUADRON, ROYAL FLYING CORPS

The son of Mr and Mrs Walrond-Skinner of 5 Brigupoyn Road, Newport, Monmouthshire. Gazetted Second Lieutenant to the 1st Battalion of the Monmouthshire Regiment (TF) on 31 May 1915. Transferred to the RFC in the late summer of 1916. Qualified for his Royal Aero Club Certificate (Number 3619) on 28 September 1916. Completed his

formal training and was awarded his 'Wings' and appointed a Flying Officer on 15 November 1916. Served on the Western Front for most of 1917, attaining the rank of Captain and Flight Commander. Taken prisoner on 5 October 1917, he would not be repatriated until 10 January 1919.

PRIVATE
FRANCIS J JOHNS,
1/KING'S SHROPSHIRE LIGHT INFANTRY AND 20 SQUADRON, ROYAL FLYING CORPS

Frank Jones accompanied the First Battalion of his regiment to France on 10 September 1914, thus earning a 1914 Star and the coveted 'Under Fire' Clasp. After serving through some of the early bloody battles of the war – the Aisne and Armentières – he was wounded and returned home for hospital treatment. After he recovered his health, he served with one of the army cyclist units before successfully seeking transfer to the RFC. Sent to 20 Squadron as a probationary air gunner (Number 46558) on Bristol Fighters a short time before he was shot down by Erwin Böhme. Taken prisoner on 5 October 1917, he would remain incarcerated until 14 December 1918 when he was at last repatriated.

VICTORY NO. 17
10 October 1917 Nieuport XXVII (No.B6791) 29 Squadron 0725

Böhme claimed an SE5 as his seventeenth victory but went on to qualify the statement to some extent by adding that it may, in fact, have been a Martinsyde! SE5s were not a new type to the front but the type had continued to elude Böhme. An SE5 had indeed been shot down this date, but that one was lost in the afternoon, not the early morning. 29 Squadron had two of their Nieuport XXVIIs shot up on a morning patrol and one of these would seem to be Böhme's victim. Eight aircraft had started out at 0535 hours, led by Captain F Rose but two, troubled by mechanical problems, fell out of the formation. The Squadron patrol

report describes how their depleted force met six German fighters east of Ypres at 0620. Second Lieutenant Wigle in B6791 was shot about and forced to land behind the front lines near to a place known as 'Gloucester House' (sheet 28). The Nieuport was wrecked; its pilot slightly wounded in the face and ankle. Despite his injuries, Wigle rapidly abandoned his machine as it came under immediate shell fire from the German artillery, the shells pounding the Nieuport into matchwood.

Second Lieutenant C W Hamilton in another damaged Nieuport, made it back to the airfield. Hamilton was wounded in the

this 29 Squadron machine and pilot were the Staffelführer's opponents on this day.

SECOND LIEUTENANT
GERALD BENSON WIGLE,
29 SQUADRON, ROYAL FLYING CORPS

From Ruthven, Ontario, Canada, he was born on 31 March 1895. A student at Toronto University in 1914 and 1915, he studied electrical engineering at the School of Practical Science. He decided to curtail his studies and enlisted as a private soldier into the Canadian Army Service Corps. Served in the UK and in France before successfully applying for transfer to the RFC. Gained his Royal Aero Club Certificate (Number 4851) on 17 June 1917. His formal training completed, he was awarded his 'Wings', appointed a Flying Officer on 18 July 1917 and posted to 29 Squadron in France on 8 September 1917. Shot down into the front lines, and although wounded in the face and the ankle, he summoned up the energy to extricate himself from the wreckage of his Nieuport before it was pounded into smithereens by artillery fire. Initially reported as missing, he turned up some time later, wounded but alive. After recovering from the wounds he received at the hands of Erwin Böhme, Wigle (left) became an instructor, first with 27 Training Squadron before going on to the School of Special Flying and finally to the Canadian School of Instructing before being demobilised on 20 January 1919.

hand. His machine was in a sorry state with hits to its wings, fuel and oil tanks, struts and ailerons, fuselage and even some wires were cut through.

Böhme noted his victim going down north of Zillebeke into the British front line. His identification of his victim as an SE5 presents modern-day historians with a problem. The Type 27 Nieuport was the last of the V-strutter series. Newly arrived at the front at this time, it shared many characteristics with the earlier Nieuports. Still, weighing all the evidence, it is apparent that

---

VICTORY NO. 18
13 October 1917   Sopwith Pup (No.B1800)   54 Squadron   0850

It was a bad morning for 54 Squadron which began at 0645, six machines taking off on an Offensive Patrol to the St Pierre Capelle-Zarren area. The Pups ran into a veritable horde of German fighters from Jastas 2, 8 and 10. Four of the RFC machines were sent down with two pilots killed and two others taken prisoner. Böhme attacked his victim over

Zarren and it was seen to fall to the ground on the German side, south of Couckeleare.

SECOND LIEUTENANT
FREDERICK WILLIAM GIBBES,
54 SQUADRON, ROYAL FLYING CORPS

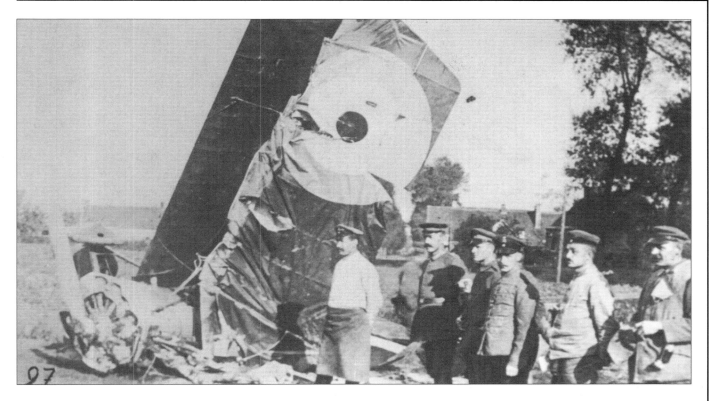

The Sopwith Pup (B1800) of 54 Squadron shot down by Böhme on 13 October 1917 for his 18th victory. Böhme's opponent, 2 Lt F W Gibbes, did not survive the crash. *(Bruce/Leslie collection)*

Fred Gibbes was born in the UK on 28 April 1889, his parents emigrating shortly afterwards to set up in business rearing sheep in New South Wales, Australia. He was educated at King's College, Goulburn and at Sydney University from where he graduated as a consultant engineer. He married Marjorie Henderson in 1914 and their son, Peter, was born on 4 April 1915. The couple were living at 46 Stanhope Gardens, London SW when Gibbes was gazetted to the RFC via the General List on 13 April 1917. Trained at Gosport, Turnberry and the CFS, Salisbury Plain, before being sent to join 54 Squadron in Flanders in August 1917. Shortly after his encounter with Böhme, a note was dropped over the British lines by the Germans which read: *'Sopwith Pup, Number WPB 1800 – occupant dead. Buried at Bovekirke'.* Gibbes's remains were subsequently re-interred at Larch Wood Cemetery, Zillebeke, Belgium (Bel 132). He was 28.

VICTORY NO. 19
14 October 1917 Nieuport XXVII (No.B6778) 29 Squadron 0742

Seven 29 Squadron Nieuport Scouts took off at 0545 on dawn patrol. The patrol was led by Captain F Rose who had also commanded the RFC machines in the combat of 10 October when Böhme gained his seventeenth victory. Shortly into the patrol two of the Nieuports turned back to base, both afflicted with rigging problems. With pit-stop efficiency, the ground crews made the necessary adjustments and the two quickly took off again, catching up with their colleagues over the front. A further fault was discovered which resulted in yet another Nieuport turning for home – the pilot having difficulties with his top wing gun-mounting.

At 0640 hours, as the patrol was heading north, seven German fighters were seen over Poelcapelle. The rapidly closing enemy aircraft engaged the 29 Squadron machines at 9,000 feet. One Nieuport was badly hit and went down to crash at position sheet 28. D. 7. c. o.o., the pilot being killed. The crash was inside British lines but close enough to the enemy trenches for front line observers on the German side actually to see the impact. The wrecked fighter was beyond salvaging and the circumstances of its destruction corresponds precisely with Böhme's claim of a Nieuport down at Wieltje at 0742.

SECOND LIEUTENANT
HENRY DOUGLAS MACPHERSON,
29 SQUADRON, ROYAL FLYING CORPS

Born in Headingley Hall, Leeds, on 6 March 1898, he was the third of the five sons of Henry and Lily MacPherson of 'Ghyllas', Sedbergh, Yorkshire. The five MacPherson brothers all attended Sedbergh School, Henry being there from 1912 to 1916. As soon as he was old enough, he applied for a commission in the RFC. Following the usual training he was awarded his 'Wings' and posted to 29 Squadron at the front just three weeks before his fatal encounter with Erwin Böhme. Henry Douglas MacPherson is buried in Mendinghem Cemetery, Belgium (Bel 18). Age 19.

VICTORY NO. 20
16 October 1917 Nieuport XVII (No.B3578) 29 Squadron 0925

Another 29 Squadron Nieuport Scout brought Böhme's score to the magical total of 20, bringing with it the probability of the award of the prized Pour le Mérite. It was a remarkable victory in another sense – for Böhme forced his opponent to surrender in the air.

The surrender was perhaps doubly unfortunate for the RFC pilot as he was of German descent, and he did little to enhance his reputation by embroidering the circumstances of his last combat flight in the post-war debriefing following his return from captivity. At 0735, Frederick Ortweiler – in company with Lieutenant C W Hamilton – had been sent off to intercept a German two-seater over the front. Rather than the ponderous and vulnerable two-seater wireless machine they were seeking, they saw five German single-seaters in the distance over St Julien. Shortly afterwards they stumbled upon a single German machine which Ortweiler immediately tried to engage but it quickly broke away and headed east. Already lured deep into Germany territory, a strong west wind

pushed him even further. Alarmed, Ortweiler broke off the chase and headed back to the lines. Almost simultaneously he was attacked by five scouts. Perhaps this was the same quintet they had seen in the distance over St Julien?

In his debriefing, Ortweiler said that his opponents were from Jag (sic) Boelcke, led by Captain Böhme. He (Ortweiler) had turned to out-climb the Albatros Scouts but after only two shots from his machine gun he got a double feed in his Lewis gun and, in his frantic attempts to un-jam it, stalled. The Nieuport hurtled down in a spin from 7,000 to 3,000 feet. At 3,000 feet he recovered control only to find the German aircraft were still with him and firing. He spun his machine down again, this time down to ground level and set off contour chasing for about three miles. However, after zooming over some trees, his engine suddenly stopped and the machine dropped into a field in amongst telegraph wires strung between poles. He went on to say that he had landed near to a German Battalion HQ and was physically thrown to the ground onto his back by a German soldier just as he was about to fire a Verey light into a pool of petrol which had leaked from his crash-landed machine. He also claimed that apart from some bullet holes and a bent undercarriage, his Nieuport was otherwise intact.

Compare this story with Böhme's version of events, written in a letter to his girlfriend: *'I once again had the opportunity ..... to make the acquaintance of a merchant, this time an English merchant. His name is Mr Ortweiler. His family comes from Frankfurt and he is now biding his time in a German PoW camp. I recently came upon an English Nieuport single-seater at the front, in which our friend was sitting. Naturally I invited him to pay us a visit. As he did not promptly begin to descend, I became somewhat more urgent in my efforts to compel him to descend. Yet, as he continually waved at me 'with his hands'* [presumably the sign of surrendering – hands up and over the head] *I did not want to do anything to him. He then landed safe and sound <u>at our airfield</u>. We laughed until we were blue in the face. I had never had anything like this previously happen to me.'*

Jasta 2's home field was at Rumbeke at this time, some 17 kilometres north-east of Ypres and the front lines. Not *'the three miles'* into enemy territory reported by Ortweiler. Nor does Böhme make any mention of a low-level, contour-hugging chase towards the lines. Significantly, Ortweiler fails to make it clear that the 'field' in which he *'force-landed with his engine stopped'*, was an enemy aerodrome, nor that the *'German Battalion HQ'* he landed close to, was, in fact, the HQ of a German fighter squadron. The photograph subsequently taken of his Nieuport by the Germans, shows no sign of a bent undercarriage. In being 'economical with the truth', he also had to give a reason as to why he did not take off again – presumably the bent undercarriage explained that omission – not to mention having been wrestled to the ground by an enemy soldier!

We mention these contradictions not to demean or disparage Ortweiler but to illustrate the oft-repeated but unspoken fear of a possible court martial exhibited by returning POWs who, understandably in the circumstances, had effectively surrendered themselves and their machines in the heat of battle. Imagine Ortweiler's dilemma on 16 October 1917 – new to combat flying, alone and miles behind enemy lines with no less than five German fighters surrounding him. Facing certain death, he gave himself up. Subsequently, he displayed great bravery in various escape attempts, becoming one of the few who actually succeeded in breaking out to freedom.

SECOND LIEUTENANT
FREDERICK JOHN ORTWEILER,
MC, 29 SQUADRON, ROYAL FLYING CORPS

The son of leather goods manufacturer Simon Ortweiler and Mrs Matilda Ortweiler of 13 Cavendish Road, Brondesbury, London NW 6, Frederick was born on 25 February 1898. He was educated at Brondesbury Preparatory School and at St Paul's,

Westminster (1911-16). Ortweiler's parents were both German born, coming to England in 1886 before being 'naturalised' on 27 February 1897, the year before Frederick's birth. A note in his personal file – now in the PRO – suggests that 'Intelligence' sources were satisfied that the senior Ortweilers were British sympathisers. On leaving St Paul's in December 1916, he volunteered for service with the RFC, being accepted as a cadet in March 1917 and sent to Oxford for training in the following month. Gained the Royal Aero Club Certificate (Number 4681) on 19 May 1917. Served with both 69 and 81 Squadrons in the UK before being sent out to join 29 Squadron in France on 29 September 1917. Less than three weeks later and still learning his trade, he had the misfortune to fall to Erwin Böhme – the German ace's twentieth victory. He was not, however, content to remain a prisoner for the rest of the war. Following his capture, he was first taken to Lendelede for interrogation before going on to a series of camps including Karlsruhe and Bruf before finally arriving at Halle on 16 December 1917. His first break for freedom – on 7 January 1918 – was short-lived, he was re-captured at the Dutch border on the following day. He was detained at Aachen for three days before being sent to Halle civil prison where he was kept for another three days. From Halle he was shuttled to Fort Zorndorf and then on to Causthal, to be the scene of his second failed escape bid in April 1918. Not surprisingly, he was sent to Holzminden in the following July and then on to Stralsund in August. His third escape attempt – on 12 October 1918 – was entirely successful and for this he was eventually awarded the Military Cross, the announcement of which appeared in the 'Escapers Gazette' – the *London Gazette* of 16 December 1919. After completing his war service in April 1919, he took a shortened degree course at King's College, Cambridge, gaining a Batchelor of Arts in 1920. Deciding

The 29 Squadron Nieuport 17 (B3598) forced down by Erwin Böhme onto his own airfield on 16 October 1917. Its pilot, Lt F J Ortweiler, was taken prisoner. This was Böhme's all important 20th victory – qualifying him for the award of the Blue Max. *(Via Dr.-Ing Niedermeyer)*

Ortweiler's
Nieuport Scout
under camouflage
after its capture.
(Mike O'Connor)

upon a career in aviation, he became chief pilot at the Cambridge School of Flying. He flew an SE5a in the 1921 Derby aerial display and also represented the de Havilland Company, travelling to Spain for them on a number of occasions. On 14 February 1922, he was a passenger in a Bristol machine that crashed at Cuatro Vientos aerodrome near Madrid. Onlookers said that the Bristol appeared to stall in a steep turn over the airfield. Ortweiler and two other men were killed. His body was returned home for burial – he was just eleven days short of his twenty-third birthday.

On the 29th October 1917, the ace Max Müller arrived to fly again with Jasta 2 (Boelcke). He had 31 victories at this time.

VICTORY NO. 21
31 October 1917 SE5a (No.B544) 84 Squadron 1715

Erwin Böhme arrived back at Rumbeke this afternoon following a brief visit to Dessau to attend a ceremony commemorating the first anniversary of Oswald Boelcke's death. Given his part in the great ace's demise, it is hard to imagine the emotions the anniversary must have evoked. After the grave-side ceremony ended, he diverted to Hamburg to visit his girlfriend on 29 October. He proposed, was accepted and left behind a fiancée rather than a girlfriend as he returned to the front. A fiancée, however, he was destined never to see again.

An 84 Squadron patrol, heading for the Roulers-Menin-Courtrai area, took off at 1400 hours – the six aircraft involved led by Captain K M StC G Leask. Although an experienced pilot, having flown two-seaters and later FE8s, he had yet to claim his first victory. In the fighting during this afternoon

Leask claimed to have forced a German machine down out of control but, unfortunately for him, it was not confirmed. 84 Squadron had more than one combat on this day, losing one SE5 at around 1510 over the Roulers-Menin road and another more than an hour later at 1615. Because these were the only two SE5s lost this date, it appears that once again disparities in the Allied and German timings have come down to us.

Böhme had called in to visit Manfred von Richthofen before returning to his Staffel and it was after leaving the Red Baron's base that he coincidentally came across his own command out on patrol. Intending to fall in with his men as they mounted an attack upon Leask's 84 Squadron SE5as, Böhme climbed hard towards the main group. Seeing the isolated Albatros, one of the RFC pilots turned and dived upon it. It was a mis-match, however, an experienced ace against a comparative novice. The contest was soon ended.

Böhme claimed his success south-east of Zillebeke Lake, the SE5a falling either in the front lines or just inside the British lines. The other SE5a lost on the day fell victim to Jasta 36 (Leutnant Heinrich Bongartz's twentieth victory) which fell in German territory south of Roulers.

SECOND LIEUTENANT
GEORGE ROBERT GRAY,
84 SQUADRON, ROYAL FLYING CORPS

Born on 7 May 1898, he was the son of iron foundry owner Andrew Gray and Mary E Gray of 1135 Catherine Street, Victoria, British Columbia, Canada. After the usual training, he was awarded his 'Wings' and appointed a Flying Officer with effect from 27 September 1917. Shot down by Erwin Böhme between Roulers and Menin, he was found to have gun shot wounds to the chest and upper arm as German soldiers pulled him from the wreckage of his SE5a. He was still alive when an ambulance carried him to Kr Laz Burger Hospital but died shortly after arriving there. The announcements concerning his fate were contradictory and must have added to the agonies of his parents. First reported as wounded and prisoner of war, his father actually received a letter from the War Office on 3 January 1918 (more than two months after his death) congratulating him most warmly on his son's safe deliverance and expressing the hope that he would soon recover from his wounds. Furthermore, news was received from the Red Cross on 18 January 1918 to the effect that Gray's name was on a list of POWs incarcerated at Limberg Camp and that he was suffering from wounds to the chest and upper arm. This statement was changed in the following month when he was finally pronounced as having died of his wounds on 31 October 1917. To add to the family's distress and bewilderment, the German announcement in the *Norddeutsche* whilst correctly showing him to have died on 31 October 1917, misspelt his name as 'Grey' and incorrectly identified his machine as a 'Sopwith'. Because of these inaccuracies, Andrew Gray clung, for many months, to the hope that his son was still alive before finally having to accept the fact of his death. The pain and grief appears to have shortened his life as he was dead before the war's end. George Robert Gray is buried in Tourcoing Cemetery, France (Fr1029). Age 19.

VICTORY NO. 22
6 November 1917 Sopwith Camel (No.B2408) 65 Squadron 1150

William Harrison was leading a defensive patrol over Ypres on this winter morning. In his post-war debriefing report following his return from prison camp, he recalled that the weather was very misty and that he and his colleagues had got themselves too far beyond the lines. Before they could get back they were attacked by a veritable flock of

seek where who spied first got in the first fusillade. Harrison may have thought that he had hit Böhme but he was mistaken, Jasta 2 suffered no losses or serious damage.

After his capture, Harrison was taken to Jasta 2's airfield and took coffee with the pilots. Böhme later described him as a very nice person who had defended himself valiantly to the end.

Three of 65 Squadron machines had been brought down in the battle of the clouds, a fact that Harrison could not believe until the names of the other two were read out to him – Second Lieutenant E H Cutbill and Lieutenant E G S Gordon, both, like Harrison, taken prisoner. All three had fallen to Jasta 2 – Leutnant Richard Plange and Vizefeldwebel Paul Bäumer being the other successful pilots. These were 65 Squadron's first losses since arriving in France on 27 October 1917.

SECOND LIEUTENANT
WILLIAM L HARRISON,
CANTERBURY MOUNTED RIFLES AND 65 SQUADRON, ROYAL FLYING CORPS

Originally from Rakaia, Canterbury, New Zealand, he was with his regiment, the Canterbury Mounted Rifles, in Egypt when he was selected for a commission – gazetted on 24 June 1916. An application for transfer to the RFC was approved in the early summer of 1917. An exceptional pupil, he took his flying training in his stride, was awarded his 'Wings' and joined 65 Squadron in Wyton on 22 August 1917. Such was his prowess that he was briefly attached as an assistant instructor on Camels to 85 Squadron before returning to his own 65 Squadron just prior to their departure for France on 27 October 1917. As good a pilot as he undoubtedly was, his operational flying was abruptly ended by Erwin Böhme just ten days after his arrival at the front when he was shot down and taken prisoner on 6 November 1917. Repatriated to the UK on 27 November 1918, he finally relinquished his commission on 30 December 1918 and returned to his native New Zealand.

German fighters. During the ensuing combat the controls of his Camel were disabled but not before he claimed to have downed one of the enemy. His Camel crashed heavily and he suffered back injuries. Böhme recorded a fight in cloud and mist – a game of hide and

VICTORY NO. 23
20 November 1917 Nieuport XVII 5me Escadrille 1030

Clashes with aircraft of the Belgian Aviation Militaire were inevitable over this section of the front. On this occasion, Böhme was leading five aircraft of his Staffel on a mid-morning patrol and encountered Belgian Nieuport Scouts near

Dixmude. As he later wrote, he first saw his victim attempting an attack upon a German observation machine. Despatching the Nieuport with his usual ruthless efficiency, he watched as it fell into the flooded area to the west of Dixmude, between Caeskerke and Oudecapelle. Belgian records show that the pilot had flown as many as fifty-five patrols but that this was only his second actual combat. He was hit twice in the head and three times in the heart – mute if terrible testimony to the German ace's marksmanship.

1ST SERGENT
LEON ANDRÉ ROBERT CISELET,
5/(BELGIUM) ESCADRILLE

Born in Antwerp on 23 May 1892, Robert was one of four brothers all of whom would die as a consequence of their flying service. Robert volunteered early in the war and after serving in the infantry was accepted into the aviation service in 1916. Following training, he arrived at a front line squadron on 24 July 1917 and was promoted to Sergent three days later. A further promotion to 1st Sergent followed on 24 September 1917. Robert's brother, Marcel, flying a Nieuport XVII (6/Escadrille) was killed in action on 18 May 1918, shot down over Houthulst Forest. Brother Maurice was severely injured in the flying service and was invalided out – only to die shortly after the Armistice as a consequence of his injuries. The fourth brother, Charles, would be killed in a flying accident near Antwerp on 1 April 1931. In all, Robert flew 55 combat sorties and was awarded the Croix de Guerre before his fatal last fight with Erwin Böhme. He was also awarded – posthumously – the Chevalier l'Ordre de Leopold. Age 25.

VICTORY NO. 24
29 November 1917 Sopwith Camel ? 1255

This was a particularly busy time over the front and Böhme knew that he would not be able to get leave until the following month. He wrote almost daily to his fiancée, Annamarie. The Third Battle of Ypres had raged since 31 July 1917 and now the Battle of Cambrai was in full swing. On the afternoon of 28 November he again visited his friend and colleague, Manfred von Richthofen, at Avesnes-le-Sec. His last note to Annamarie was on the morning of the following day: *'My love. Now just a quick affectionate morning greeting! The Staffel is already waiting for me. This evening I will write a proper letter to you. Your Erwin.'*

He apparently flew two sorties on this day, the second – his last – during the afternoon.

According to Professor Johannes Werner, the author of a book on Böhme (he also wrote – *Knight of Germany* – with Oswald Boelcke as its subject), the ace gained his 24th victory beyond the front lines above Lake Zillebeke, close to Ypres. The problem here is that the victory was timed at 1255 German time. While this is, patently, in the afternoon, the sortie may well have started in the late morning or soon after noon.

Jasta 2 indeed saw action, but just who their opponents were, remains something of a mystery. It seems that members of his Jasta saw their leader either shoot down an Allied aeroplane, or at least reduce one to a state of serious trouble and apparently going down. Previously speculative references to the victim being a Camel confuse the issue further for, in fact, no

AWFK8 'Big Ack' – the type of machine flown by Lieutenants J A Pattern and P W Leycester (10 Squadron RFC) in the shooting down of Böhme on 29 November 1917.

Erwin Böhme's portrait. The Blue Max was added later. The actual prized insignia of the Pour le Mérite lay undisturbed in its unopened box, awaiting in vain the return of its owner.

victory to Jasta 36. Passchendaele is a little further east than Ypres and inside German lines, hence the Spad had crossed the lines before crashing. There is no obvious connection between the fall of the Spad and Böhme's 'victim' but, equally, it would not be the first – or the last – time a Spad would be confused with a Camel and therefore the vaguest of possibilities exists that this was the one. However, if Böhme's claim time of 1255 (1155 British time) is correct, he must have scored it on his first sortie of the day, for he would not possibly still be in the air by the time the 10 Squadron crew shot him down over three hours later. Nothing quite fits.

Böhme is said to have been shot down by a <u>single</u> 'Big Ack' of 10 Squadron but, again contradictorily and confusingly, a contemporary statement describes how: '... he was enveloped by an enemy fighter squadron and fatally wounded over Zonnebeke.'

The 10 Squadron AWFK8 (B324) credited with Böhme's destruction was crewed by Second Lieutenants John Arthur Pattern, from Leeds, and Philip Wrey Leycester, from Ennismore, Cork. Both would go on to survive the war. They had left their base at 1445 to take panoramic photos of Polderhoek Chat and Becelaere. By 1500 hours, they had exposed 14 photographic plates but were interrupted in their labours by the arrival of three German fighters swooping down upon them from clouds at 14,000 feet above Zonnebeke. Leycester immediately left his camera, grabbed his Lewis gun and commenced firing. After just one short burst, the leading Albatros erupted into flames. The two other German scouts sheered away, before following their burning colleague down until he crashed into the ground below. The smashed and burnt Albatros DVa was recorded and located by the British as number G.92, map reference D.23.c. Erwin Böhme was buried in the cemetery at Keerslaarhoek, and accorded full military honours by the British.

Camels were lost or seriously damaged on the day. A DH5 was shot-up in the air but managed to land at its base at 0925 hours – too early to be placed in the frame as a possibility.

Only two single-seaters failed to return on this day; a Spad in mid-afternoon and an SE5 in mid-morning. The Spad, a 19 Squadron machine (A6758), fell at 1535 British time inside British lines near to Passchendaele and was credited as a

Böhme's conquerors were:

SECOND LIEUTENANT
JOHN ARTHUR PATTERN,
10 SQUADRON, ROYAL FLYING CORPS

Born in Leeds on 31 July 1892, he was the son of electrical engineer Miles Pattern and Mrs Pattern of 86 Churchill Road, Great Yarmouth, Norfolk. Educated at St Paul's College, Cheltenham. After completing his education, he became an assistant school master, teaching at Cobham School, Yarmouth. Enlisted as a private soldier (Number PS 6089) into the 19th (2nd Public Schools) Battalion, Royal Fusiliers. Served in France from November 1915 but then, in May 1916, the battalion was brought back to the UK with most of the men dispersed to Officer Cadet Battalions. Pattern was ordered to Number 5 OCB, then at Trinity College, Cambridge, from whence he was gazetted Second Lieutenant to the Special Lists on 26 September 1916. An application to join the RFC successful, he was ordered to Reading on 9 October 1916. Awarded his 'Wings', he was sent out to join 10 Squadron at the front on 2 May 1917. On the day before their encounter with Erwin Böhme, Pattern and Leycester, flying AWFK (B227), received damage to their machine from ground-based machine-gun fire although they themselves were uninjured (this was Philip Leycester's first operational flight!). Transferred briefly to 21 Squadron as a Flight Commander in December 1917 before returning to 10 Squadron in the following month. Slightly injured on 16 February 1918 when he hit some trees returning from a night bombing raid. Wounded in action on 25 February 1918, he was finally relieved of operational flying duties in May 1918, spending the remainder of the war instructing.

LIEUTENANT
PHILIP WREY LEYCESTER,
(LATER MBE, MA), ARMY SERVICE CORPS
AND 10 SQUADRON, ROYAL FLYING CORPS

The third son of Joseph William Leycester DL and Mrs Leycester of Ennismore, County Cork, Ireland, he was born on 16 November 1894. Educated at Rugby School (1908-13) and at Oriel College, Oxford. Gazetted Second Lieutenant to the Army Service Corps on 24 October 1914. Served for two years with the 1st Cavalry Division in France. Successfully applied for transfer to the RFC and was posted to Reading on 12 August 1917. Completing his observer training, he joined 10 Squadron at the front on 28 November 1917. On only his second operational flight, he shot down and killed the German ace, Erwin Böhme. Returned to the Home Establishment in May 1918. Promoted to the rank of Captain, he spent the remainder of the war training aspiring observers. After the Armistice, he was sent to the British Military Mission in South Russia and gazetted a Staff Officer. Relinquished his commission on 14 March 1919. Awarded the MBE for valuable services in South Russia, *London Gazette* of 11 November 1919. Entered the Civil Service and married Aileen Lilian Goold-Adams of Glanmire, County Cork in 1921. Served again in the Second World War, appointed as an adviser to the Military Mission in Egypt with the local rank of Lieutenant Colonel. Relinquished his commission on 20 November 1946 – granted honorary rank of Major. Lived, post-war, at 'Perry's', West Hill, Ottery St Mary's, Devon. Died 1963.

Erwin Böhme had been notified that he had been awarded the Pour le Mérite on 24 November 1917. Still lying unopened on his desk back at the airfield was the case containing the insignia of the Blue Max he had fought so long and so hard for. Death had cheated him of the opportunity of ever wearing it or of marrying his dear fiancée, Annamarie Brüning.

CHAPTER 2

OBERLEUTNANT MAX MÜLLER

Vizefeldwebel Max Müller before he became a fighter pilot. He wears the insignia of the Iron Cross 2nd Class and the Bavarian Military Merit Cross with Crown and Swords. The ribbon on his breast signifies the Prince Regent Luitpold Medal in Bronze. *(Neal O'Connor)*

Max Müller was born in Rottenburg, Lower Bavaria, on the New Year's day of 1887. He enlisted into the German army some time before the commencement of the Great War and as a highly skilled motor mechanic and driver was, in 1913, appointed to act as chauffeur to the Bavarian War Minister. Physically, he was unusually small in stature, being only 5 foot 1 inch tall. Avidly interested in aviation, he began to pester his illustrious passenger with requests that he be allowed to transfer into the air service.

Müller's overtures finally succeeded and he was sent to the flying school at Schleissheim on 1 December 1913, one month before his 27th birthday. He soon picked up the art of piloting an aeroplane, being awarded his Bavarian pilot's badge on 4 April in the following year. Once war began in August, he was sent to join Flieger Abteilung 1b (the 'b' denoting a Bavarian unit). On the evening of 18 August, his engine failed on take-off and the resulting crash caused both his legs to be broken.

Eventually recovering from his injuries, he returned to FA1b but, whilst piloting an Otto CI pusher-type two-seater, he and his observer were forced down in a fight with a French Farman. Once again he found himself in hospital with yet more broken bones. This time, however, he had the consolation of receiving the Iron Cross 2nd Class on 13 September 1915 – the first of many awards.

1915 saw Müller promoted twice, but remaining within the non-commissioned ranks. Further decorations came his way, first the Iron Cross 1st Class was followed by the Bavarian Military Merit Cross, 3rd Class with Crown and Swords. Following an important photo-reconnaissance sortie in difficult circumstances on 13 December

1915, he was awarded the Bavarian Bravery Medal in Silver – one of only 17 airmen to receive this decoration during WW1 (five airmen received the Gold award). The Bavarian Government had obviously taken particular note of this NCO and marked him out for distinction beyond the norm. The reconnaissance was necessary in order to secure urgently needed photographs of the French positions west of Péronne, along the banks of the Somme. Müller would have to fly at an extremely low level to be sure of pinpointing them exactly. Inevitably this low-level flying exposed him to heavy and almost continuous ground fire but despite the danger and difficulties Max brought home the bacon! The photographs were later deemed extremely valuable for the furtherance of ground operations in this sector. It is unclear whether or not he flew with an observer – no one else is mentioned in connection with the sortie – and bearing in mind the high level of award considered appropriate, it seems probable that he did, indeed, fly out alone. His coolness in taking precise photographs whilst at the same time piloting his machine at extreme low level under fire was quite remarkable.

Having made a name for himself as a skilled and aggressive airmen, Müller was soon switched to single-seaters. He was amongst the first to fly operationally the Fokker Eindecker, a fighter now being sent to FA units for scouting and protection. This switch led to a posting to Kampfeinsitzer-Kommando B, which, in May 1916, would become Abwehrkommando Nord of FFA32. Despite not scoring an official victory with this unit, Müller's record was still good enough to get him a posting to Jasta 1 in August 1916, at the time when the 'talent spotters' were combing the air service for the élite which would populate the newly formed Jasta units.

However, before he could take up this new position, the movement order was changed and he was instead directed to Oswald Boelcke's Jasta 2, reporting for duty on 1 September. Scout machines were still few in number in the early days and had to be shared around, but the experience Müller would gain by rubbing shoulders with the likes of the great Boelcke himself, not to mention emerging talents like Manfred von Richthofen, Erwin Böhme, Hans Imelmann, Otto Höhne, Leopold Rudolf Reimann and Erich König, would stand him in good stead in the future.

Oswald Boelcke deliberately imbued a hunting, sporting, ethos into the proceedings of the Jasta, encouraging the natural competitive instincts of the young men under his command to look upon their grim and deadly purpose as some sort of game, with 'scores' to be accumulated and glory and accolades accruing to the swiftest, the strongest, the bravest.

Max Müller achieved his first 'kill' on 10 October, the second falling ten days later. By the end of November his score had risen to five. In the new year of 1917, he was posted to Jasta 28(w), essentially a Würrtemberg unit but one commanded by a fellow Bavarian, Oberleutnant Rudolf Lang. Lang had commanded Jasta 11 before being relieved by Manfred von Richthofen. Regrettably, from the German Air Service's point of view, Jasta 11 had enjoyed little success under Lang's bailiwick, in fact its record was frankly dismal. Now Jasta 28 was also under-achieving under Lang, indeed the first ever victory gained by the squadron fell to Max Müller – his sixth – on 7 April 1917.

Lang was again relieved, this time by yet another Jasta 11 success-story, Karl-Emil Schäfer, one of von Richthofen's star pupils, who had achieved a startling 23 victories thus far. Under the new leadership, Müller in particular began making frequent claims and by mid-June had been credited with 18 victories. The relatively newly arrived Commanding Officer, Schäfer, was killed in action on 4 June 1917, brought down by the FE2ds of 20 Squadron shortly after registering his 30th victory.

Opposite: Max Müller in combat with a 23 Squadron Spad on 7 June 1917. Second Lieutenant G C Stead survived as a prisoner of war, and the German ace had secured his 15th victory.

Müller's star continued in the ascendancy and even further rewards came to the Bavarian NCO; the next to arrive being the Würrtemberg Gold Military Merit Medal, announced on 28 June 1917. A month later came one of the most unique and exclusive awards of the First World War. On 14 July 1917, the State of Prussia gave Müller the Member's Cross with Swords of the Royal Hohenzollern House Order. This should not be confused with the more usual officers' 'House Order' – the Members' Crosses was meant exclusively for NCO recipients. In all, only 16 Members' Crosses with Swords were presented throughout the war, ten of which went to airmen.

Through August 1917 Müller's successes continued and on three separate occasions he achieved two victories on a single day, bringing his total to 26. A unique distinction followed this singular achievement when he became the first NCO, ever, to be given a Regular Army commission. Up until then, rankers were given commissions only in the Reserve Army. Now, too, with his score well over the twenty mark, he was recommended for the ultimate award – the Orden Pour le Mérite, which was almost immediately approved, the announcement coming on 3 September 1917.

Müller continued to break new ground when, shortly afterwards, he was awarded the Bavarian Gold Bravery Medal which, although only usually bestowed upon NCOs, was, exceptionally, presented to him as an officer. The recommendation had taken time to find its way through the system and, when it was approved, he had already been commissioned. Thus Müller became the first – and only – airman in WW1 to hold both the Silver and Gold Bravery Medals.

Viewing the little maestro's victories in retrospect, it has to be said that there are an unusual number of the questionable variety. Given all of the well known difficulties and confusion involved in attributing individual successes to particular pilots, still, as a general rule, the Imperial German Air Service was careful – meticulous even – in assembling evidence before awarding confirmation. Two German aces whose victories have given us recurring and often insoluble problems are Herman Göring (see *Under the Guns of the German Aces*) and Max Müller. Perhaps the fact that the Bavarian NCO had been built up as a working class 'super-star' by the propaganda peddlers – his career attracting more than its fair share of attention – made for a lessening in the normally strict application of criteria for the confirmation of claims.

After bringing his score to 29 in October 1917, he was sent back to his old unit, Jasta 2, now more familiarly known as Jasta Boelcke, after its late and great first commanding officer. Müller was, by this time, amongst the first ranks of fighter pilots of the Imperial German Air Service, a national hero. When Heinrich Gontermann was killed at the end of October 1917, it left Manfred von Richthofen and Müller as the leading living aces, although Richthofen, having by then scored 61 confirmed victories, was way ahead of the Bavarian's 29.

Erwin Böhme was, currently, the commander of Jasta Boelcke. Given his fine record, it was perhaps surprising that Müller had not been given his own command, but then, his was only a very recent commission. Müller began scoring with his new unit during November. Then Böhme was killed on 29 November 1917 – an event which undoubtedly had a sobering effect on Müller as, indeed, it did on so many others of the air fighting clique. Müller had seen the great Boelcke fall and now Böhme had gone, revered comrades forever enjoined in the events of 13 months earlier when the collision between the two men's machines had resulted in the former's death. Walter von Bülow-Bothkamp arrived to take over command of Jasta Boelcke. He already had 28 victories and held the Blue Max. Müller brought his score to 36 in

Opposite: Müller
was shot down
and killed on 6
January 1918
whilst attacking an
RE8 of 21
Squadron, flown
by Captain G F W
Zimmer and
Lieutenant H A
Sommerville MC.

December 1917. The Bavarian military authorities now contemplated bestowing the Military Max-Joseph Order on their famous compatriot. There is anecdotal evidence that a Knight's Badge of the Order was actually selected from the stock within the Orders Chancery in anticipation of the announcement. However, Müller had yet to receive the intermediate Bavarian Military Merit Order – normally a pre-requisite prior to the bestowal of the ultimate award. To correct this procedural chain, Müller was awarded the Military Merit Order, 4th Class with Swords on 18 December 1917. The way was now clear for the eventual award of the ultimate tribute.

Then von Bülow-Bothkamp was shot down and killed six days into the new year. Müller, still with no further advance on his 36 victories, was given command of the Jasta, at least in the air. Apparently, some Prussians were reluctant to accept a Bavarian as commanding officer of one of their crack squadrons and so he was given temporary command until matters could be resolved, one way or another. Either another (Prussian) Staffelführer would be brought in or the problem would be solved by moving Müller to the command of a Bavarian Jasta, thus sparing the blushes of all concerned.

The issue would be resolved with cruel finality on the morning of 9 January 1918, when the Bavarian's body was moved to St Joseph's Church in Courtrai and placed under a guard of honour. From there it was taken to his home town of Rothenburg ob der Tauber, before being laid to rest in the local cemetery.

Not so clear cut, however, were the circumstances surrounding the outstanding matter of the award of the Max-Joseph Order. The resolution of this event had to wait until after the war had ended. The actual date of the award remains unclear but it occurred some time during the early months of 1919, although, of course, it was actually back-dated to November 1917 – to the time that Max Müller had achieved his 30th victory, in fact. (This has sometimes led historians to the mistaken belief that he received the award whilst he was still alive.) And so, albeit belatedly, Max Müller – the former Bavarian NCO airman who, exceptionally, had been raised to the rank of Leutnant in the Regular Army – posthumously became Max Ritter (Knight) von Müller.

Müller had been one of the most highly decorated men in the Imperial Armed Forces of the Kaiser. In fact, only Manfred von Richthofen amongst the fighter pilot élite, received more honours. The little Bavarian was awarded twelve distinctions of one sort or another, including (not previously mentioned) the Prinzregent Luitpold Medal in Bronze from Bavaria, and the Long Service Distinction, 3rd Class, also from Bavaria.

VICTORY NO. 1
10 October 1916 DH2 (No. A2540) 24 Squadron 1100

Norman Middlebrook, the captured pilot of this machine, was repatriated in December 1918. In his post-war debriefing he said that he and the patrol had taken off from Bertangles and, once over the lines, he had followed his squadron commander in an attack upon enemy aircraft. In the ensuing action, Middlebrook, was, in turn, counter-attacked from the rear, receiving a hit in the emergency fuel tank upon which his engine was currently running – the main (bottom) tank having already run dry. Starved of fuel, the engine stopped and he was forced to make a landing behind the German lines and give himself up as a prisoner.

Middlebrook's squadron commander was none other than Major Lanoe Hawker VC DSO, although the patrol on 10 October was

SECOND LIEUTENANT
NORMAN MIDDLEBROOK,
6/RIFLE BRIGADE AND 24 SQUADRON, ROYAL FLYING CORPS

The younger son of solicitor E H Middlebrook and Mrs Middlebrook of 4, Woodrhydding, Ilkley, Yorkshire and the nephew of Sir William Middlebrook MP, he was born on 8 August 1897. Educated at Starncliffe Hall Preparatory School, at Repton (1911-14), where he was a member of the OTC and at Pembroke College, Cambridge. He left Cambridge prematurely to join up and was commissioned to the 6th (Reserve) Battalion, Rifle Brigade on 28 January 1915. Norman's older brother, John, also an officer in the Rifle Brigade (12th Battalion) would be awarded a Military Cross in the *London Gazette* of 3 June 1918. Accepted for training with the RFC, Norman first reported to Reading on 19 June 1916. Gained a Royal Aero Club Certificate (Number 3352) on 16 August 1916. After formally qualifying, he was awarded his 'Wings' and posted to 24 Squadron in France on 28 September 1916. A mere twelve days later he had the misfortune to run into Max Müller, so to become the ace's first victim. Initially reported as 'Missing in Action', his parents were delighted to learn more than two weeks later on 26 October 1916 that he had been taken prisoner. Repatriated on 18 December 1918, he was finally demobilised on 12 April 1919. Entered the motor trade in the early post-war years, working for Castlehouse, Vasey and Company, motor engineers, of Scarborough, taking up residence at 75 Norwood Street in that town. Volunteered for the RAFVR in October 1941.

actually led by Captain J O Andrews MC. Records indicate that the patrol had reached Beaulencourt when the engagement began. During the fight, Hawker, who was present, saw a German machine dive on one of the De Havillands which went down too quickly for him to attempt to come to its aid, the attacking German pilot diving away eastwards and beyond his range.

Middlebrook's DH went down at around 10 am British time – 11 am German time. German time was one hour ahead of Allied time and would remain so until 25 March 1917.

VICTORY NO.2
20 October 1916 BE12 (No. 6608) 21 Squadron 1750 (?)

A patrol from 21 Squadron, operating with the fighter version of the BE2c (the observer's cockpit covered over and with a Lewis machine gun mounted on the top wing) took off at 1130 hours. The occupant of '6608', Second Lieutenant Creery, was last seen diving over Bapaume and subsequently failed to return.

There is an obvious discrepancy in the times, for there is certainly no way that Creery could still be airborne at 1750 (1650 Allied time) – over five hours after he took off. Müller's victim did come down inside German lines and so there must have been a wreck to inspect and, as there are no apparent British losses in the afternoon, it would appear that the recorded German time of 1750 is in error. The kill was reported down south-west of Grevillers Wood, which is just to the west of Bapaume. In the circumstances, one suspects that the '1750' was, in reality, '1250', a badly written '2' becoming, in transcription, a '7' – no other scenario fits. Jasta 2 had also been in action earlier that morning, Boelcke and Böhme claiming two 11 Squadron FEs.

SECOND LIEUTENANT
CUTHBERT JOHN CREERY,
21 SQUADRON, ROYAL FLYING CORPS

The second son of Andrew McCreight Creery and Anna Creery (née Hulbert) of 1389 Jervis Street, Vancouver, British Columbia, Canada. Educated at University School, Victoria and at McGill University, Toronto, Canada. Cuthbert's father, a relative of the Bell-Irvings, was employed by H Bell-Irving and Company, insurance and real estate brokers in Vancouver. Cuthbert decided to volunteer and enlisted as a trooper in the 11/Canadian Mounted Rifles. Initially, he had intended to join the Royal Naval Air Services and consequently learnt to fly at his own expense, gaining the North American version of the Royal Aero Club Certificate (Number AM363) on 24 November 1915 – the certificate of competence signed by no less an aviation personage than Orville Wright. In the event, however, Cuthbert was gazetted Second Lieutenant to the RFC on 15 December 1915, arriving in London from Canada on 4 January 1916. Joining 21 Squadron in Netheravon, he accompanied the unit on its first entry into France on 23 January 1916. He was injured in a flying accident in early

Memorial Service to commemorate 'Cuthy' (far right) and his cousin, Sam. *(Elizabeth O'Kiely/John Creery, Vancouver)*

ST. PAUL'S CHURCH
VANCOUVER

✝

𝔐emorial 𝔖ervice
AT 4.30 P.M.
WEDNESDAY, NOVEMBER 1, 1916
ALL SAINTS' DAY

Cuthbert John Creery,
2nd Lieut., 21st Squadron, Royal Flying Corps,
Killed in action on the Somme Front, October 20, 1916.
and his cousin,

Samuel Bristow Stevenson
2nd Lieut., 138th Siege Battery, R.G.A.
Died of malaria at Saloniki, September 29, 1916.

*"Why seek ye the living among the dead?
He is not here, but is risen."*

May 1916 – cut lip and slight facial abrasions – recovering in the Red Cross Hospital at Le Touquet before returning to his Squadron on 21 May 1916. After his fatal crash, the Germans buried Creery and carefully recorded his grave site. Given precise information including the map reference – Map Sheet Albert (1/40,000) :

J13/B.7.5. the area of Heilly, Méricourt l'Abbé – it was hardly surprising that the grave was subsequently located by Captain (later Lieutenant Colonel) Duncan Bell-Irving MC, Gordon Highlanders attached RFC, acting on behalf of the Creery family. The remains were re-interred in Heilly Station Cemetery, France (Fr833). Age 21.

VICTORY NO.3
3 November 1916 FE2b (No. 7026) 22 Squadron 1520

This 22 Squadron 'pusher' took off at 1337, a member of a photographic reconnaissance mission. A letter later received from the captured observer advised that their machine had been attacked by three German aircraft and riddled with machine-gun bullets. The pilot, Lord Lucas, was hit in the back of the head and in the left leg, causing him to lapse into unconsciousness. The FE's engine stopped and the machine began to side-slip towards a headlong crash. The observer letter-writer, Irishman Lieutenant Alex Anderson, survived the impact with just a slight injury over one eye and a strained back. His pilot never regained consciousness and died at about 4 o'clock in the afternoon (ie. 5 pm German time). In March 1917, the noble Lord's grave – marked with the classic Germanic cross – was located by soldiers of the 5th Australian Division (Map reference -Sheet 57 CSW, 0.9.d.8.5.).

Müller recorded his victim as having fallen south-east of Bapaume, near Haplincourt. Two other of the escorting squadron FEs were also shot down by varying claimants. The British Official History states that Anderson somehow took over the controls and brought the machine in to land but it has to be pointed out that he signally fails to mention this important fact in the letter describing the circumstances of the shooting down – surely he would have been only too proud to have claimed the credit for any such action?

CAPTAIN
THE RIGHT HONOURABLE LORD LUCAS (AUBERON THOMAS HERBERT)
MID, HAMPSHIRE CARABINEERS YEOMANRY AND 22 SQUADRON, ROYAL FLYING CORPS

The 8th Baron Lucas and the 11th Baron Dingwall, Auberon Thomas Herbert was born on 25 May 1876, the second son of Hon Auberon Edward William Molyneux Herbert MP and Mrs Herbert of Picket Post, Ringwood, Hampshire and the first cousin of the 6th and 8th Earls of Portsmouth. He was educated at Bedford Grammar School and at Balliol College, Oxford (1895-99) where he captained the College Eight and rowed 7 in the Oxford boats of 1898 and 1899. Soon after leaving Oxford he was gazetted to the Hampshire Yeomanry and was a *Times* correspondent in the South African War where he was wounded and, as a consequence, had a leg amputated below the knee. After the Boer War he entered politics. In 1905 he succeeded his uncle, the 7th Earl Cowper KG, as 8th Baron Lucas (England) and 11th Baron Dingwall (Scotland). Appointed Private Secretary to the Secretary of State for War (Mr Haldane) in 1907. Served as Under-Secretary of State for War from 1908 to 1911 and as Under-Secretary for the Colonies in 1911. Next he was appointed as Parliamentary Secretary to the Board of

LORD LUCAS AND DINGWALL.

14 Squadron, he accompanied the unit to its first operational posting with the Mediterranean Expeditionary Force in Egypt in November 1915. He built up his flying hours considerably in the Middle East, receiving a Mention in Despatches for his outstanding service. Upon his return to England, he spent some months instructing new flying aspirants at Dover before being offered command of his own squadron. He refused the offer of a command, feeling that he had insufficient experience of flying on the Western Front – something, he realised, that was an entirely different proposition to operational aviation in Egypt. Joined 22 Squadron in France as a Flight Commander in October 1916 and very soon afterwards his self-proclaimed inexperience was fatally exposed to the still emerging but extraordinarily deadly talents of Max Müller. In the words of the Official History, *The War in the Air*, page 314: *'Bright intervals on 3 November, brought out many German fighters. Five of our aeroplanes were shot down during the day, three of them from a photographic formation of Number 22 Squadron led by Captain Lord Lucas who it was afterwards known, had been attacked by three enemy pilots and shot in the head and leg. His aeroplane was landed by the wounded observer, Lieutenant A Anderson. Lord Lucas never regained consciousness after he was hit, and died the same day. He had lost a leg from wounds received in the South African War........He was the oldest in years, but youngest in heart, of all the pilots of his squadron. Of the four officers in the two aeroplanes shot down with him, one was killed and two were wounded. Two of them had fallen, with their machine, on to an enemy kite balloon on the ground and set it on fire'*. A footnote to this tells us that the death of Lord Lucas is commemorated in a poem, In Memoriam. A H, by the Hon Maurice Baring, Aide de Camp to Lord Trenchard:

O liberal heart fast-rooted to the soil,
O lover of ancient freedom and proud toil,
Friend of the gipsies and all
wandering song,

Agriculture, 1911 to 1914. Made Privy Councillor in 1912. A member of Prime Minister Herbert Asquith's Cabinet in 1914, he held the office of President of the Board of Agriculture. In May 1915, when the coalition government was formed, he was one of the ministers who resigned. Immediately after his resignation and despite his infirmity, he sought an appointment to the Royal Flying Corps. Qualified first as an observer before gaining his Royal Aero Club Certificate (Number 1747) on 2 September 1915. Following completion of his formal pilot training, he was appointed a Flying Officer later in the same year. A founder member of

*The forests' nursling and the
favoured child
Of woodlands wild –
O brother to the birds and all things
free,
Captain of liberty!*

*Deep in your heart the restless seed
was sown;
The vagrant spirit fretted in your feet;
We wondered could you tarry long,
And brook for long the cramping street,*

*Or would you one day sail for shores
unknown
And shake from you the dust of towns,
and spurn
The crowded market-place –
and not return.*

*You found a sterner guide;
You heard the guns. Then, to the distant fire,
Your dreams were laid aside;
And on that day, you cast your heart's
desire
Upon a burning pyre;
You gave your service to the exalted need,
Until at last from bondage freed.*

*At liberty to serve as you loved best,
You chose the noblest way.
God did the rest.*

The German Air Service confirmed his demise early in December 1916. Advancing Australian troops found his grave in the spring of 1917 and he was eventually re-interred in the Honourable Artillery Company Cemetery, Ecoust-St Mein, France (Fr568). Age 39.

The democracy of death. The 8th Baron Lucas and 11th Baron Dingwall, the Right Honourable Auberon Thomas Herbert lies alongside Gunners of the Royal Artillery in the HAC Cemetery. An equality of sacrifice.

LIEUTENANT
ALEXANDER ANDERSON,
4/CONNAUGHT RANGERS AND 22 SQUADRON, ROYAL FLYING CORPS

Born on 30 September 1895, he was the son of Alexander and Mrs Anderson of Galway, Ireland. Gazetted Second Lieutenant to the 4th Reserve Battalion of The Connaught Rangers on 20 November 1914. Promoted to Lieutenant on 10 March 1916 and seconded for service at the front with a trench mortar battery shortly before successfully applying for a transfer to the RFC which occurred on 7 June 1916. Sent to 22 Squadron in France as a probationary upon completion of his training, he was formally appointed and confirmed as a Flying Officer (observer) on 2 November 1916 – the day before he was shot down and taken prisoner. He was eventually repatriated on 16 December 1918, arriving in the port of Leith on the following day. Served in a number of capacities, being posted to various training units until, in August 1919, he was seconded to administration duties at the Inter-Allied Control Commission with which organisation he served until leaving the RAF on 10 September 1921.

VICTORY NO.4
16 November 1916 BE2e (No. 7080) 9 Squadron 1045

The crew of this BE were engaged on an artillery observation mission (ArtObs), having taken off at 0830. They were flying at 5,000 feet in a cloudless sky – a mixed blessing for although they could see perfectly well to carry out their duties, so too could they be seen from a distance by marauding enemy scouts. Furthermore, clouds were often very handy bolt holes and hiding places!

Arriving over the front, they called up the 145th Siege Battery to orchestrate a shoot against a German gun position. Only one round had been fired – its fall remaining unobserved – when the BE was attacked by a German fighter over Le Transloy. The two-seater was hit in many places and the observer wounded. The pilot had no choice but to dive steeply for the lines and British air space.

During the whole episode several other hostile aircraft had been observed flying around Le Transloy and over the Bapaume-Péronne road, then westward towards the British lines. Somehow, Hyde managed to evade them all and succeeded in getting his damaged machine down inside friendly territory where his observer's wounds could be seen to.

Müller timed his fight at 1045, noting the fall of the aircraft to be inside British lines near Flers. Hyde landed at 0955 (1055 German time) which gave him ten minutes to get back and down. German front-line observers could confirm that the BE had, indeed, come down and although the claim was originally formally noted as 'zwdl' (forced to land) this must have been changed as the Bavarian's fourth victory was soon afterwards duly confirmed. (Suggestions that Müller may have shot down a 7 Squadron BE have been discounted by the writers because that machine's last wireless message was timed at 1032 (ie. 1132 German time), a long way past Müller's 1045. Furthermore, Beaumont Hamel, where the 7 Squadron machine came down, is a long way west of either Le Transloy or Flers.)

LIEUTENANT
CHARLES WALTER HYDE,
ROYAL GARRISON ARTILLERY AND 9 SQUADRON, ROYAL FLYING CORPS

Born in Olwin, Birmingham on 29 July 1895. Gazetted Second Lieutenant to the Royal Garrison Artillery on 25 November 1914.

Lt Charles Walter Hyde.

LIEUTENANT
JAMES VINCENT BARRY,
ROYAL ARMY SERVICE CORPS AND
9 SQUADRON, ROYAL FLYING CORPS

Born in Dulwich, London, on 1 December 1892, he was the son of H and Mrs Barry of 50 Castletown Road, West Kensington, London. Educated at Felsted School (1905-06) where he was a member of the OTC. After completing his schooling he trained as an accountant at the Southampton offices of the United Dominions Trust Ltd. Very soon after the war started, he enlisted in the 16th (Public Schools) Battalion, Middlesex Regiment on 11 September 1914. Gazetted Second Lieutenant to the Army Service Corps on 16 November 1914, serving in the UK at Aldershot, Pangbourne, Hyde and Borden before proceeding to France on 25 August 1915, joining the Headquarters (190) Company, 23rd Division. His application to join the RFC successful, he was next sent for observer training on 27 July 1916. Barry was severely wounded in the clash with Max Müller which resulted in the amputation of his right leg on 3 January 1917. Because a number of limbless men continued to serve in combat roles with the RFC, the authorities were at first apparently reluctant to assume that Barry could not. Finally, on 14 January 1918, it was accepted that he was permanently incapacitated and fit only for office work. Awarded a gratuity of £250, he was posted as Acting Adjutant to Number 1 (T) Wireless School at a training division on 18 January 1918. He was, at this time, living at 8a Longridge Road, Earl's Court, London. After leaving the service in 1919, he returned to his job with UDT, married and fathered a son, Harry Vincent Barry, who, eventually, also attended Felsted (1932-36). James Vincent Barry never fully recovered his health after his encounter with Max Müller and died at Bournemouth on 6 June 1931 at the early age of 38.

Qualified for the Royal Aero Club Certificate (Number 2246) on 16 November 1915. Subsequently awarded his 'Wings' and sent out to join 9 Squadron in France. Unhurt in the clash with Max Müller, he was shortly afterwards promoted to the rank of temporary Captain and Flight Commander (25 November 1916). By the war's end Hyde was a Major in the Royal Air Force.

VICTORY NO. 5
27 November 1916 Nieuport XVII (No. A281) 60 Squadron

As we progress through the Müller victory list, we will come to claims that prove difficult or even impossible to reconcile with records of Allied losses, circumstances or events. This next, number five on the list, is just one of those irreconcilables.

Whilst there is no doubt that Jasta 2 aircraft were in combat with the Nieuport Scouts of 60 Squadron on this day, the RFC squadron losing Captain G A Parker DSO MC in the fight, Parker's scalp, however, was justifiably claimed by Werner Voss (see our *Under the Guns of the German Aces*). Parker's machine fell near to Miraumont, in the German lines. Müller's claim specified an aircraft going down into the Allied lines,

thus eliminating any possible confusion with Parker's exit. It has to be assumed that Müller must have thought that the machine he engaged dived away so desperately to escape his unwelcome attentions, that it had to have been critically damaged. The location he gave for his imagined victim's crash-site was Hébuterne, some eight kilometres north-west of Miraumont, some way inside British lines.

In point of fact, Parker's was the only Nieuport to be lost (or even damaged) on this date – the grand total of losses for the day being just three. Parker's Nieuport aside, the other two were a BE and an FE – both of which went down after mid-day.

VICTORY NO 6
7 April 1917 FE2d (No. A6400) 20 Squadron 1820

Müller had been sent to Jasta 28 on 24 January 1917, moving from Böblingen to Marcke aerodrome, near Courtrai, on the same day. His new CO, Oberleutnant Rudolf Lang, a former Jasta 11 man, felt he needed time to fashion his new unit into a fighting team and was, apparently, not particularly anxious to seek out trouble in the meantime. It was not, therefore, until 26 March 1917 when Jasta 28 moved to Wasquehal (under the aegis of the German 6th Army) that seriously aggressive operations began.

On 7 April 1917, 20 Squadron mounted a bomb raid during the afternoon. Their return route took them over the Tourcoing – Ploegsteert area where they ran into a group of German fighters, one of which was distinctively coloured red with green wings.

The bombing raid had been led by Captain G J Mahony-Jones (A1961) and he had actually re-crossed the lines at the head of his returning group when he saw, behind him, one of his machines in trouble. He immediately turned back into German

territory and helped to drive off the attacking Albatros (Müller's it transpired) but in doing so left himself wide open to attack by a Jasta 18 Albatros flown by Leutnant Walter von Bülow. Mahoney-Jones and his observer, Lieutenant W B Moyes, went down in flames, both being killed.

Yet another of the 20 Squadron pilots, Lieutenant Robertson, subsequently reported seeing three Albatros Scouts during his return flight from the bombing raid on Mouveaux aerodrome north-east of Tourcoing. Robertson and his observer, Second Lieutenant L G Fauvel, attacked one of the scouts. Later reports said that a red and green Albatros was seen low down and trailing smoke.

The combined efforts of their comrades had, partially at least, saved Lawson and Hampson. Both crewmen were wounded – Hampson mortally so. Despite his wounds, Lawson brought down his FE inside British lines, crash-landing south of Ploegsteert Wood.

Müller in front of his Jasta 28 Albatros DV prior to being awarded the Blue Max.

This was Max Müller's first victory as a member of Jasta 28; indeed, it was the entire Jasta's first victory – confirmed as such even though the FE went down on the British side of the lines. It was also the first successful action by the Bavarian during the terrible month which the RFC would always remember as 'Bloody April'.

SECOND LIEUTENANT
JAMES LAWSON,
20 SQUADRON, ROYAL FLYING CORPS

The son of Mr and Mrs Lawson of 10 Sunnyside Road, Smithills, Bolton, Lanca-

shire, he was born on 15 September 1895. Educated at Bolton Grammar School. After completing his education, he obtained a position with a local firm as an apprentice raw cotton salesman. He enlisted into the 21st (4th Public Schools) Battalion of the Royal Fusiliers (Number 2942) on 6 October 1914. Accompanied his battalion to France in November 1915. The whole battalion was withdrawn from the line in March 1916 and upon returning home, was posted to Pembroke College, Cambridge, to form what was, in effect, an officer cadet training unit. Gazetted Second Lieutenant to the Special List to be employed with the RFC on 5 August 1916. Awarded his 'Wings' and appointed a Flying Officer on 25 January 1917. On 7 April 1917, he and his observer were on a bombing raid over Lille when they were engaged by a covey of enemy fighter planes which included one piloted by Max Müller. Lawson was hit by machine-gun fire – a bullet lodging in his left shoulder, another passing through his right arm whilst a third furrowed through the flesh of his side. His observer, Harold Hampson – a former Liverpool Jock who had first arrived at the front in November 1914 – despite receiving what would prove to be mortal wounds, fought on valiantly. So valiantly, in fact, that the crippled pair were able to hold off Müller sufficiently to effect not only their escape but also a return to base. After landing, both wounded men were taken to hospital. Happily, Lawson would survive. His wounds healed, he was next posted to 72 Squadron then in Netheravon. At first he was employed in a non-flying capacity but later, with effect from 10 August 1917, he was declared fit for home flying service and took up duties as a flying instructor – still with 72 Squadron. Did not return to operational flying and survived the war.

SECOND LIEUTENANT
HAROLD NORMAN HAMPSON,
4/SOUTH LANCASHIRE REGIMENT AND
20 SQUADRON, ROYAL FLYING CORPS

Harold Hampson's war grave – Bailleul Cemetery Extension, France.

From Wallasey, Cheshire, he was a pre-war volunteer in the 10th (Scottish) Battalion, King's Liverpool Regiment, having attested on 11 November 1912. Mobilised in August 1914, he accompanied – as a piper – the original contingent of the Liverpool Scottish to France on 1 November 1914, thus qualifying for the award of the 1914 Star. After service at the front, during which time he was wounded, he was selected for officer training with the Inns of Court OTC (Number 6/3/7637) on 18 November 1915, being eventually gazetted Second Lieutenant to the 4/South Lancashire Regiment on 20 June 1916. An application to transfer to the RFC was granted in February 1917 and shortly after completing his observer training, he was sent out to join 20 Squadron at the front. The official history, *The War in the Air* and Alan Morris's, *Bloody April*, both relate the circumstances of Hampson's last fight, '.....*recklessness was verbally condemned and privately rewarded. There were, for instance, the cases of 2 Lt Smart (sic) and 2 Lt Harold Hampson of 20 Squadron, officially on a bombing raid, they sighted three HA and promptly attacked despite the unsuitability of their FE. A wild dogfight ensued and Hampson was shot through the body. Ignoring the pain he clambered about the exposed pulpit from gun to gun. His bullets stripped the wings from one Hun, sent another into an uncontrolled spin, the third dived steeply to escape. Hampson, 21, died a few hours after making his report'*. In fact, Harold succumbed to his wounds on the following day. He is buried in Bailleul Cemetery Extension, France (Fr285). Age 20.

VICTORY NO. 7
30 April 1917 Sopwith 1½ Strutter (No. A1080) 45 Squadron 1005

Although this was the month which saw the almost wholesale slaughter of British and French flying units by the Imperial German Air Service fighter squadrons, exceptionally, Jasta 28 did not score another victory until the 22nd day. Müller, himself, failed to

register until April's very last day, by which time Jasta 28 had acquired a new leader. Lang had given way to Leutnant Karl Emil Schäfer (ex Richthofen's Jasta 11), an ace with no less than 23 victories.

The Sopwith two-seaters of 45 Squadron

Awards and Decorations of Ritter Max Von Müller

In recognition of a
great fighter pilot.
(Via Roger Bragger)

which jammed an aileron. The defenceless pilot, Lieutenant Wright, attempted to shelter beneath the canopy formed by his fellow Strutters. In the meantime, three more enemy aircraft, thought to be Halberstadts, arrived on the scene.

Wright remained below the British formation until well over the lines and then made a forced landing near Robecq. Given the problems posed by the jammed aileron, it was hardly surprising that he came in hard and heavy. Only when Wright extricated himself from the wreckage and turned to see the extent of Perrott's injuries, did he realise that his observer was beyond help.

Müller claimed his victory as coming down inside British lines east of Armentières. Obviously the falling machine was within clear sight of German front-line observers who confirmed that the Sopwith had indeed come down – and crashed.

SECOND LIEUTENANT
WILLIAM ALLAN WRIGHT,
(LATER CIE, AFC, CDEG (BELGIUM), CHEV. ORD. CROWN OF BELGIUM), 6/LEICESTERSHIRE REGIMENT AND 45 SQUADRON, ROYAL FLYING CORPS

Born on 27 November 1895, he was educated at Oundle (1904-14). Gazetted Second Lieutenant to 6th Battalion, Leicestershire Regiment on 4 January 1915. Successfully sought transfer to the RFC in May 1916. Following his brush with Müller, Wright went on to become a minor ace himself, achieving four victories in Sopwith 1½ Strutters and four more in Camels. Created Chevalier of the Crown of Belgium (London Gazette of 24 September 1917) before subsequently adding a Croix de Guerre (Belgium). Returned home to instruct in late 1917 and never again returned to operational flying. In recognition of his valuable services as an instructor, he was awarded the Air Force Cross in the New Year honours of January 1919 (London Gazette 1 January 1919). In 1921 he joined the Indian Civil Service, serving mainly in Burma. Worked in the

were up and over the front flying escort to a photo reconnaissance machine. Above Roubaix at 1040, a lone German fighter was seen trailing the formation at some distance and quite high-up. Shortly after this initial observation, the solitary enemy scout was seen to have been joined by two others.

One of the trio, an Albatros Scout, made a series of short diving swoops at the formation, firing as it did so. The observer in A1080, 2AM George Perrott, returned the fire, expending the best part of a drum of ammunition in the process, but was then hit in the head by machine-gun fire. With the observer silenced, the unthreatened German fighter remained on the Sopwith's tail, shooting away two flying wires, one of

Government of India War Department during the Second World War. Appointed Director of Civil Affairs (Burma) with the military rank of Brigadier in 1945. Created Companion of the Order of the Indian Empire. Retired in 1948 and settled in Australia. Died at his home in Hawthorn, Victoria, Australia on 26 April 1990 in his ninety-fifth year.

2AM
GEORGE BURNSBY PERROTT,
45 SQUADRON, ROYAL FLYING CORPS

Originally from South Harrow, London, he is buried in Lillers, France (Fr201).

VICTORY NO.8
2 May 1917 BE2e (No. 6281) 12 Squadron 1615

The month of May would prove more successful for Müller. During this phase, his victories seemed invariably to fall inside British lines, albeit apparently close enough for observers in the German trenches to confirm their destruction. Victory number eight, however, is yet another of Müller's claims that is difficult or even impossible to 'match up' with British or Allied losses on the day.

Müller timed his BE claim at 1615 (ie 1515 British time) and said that it had gone down near to Ploegsteert Wood. There were, in relative terms, only a handful of casualties this day – one BE 'shot up and forced to land', one FE8 'possibly hit in the engine' and one of the new Bristol Fighters 'shot about' a bit.

Matching the timing of the BE claim is the bug-bear. The subsequently 'shot up and forced to land' BE took off to fly an artillery observation patrol at 1030. The pilot, John Turner, got himself, his machine and his observer, Percy Laughton, down on the right side of the lines. Although both men were badly shaken by the experience, they were heading for treatment in hospital by quarter past three in the afternoon when Müller claimed to be shooting down a BE.

Damage to the two-seater was extensive. Front longerons and cross-members were smashed; centre section struts and bracing were smashed; undercarriage completely smashed; all wings and ailerons smashed, rudder twisted and tail elevators badly

strained; flying wires damaged, petrol tanks wrecked, cam-shaft bent, breather broken. Small wonder that German observers were happy to confirm the machine a wreck! British records note the BE as struck off charge after coming down at map reference Sheet 51b (N.13.b.1.7.). This location is some way south of the combat area, to say the very least, but we can find no other action which even remotely fits the circumstances.

LIEUTENANT
JOHN FRANCIS TURNER,
7/CHESHIRE REGIMENT (TF) AND
12 SQUADRON, ROYAL FLYING CORPS

Born in Wintaton, Warwickshire, on 14 November 1891, he was the son of Mr and Mrs Turner of Esthwaite Lodge, Hawkshead, Ambleside, in the Lancashire section of the Lake District. Leaving school at the age of sixteen, he secured a position as a clerk in the Admiralty where he remained until September 1911, leaving to become a student. When war came in August 1914, Turner was studying for entry into the Canadian Dominion Land Surveys Department. Enlisted into the 9th Battalion of the Royal Fusiliers at Westminster on 3 September 1914. Gazetted Second Lieutenant into the 1/7th (TF) Battalion, Cheshire Regiment on 3 July 1915. In early

1916 he was sent out to join his battalion – recently evacuated from Gallipoli – in the Middle East. Next he applied for transfer to the flying service, reporting for training with the RFC in Egypt on 26 September 1916. Turner first qualified as an observer, being appointed Flying Officer (observer) on 10 November 1916. Briefly, he served operationally with 14 Squadron before returning to England for pilot training. Qualified for his 'Wings' in April 1917 just days before being sent out to 12 Squadron on the 11th of that month. Apart from being severely concussed, he was otherwise physically unhurt in Max Müller's attack of 2 May 1917. However, a subsequent medical report declared him, 'unfit as a pilot or observer due to stress'. He had, apparently, lost all confidence in himself. After recovering from the effects of the concussion in Number 3, General Hospital, he was sent to the Cheshire Regiment base depot for light duties. Next he was transferred to the RFC base depot, still to be used for light duties. By September 1917, he was requesting a release from the RFC and either a return to the Cheshire Regiment or a transfer to the Tank Corps. Served out the war with the 4th Battalion, Cheshire Regiment, first in Egypt and finally, from July 1918, back in France.

LIEUTENANT
PERCY STOTHARD LAUGHTON,
7/NORTH STAFFORDSHIRE REGIMENT AND 12 SQUADRON, ROYAL FLYING CORPS

Born on Christmas Day 1891, he was the son of Mr and Mrs Laughton of 35 Cloudesdale Road, Upper Tooting, London SW17. A commercial clerk with Polenghi Brothers, provision importers of 72/74 Tooley Street, London SE, he enlisted as soon as war was declared. Served in the trenches in the early months of the war, thus earning the coveted 1914 Star. Gazetted Second Lieutenant to 1/North Staffordshire Regiment on 4 September 1916, shortly afterwards being posted to the 7th Battalion of his regiment. A successful application for transfer to the RFC was followed by an order to report for training at Reading on 27 February 1917. Sent to France and 12 Squadron as a probationary observer in March 1917. Wounded in the action with Max Müller, he eventually recovered sufficiently to be appointed to a training position at the Number 1 School of Aviation in 1918. Returned to the North Staffordshire Regiment in the summer of 1919 before relinquishing his commission and returning to business in the City of London on 28 November 1919.

VICTORY NO.9
7 May 1917 FE2d ? 1215

This claim is even more difficult to reconcile than the last – impossible, in fact. If we can – safely – assume that Müller knew the difference between a pusher and a tractor aeroplane, then there can be only two pusher casualties to chose from. Both were FE2s, one from 18 Squadron, the other belonging to 20 Squadron. The 18 Squadron machine was brought down mid-morning on the 5th Army front west of Cambrai and so is way out of the area under scrutiny. The 20 Squadron FE – part of a bombing raid – seems, on the face of it, a likely candidate until it is realised that it was claimed and credited to Jasta 18's Walter von Bülow as a victory inside German lines. Müller reported his victim down in British lines, so it seems that at best, it was a 20 Squadron machine that dived away precipitately from his unwelcome attentions towards the front-line trenches at Boesinghe – and that wishful thinking by the Bavarian ace did the rest.

VICTORY NO. 10
12 May 1917 RE8 (No. A3243) 53 Squadron 1525

This Müller victory, timed at 1525, came down in the front-line trench area, south of Ypres, near to Hollebeke. Records for 53 Squadron are sadly sparse, however we do know that this crew were flying a reconnaissance sortie and had taken off at 1345. They were shot down in enemy air-space above the Messines Ridge. A past suggestion that they may have been brought down by anti-aircraft fire has been discounted as the time and location coincide with the details of the Müller claim.

SECOND LIEUTENANT
FREDERICK ADAMS,
53 SQUADRON, ROYAL FLYING CORPS

The son of W H and Mrs E Adams of Allesley Old Road, Coventry, he was born on 24 October 1888 and educated at Bablake School, Coudon, Coventry (1895-1900). Served an apprenticeship as a mechanic before enlisting as one of the earliest members of the newly formed Royal Flying Corps in 1912 (Number 341). Having achieved the rank of Corporal, he qualified for his Royal Aero Club Certificate (Number 903) on 20 August 1914, flying a Maurice Farman biplane at the Central Flying School, Upavon. Promoted to Sergeant, he was sent out to join 1 Squadron in France on 3 March 1915. Further promotion to Flight Sergeant followed before he was gazetted Second Lieutenant to the RFC on 16 December 1916. Next he was sent to join 53 Squadron on the Western Front at the turn of the year. On 7 April 1917, armed

Below: Fred Adams – then a Corporal, RFC – on 20 August 1914, the day he qualified for his Royal Aero Club Certificate piloting a Maurice Farman. Note false 'wings' drawn on the photograph.

Below right: Adams as an officer.

with two 112lb bombs, he was engaged on a bombing raid – one he dropped near a moving train, the other on a surprisingly well illuminated Wervicq aerodrome. During May, 53 Squadron increased the frequency of their artillery duties, often working from a dangerously low altitude. Müller's fierce attack caused the RE 8 – built by the Austin Motor Company in Birmingham – to break up in the air, precipitating both occupants to their deaths. Buried originally by the Germans, Adams' remains were re-interred in 1924 by the then Imperial War Graves Commission and he now rests in the Oosttaverne Wood Cemetery, Wytschaete, Belgium (Bel 152). Age 28.

SECOND LIEUTENANT
OSCAR RAPHAEL KELLY,
20/NORTHUMBERLAND FUSILIERS (1ST TYNESIDE SCOTTISH) AND 53 SQUADRON, ROYAL FLYING CORPS

The son of Mr and Mrs Kelly of 441 Sauchihall Street, Glasgow and 10 Wodehouse Road, Middle Colaba, Bombay, India, he was born in Arsikere, India on 24 October 1896. Educated at Mount St Mary's School, Chesterfield, Derbyshire. Joined the Inns of Court OTC (Number 6/3/5855) on 26 August 1915 and, following training, was gazetted Second Lieutenant to the 20th Battalion, (1st Tyneside Scottish) Northumberland Fusiliers on 1 June 1916. Next he successfully applied for a transfer to the RFC, qualified as an observer and accompanied 53 Squadron to France in February 1917. After his son's death, Mr Kelly Senior received a bill for £15 5s 3d from Oscar's former tailor, Messrs Herbert Chappel and Company. The War Office eventually settled this bill for uniform from funds owed to Oscar's estate before sending the modest balance to Mr Kelly in India. Oscar is buried in Oosttaverne Wood Cemetery, Wytschaete, Belgium (Bel 152). Age 20.

VICTORY NO. 11
23 May 1917 FE2d (No. A6468) 20 Squadron 1615

In his debriefing following his return from captivity after the war's end, Lieutenant Richard Johns described in detail the circumstances of how he and his observer were brought down. Theirs was one of four FEs on an Offensive Patrol near to Comines as nine German fighters of the Richthofen squadron attacked them at 12,000 feet.

The opposing machines traded machine-gun fire for several minutes. Johns was busy engaging an enemy scout in front of him when his FE's engine and fuel tanks were shot through by a fighter coming from the rear and this despite his observer's good and resolute defence. The stricken FE began to burn and Johns was unsuccessful in attempting to extinguish the flames by side-slipping. In a last desperate measure, he opened the throttle fully and at the same time turned the petrol switches off. Johns managed a forced landing but suffered severe burns in the process.

His observer had been mortally wounded and died two days later in a Field Hospital at Bousbecque, a small village six miles south of Comines. Johns considered his observer's behaviour was worthy of special mention for gallantry. It seems that throughout the time Johns was trying to extinguish the fire Sergeant Aldred, although wounded in the stomach, strove to help his pilot to bring the FE safely to the ground.

Müller noted the fall of Johns' FE as being south-west of Houthem – for once on the German side of the lines. His Staffelführer, Karl Schäfer, also downed a second machine from 20 Squadron, a victory which brought his total to 28.

LIEUTENANT
RICHARD ALLAN PENDARVES JOHNS,
20/HUSSARS AND 20 SQUADRON, ROYAL FLYING CORPS

The son of Richard Bragington Johns and Mrs Johns of 'Princess House', Princess Square, Plymouth, he was born on 20 July 1892. He was educated at Marlborough (1906-08) where he was a member of the OTC. After leaving school he entered his father's Plymouth-based practise to study law, living at 71 The Terrace, The Hoe, in that city. Gazetted Second Lieutenant to the 20th Hussars on 15 November 1914, he served with the 13th Reserve Regiment of Cavalry in the UK. Promoted Lieutenant on 11 October 1915. A successful application for transfer to the RFC led to him reporting to Oxford to commence pilot training on 9 August 1916. Gained the Royal Aero Club Certificate (Number 3745) on 18 October 1916. Formally awarded his 'Wings' and appointed Flying Officer on 3 December 1916, he was sent out to join 20 Squadron at the front on 7 March 1917. Shot down, wounded and taken prisoner just over two weeks after his arrival in France. Repatriated on 5 January 1919, he relinquished his commission on 31 May following. 'Rich' completed his articles and went out to India to practise. Died at Adra, India, on 26 October 1922 at the age of 30.

SERGEANT
BERNARD ALDRED,
MM, NUMBER 77449, 220 SQUADRON, ROYAL FLYING CORPS

One of the six sons of Mr and Mrs P Aldred of the Locomotive Inn, Union Street, Long Eaton, Derbyshire. Adding a couple of years to the mere sixteen he had already lived, he enlisted into the 9/Battalion, Notts and Derby Regiment, in September 1914. All six Aldred boys were, within weeks of the war starting, serving with various branches of the services. Bernard (right) accompanied his unit to Gallipoli, landing at Suvla Bay on 7 August 1915. He received two wounds during the Dardanelles campaign but just as soon as he recovered, he was immediately sent to serve in the trenches in France. A successful request for a transfer to the RFC followed and by the end of 1916 he was flying with 20 Squadron at the front. He was involved in a number of aerial combats, displaying great resource and courage for which he was awarded the Military Medal – the formal announcement of which appeared after his death in the *London Gazette* of 9 July 1917, page 6825. The Germans sent one of their airmen over the British lines to drop a message advising of Bernard's death in action. He is buried in Pont-du-Hem Cemetery, France (Fr705). Age 19.

VICTORY NO. 12
24 May 1917 Nieuport XVII (No.B1642) 40 Squadron 2050

Captain C L Bath led an evening Offensive Patrol of six aircraft out at 1805 hours. During the course of the patrol, a number of German aircraft were observed in the distance. There was also some very active AA fire to the east of Arras. Indeed, it was later suggested that at around 1935, Lieutenant Morgan was a victim of anti-aircraft fire, although the exact circumstances have never been entirely clear.

Mick Mannock's diary states: '*Morgan got the MC on the 23rd, and was brought down by one of our own shells on the 24th. It appears that a shell struck his machine at six thousand feet (he was flying too low) and knocked the engine out, broke his right thigh and left ankle. The undercarriage was also blown away. Notwithstanding this, he kept his head and planed down into our own lines, but the machine – or what was left of it – broke up on touching earth. He crawled unaided from the wreckage and was inevitably taken to hospital. He said that the only thing which worried him when coming down, was that he might faint before reaching the ground. Some lad!*'

So we have a slight difference of opinion as to the cause of Morgan's downfall. The first suggests AA fire and the second as an accidental collision with a British shell. If Morgan was flying too low, as Mannock opines, was he on his own or still with the patrol? Had Captain Bath led his patrol into either a British barrage, or down to an altitude low enough to be within the range of AA guns – both unlikely scenarios. It was, in fact, much more likely that Morgan was alone – indeed, he had a deserved reputation for being a 'loner'.

An unusually aggressive pilot – known affectionately but pointedly as, 'the Air Hog' – he may very well have been looking for trouble at an altitude considerably below the remainder of his patrol, perhaps seeking out yet another balloon to add to his score.

These circumstances could legitimise Müller's claim as the German ace later reported the Nieuport he attacked as going down inside British lines at 2050 in the St Eloi-Wytshaete-Bogen area. 40 Squadron reported Morgan down north of Athies at 1935 (2035 German time) – close enough. There were no other Nieuports lost on this particular day.

SECOND LIEUTENANT
LEWIS LAUGHARNE MORGAN,
MC, MID, 6/WELSH REGIMENT (TF) AND 40 SQUADRON, ROYAL FLYING CORPS

The son of William Laugharne and Alice Emily Morgan of Underwood, Mumbles, Swansea, Glamorgan (later 10 Kingsbury Street, Marlborough, Wiltshire), he was born in Swansea on 11 December 1896. Educated at Llanyre Hall Preparatory School, Radnorshire and at Highgate School, London (1911-13) where he gained his colours in the rugby XV. On the second day of the war, he volunteered to serve as a motor cyclist. Gazetted Second Lieutenant to 6th (Glamorgan) Battalion, The Welsh Regiment (TF), on 6 August 1916. Successfully sought transfer to the RFC in late 1916. Gained his Royal Aero Club Certificate (Number 4148) on 17 January 1917 and, following his formal pilot training, was appointed Flying Officer on 15 March 1917. Within days of being awarded his 'Wings', he was sent out to join 40 Squadron in France. He was Mentioned in Despatches for gallant services with his Squadron in a balloon attack. Crossing the lines at 100 feet, the Squadron brought five balloons down in flames. The Commander-in-Chief of the BEF, Sir Douglas Haig, sent the following signal to the Squadron CO: '*A very fine performance. Please congratulate those that carried out the attack on the great success of their efforts*'. The award of the Military Cross followed – *London Gazette* 18 July 1917, page 7239: '*For conspicuous

gallantry and devotion to duty. He crossed the lines at a height of under 100 feet, and destroyed a hostile kite balloon. Previously he attacked a hostile scout at close range and brought it down in flames. He has shown great gallantry in many combats'. The Squadron chaplain wrote a congratulatory note to Morgan's parents: *'.......his work has been characterised not only by brilliancy but also by steadiness. He got his balloon in the first of the two special balloon attacks although when he went up in his machine he found that only eight of his nine cylinders were working – to have still gone on and carried out his job successfully under these conditions was a splendid and brilliant achievement. Although he was not 'down' to take part in the second balloon expedition, he would not be out of it, but went off and got a balloon on his own in magnificent style. One typical story I must tell you – when he got his balloon the German observer descended in his parachute, and when someone asked your son if he had shot him as he came down, he said, 'No, I couldn't* shoot at the poor chap when he was like that, I just flew close past him and made a face at him'. *So typical of his chivalrous and generous spirit. Never was a Military Cross more deservedly awarded than in the case of your son'.* A version of the events of 24 May 1917, were reported in *The Daily Telegraph* as follows: *'A still more wonderful experience has just come to a British pilot who, while flying at four thousand feet across the lines, was hit by an artillery shell! The shell crashed through the body of his machine, but did not explode until it struck the engine. It tore away two cylinders and smashed the engine bearers. Hit by splinters, the pilot's right leg was fractured in two places. Despite this, however, he brought the machine down in his own lines.....'.* After he was extricated from a hole in the side of the machine, his right leg was found to be shattered below the knee and had to be amputated – again below the knee. A mere two hours later he found the strength to write a reassuring letter to his parents: *'I made certain I was killed, so to find that after all I was only a foot missing, hardly seems any punishment at all ....My leg gives me very little pain, I hardly notice it'.* A contemporary book entitled, *An Airman's Wife*, made several allusions to Lewis Morgan: *'I haven't told you about the 'Air Hog'. He is simply crazy to get Huns. After going up a few times he developed a habit of going up and tearing about the sky all alone. At last he was put on a 'Roving Commission Game', and since then he has spent at least eight hours a day in the air'.* And, later on in the book: *'The 'Air Hog' had to lose one leg just below the knee. I don't think many people so well deserved an MC'.* Fitted with an artificial limb, he rejoined in March 1918, being posted to 50 Squadron, then in Bekesbourne, Kent. Appointed Aerial Fighting Instructor to the Squadron, he was accidentally killed in a side-slip and sudden nose-dive at a low altitude on 26 April 1918. The engine of his SE5 (Number C5342) spluttered and coughed on take-off and he 'did a McCudden', turning back at 125 feet but hit a railway embankment north of the airfield. Buried in Canterbury Cemetery, Kent. Age 21.

VICTORY NO. 13
27 May 1917   Sopwith 1½ Strutter (No.A8226)   45 Squadron   1215

This was most definitely not Captain McArthur's day! He first took off at 0855 but within five minutes was landing again with engine trouble. The fault rectified, he took off again at 0915, only to be forced to return five minutes later — still having problems with his motor. He got away for the last time — literally — at 0925. Perhaps he was rash in not heeding these inauspicious auguries — he would have done better to have gone to the Mess for a second breakfast.

Altogether there were eight Sopwith two-seaters flying a late morning low Central Offensive Patrol, led in 'A8299' by Captain G Mountford with Second Lieutenant J A Vessey in the observer's seat. After about forty-five minutes they met seven hostile aircraft. The enemy aircraft were a multi-coloured bunch, varying from green and blue, all green, blue and red and some all red. The Sopwiths were at 1,350 feet, the Germans 500 feet lower. Mountford turned his machine to face the enemy, fired a red Verey flare and dived to attack. Firing from fifty feet with his front gun, he targeted a red machine which was promptly despatched going down out of control. Mountford then developed engine trouble and was forced to make for the British lines. He could not make it all the way back to his home field, landing instead, at Abeele, the home of 6 Squadron.

Meanwhile, Sergeant Cook and 2AM Shaw in 'A8268' claimed another of the enemy machines out of control with their front Vickers gun.

Another crew, Second Lieutenant Carleton and 2AM Pocock, were forced out of the fight and had to land at 1 Squadron's base, crashing as they did so. Second Lieutenants H E R Fitchat and R Hayes dived on a red-tailed Albatros, with Fitchat's fire causing splinters to fly from around the cockpit area before it went over and down out of control. Fitchat then spotted another Albatros attacking a Sopwith and went to

help as the British machine seemed to be in difficulty. The Albatros immediately turned away and made off towards Lille, sent on its way with a few parting shots from Hayes's machine gun.

Unfortunately, however, McArthur and Carey failed to emerge from the mêlée, and Müller's claim was timed at 1215, north-east of Ypres. The dog-fight had taken place near to Roulers. The German time appears to be an hour out, perhaps another commonly occurring error? Every other circumstance fits.

CAPTAIN
LAWRENCE WILLIAM McARTHUR,
MC, MID X 2, HONOURABLE ARTILLERY COMPANY (TF) AND 45 SQUADRON, ROYAL FLYING CORPS

Born in 1890, he was the only son of William and Constance McArthur of 'The Meadow', Chislehurst, Kent. Educated at Malvern College (1904-07) and abroad. After completing his education he entered into business in the city of London, becoming, on 17 March 1913, a pre-war volunteer with the Honourable Artillery Company. Mobilised with the rest of the Territorial Force in August 1914, he accompanied his regiment's original contingent to France on 18 September 1914, thus qualifying for the 1914 Star and 'Under-fire' Clasp. Slightly wounded in the, *shelled by day and bullet-swept by night'*, trenches near to St Eloi 15 February 1915, he was gazetted Second Lieutenant to the HAC (Infantry) six days later. Wounded again — this time severely — in the attack on Hooge on 16 June 1915, he was evacuated to a UK hospital for treatment on 21 June 1915. Awarded the Military Cross and Mentioned in Despatches for his gallantry at Hooge. Military Cross, *London Gazette* of 10 August 1915, page 7283: *'For conspicuous gallantry on 16 June 1915 at*

FLYING OFFICER MISSING.

LIEUTENANT CAREY'S FATE.

SECOND-LIEUTENANT A. S. CAREY.

His many friends will be sorry to hear that Second Lieutenant A. S. Carey, youngest son of Mr. and Mrs. W. A. Carey, of Devonshire-road, has been missing since Sunday. Mr. W. A. Carey received the official intimation on Thursday.

Lieutenant Carey, who is in the Royal Flying Corps as an aeroplane observer, went out to France about six months ago.

Hooge. When our troops were forced to retire from the 3rd line of German trenches, he rallied part of the retiring troops and re-occupied and held the vacated trench under heavy fire until he was himself forced later to withdraw owing to retirements on his flanks. He was severely wounded on this occasion'. MID : *London Gazette* of 15 October 1915. After recovering his fitness, he successfully applied for a transfer to the RFC which was granted on the same day his first 'mention' was gazetted. Gained his Royal Aero Club Certificate (Number 2758) on 3 April 1916 and, following his formal training, was given his 'Wings' and appointed a Flying Officer on 31 May 1916. By the time of his confrontation with Max Müller, he was a Flight Commander and had again been Mentioned in Despatches. Buried in Harlebeke Cemetery, Belgium (Bel140). Age 26.

SECOND LIEUTENANT
ALLAN STEWART CAREY,
45 SQUADRON, ROYAL FLYING CORPS

One of the four sons of Mr W A and Mrs Carey of 38 Devonshire Road, Bexhill-on-Sea, Sussex. A clerk in civilian life, he joined the Inns of Court OTC (Number 6/1/6241) on 16 September 1915, being eventually gazetted Second Lieutenant to the RFC via the General List on 6 July 1916. A telegram advising that their son was posted 'missing', was received by his parents on 30 May 1917. Shortly afterwards, a message was dropped by the Imperial German Air Service over the Allied lines which confirmed his death in action. Buried in Harlebeke Cemetery, Belgium (Bel140).

VICTORY NO.14
3 June 1917 Sopwith 1½ Strutter (No.A8272) 45 Squadron 1910

Taking off at 1800, eight 45 Squadron aircraft were on an evening Central OP led by Captain G Mountford. They began to meet heavy AA fire which caused the aircraft to spread out. Although a natural move in the circumstances, it was a mistake. Especially so at that particular moment as, two miles east of Ploegsteert Wood, several groups of German fighters – numbering up to 25 machines – appeared on the scene.

One group of eight attacked a single Sopwith which was seen to go down after losing both wings, crashing one mile south-east of Quesnoy. Second Lieutenant Watt and Corporal Harris in 'A8244' attacked an Albatros and saw it crash in the same vicinity. Second Lieutenant R Hayes, observer to Second Lieutenant H E R Fitchat, drove down another enemy machine. After returning to its base, the RFC patrol noted that their fallen fellow Sopwith had crashed at map reference 36.E.11.

The 45 Squadron combat reports later noted that some of the Albatros Scouts were red in colour, others had red fuselages, whilst another appeared to carry red crosses. The encounter was recorded as taking place at 11,000 feet between 1815 and 1825 hours. Whilst Harries had success-fully driven off one of the attackers, four more had latched on to the stricken two-seater of Haller and Foster, the machine's wings folding back and ripping away. As the other Sopwiths were in danger of being gradually overwhelmed, they withdrew to the safely of their own lines.

Again Müller's claim, time and locality fit the loss – Quesnoy at 1910 German time. On the other hand, there does not seem to be a German loss to link with the Watt and Harries' claim. One is left wondering if the machine they apparently saw hitting the ground was their own fellow Sopwith going in?

SECOND LIEUTENANT
EDWARD DENISON HALLER,
45 SQUADRON, ROYAL FLYING CORPS

Born in 1894, he was the son of Thomas and Laura Haller of 'Burnside', Newland Park, Kingston upon Hull. Commissioned to the Royal Flying Corps via the General List in the summer of 1916, he shortly afterwards qualified for the Royal Aero Club Certificate (Number 3420) on 16 August 1916. Awarded his official 'Wings' in early 1917, he was sent out to join 45 Squadron in France in the spring. His remains were lost and hence he is commemorated on the Arras Memorial to the Missing, France. Age 22.

SECOND LIEUTENANT
FRANK HAWLEY FOSTER,
45 SQUADRON, ROYAL FLYING CORPS

The son of chartered accountant Arthur J Foster and Mrs Helen Isabel Foster of 80 Darenth Road, Stamford Hill, London, he was born on 13 August 1898. Educated at Hackney Downs Secondary School and at St Paul's School, London (1914-15). An apprenticed clerk to a firm of chartered accountants in the City of London, he enlisted into the 28/London Regiment, the Artist's Rifles (Number 762557) on 6 June 1916 – as soon as he was old enough to do so. Following a successful application for transfer to the RFC, he was gazetted Second Lieutenant on 5 April 1917 and accepted for observer training three weeks later. He joined 45 Squadron in France on probation shortly before the fatal encounter with Max Müller. His remains were never found and hence he is commemorated on the Arras Memorial to the Missing, France. Age 18.

VICTORY NO. 15
7 June 1917 Spad VII (No.B1527) 23 Squadron 0915

Today saw the opening of the Battle of Messines. Three 23 Squadron Spads, led by Captain W J C K Cochrane-Patrick MC, were flying an Offensive Patrol to Bonjours which had begun at 0630. Three Albatros Scouts were engaged in action east of Armentières. In the ensuing dog-fight, George Stead in 'B1527' had both fuel tanks hit while at a height of 1,000 feet. Another bullet ricocheted off his skull, grazing his forehead and knocking him unconscious. He knew nothing more until he came around some twelve hours later, finding himself in a German hospital – a prisoner of war. Astonishingly, he had survived the crash with no further injury.

Cochrane-Patrick, the patrol leader, was already an ace with 12 victories and would eventually go on to achieve a total score of 21. Coincidently, two of his victories had been achieved in what, subsequently, became Stead's crashed Spad (B1527) before he took over another of the marque (B1580).

The location given by Müller with this claim was an area between Comines and Warneton, just to the north-east of Armentières. 23 Squadron would send out several small patrols during this morning and Jasta would take out two others of their machines – both pilots joining Stead in captivity.

SECOND LIEUTENANT
GEORGE CHRISTOPHER STEAD,
23 SQUADRON, ROYAL FLYING CORPS

The son of F Herbert Stead MA and Mrs Stead of 29 Grosvenor Park, Southwark, London, he was born on 6 May 1891. Educated at the City and Guilds College (University of London). Fluent in French and with a good command of German, he pursued a journalistic career becoming, at an unusually early age, the editor of *The Light Car* and *Cyclecar* and *The Motor* magazines, Temple Press Ltd., 7 – 15 Rosebery Avenue, London EC. He volunteered under the Derby Scheme on 11 December 1915 – his stated preferences for service being : 1) RFC; 2) ASC (Motor Transport) and 3) Royal Engineers. Perversely but typically, he was eventually called up into his least favoured option, the 3/1 London Divisional Signal Company, Royal Engineers (TF), on 3 April 1916. George's father used his influence at the War Office, approaching a family friend,

Lord Hugh Cecil. The string-pulling had the effect of hastening George's gazetting to the General List on 22 July 1916 and opened the door for his admission for pilot training at Oxford on the same day. Appointed a Flying Officer and awarded his Wings on 14 December 1916. Despite already having his official Wings, he still insisted on qualifying for the Royal Aero Club Certificate, which he achieved on 14 January 1917 (Number 4142). Proceeded to the front in early 1917 and was shot down and taken prisoner on 7 June 1917. Repatriated on 3 January 1919, he left the service on 6 May 1919.

VICTORY NO. 16
7 June 1917 Sopwith Pup (No.A6157) 46 Squadron 1145

46 Squadron mounted an Offensive Patrol to the area of Polygon Wood, after taking off at 0910. After they were engaged by German scouts, Andrew Mitchell, flying 'A6157' was last seen in combat with no less than ten of the enemy. Müller claimed his victory at 1145, south of Roulers – the British pilot being wounded and taken prisoner. This would be the first time Müller achieved two confirmed victories on the same day.

LIEUTENANT
ANDREW PARK MITCHELL,
(LATER CMG, 2ND CLASS ORDER OF EL ISIQIAL OF TRANSJORDAN), 10/MIDDLESEX REGIMENT (TF) AND 46 SQUADRON, ROYAL FLYING CORPS

Born on 23 August 1894, he was the son of bank official Andrew John Mitchell and Mrs Mitchell of 19 Mortlake Road, Kew, Surrey. Educated at St Paul's (1908-13) and at the City of Guilds College (1913-14). Represented England in athletics in 1914. Gazetted Second Lieutenant to the 10th Battalion (TF), Middlesex Regiment on 16 September 1914. Accompanied his battalion to India on 30 October 1914. He was serving

in Egypt in March 1917 when he was advised that his application for transfer to the RFC had been approved. Awarded his 'Wings' in time to join 46 Squadron in France on 16 May 1917. He managed just three weeks on the Western Front before being shot down, wounded and taken prisoner on 7 June 1917. Repatriated on the last day of 1918, he continued to serve in the RAF until 6 September 1919. Entered the Survey Department, Egypt in 1919. Married Evangeline Morris in 1922. In 1927 he was appointed Director of Land and Surveys for Transjordan. His next appointment – in 1940 – was Director of Surveys, Palestine. A transfer to Nigeria as Inspector General followed in 1948. Detached for special duties to Uganda in 1953. Between 1954 to 1956 he held the office of Director of Surveys, Land Office, and Commissioner for Mines. 1957-58 saw him in Malaya as a member of the Land Administration Commission. Similar posts followed in Cyprus (1958) and in the Seychelles (1959). Appointed CMG in 1948. Second Class Order of El Isiqial of Transjordan in 1959. Died at his home at 36 Penfold Avenue, Kew Gardens, Richmond, Surrey on 6 June 1975 at the age of 80.

VICTORY NO.17
8 June 1917 Sopwith Triplane (No.N6293) 1 Naval Squadron 1910

Number 1 Naval Squadron mounted an Offensive Patrol at 1700, the five Triplanes led by Flight Commander T F N Gerrard DSC, an ace with nine combat victories. The patrol was joined a little later by two further Triplanes which took off at 1735. Shortly after 1800, Teddy Gerrard suddenly noticed that one of his patrol was missing and, as all appeared calm, quiet and peaceful, he assumed – reasonably enough – that the pilot had broken away with engine trouble. When, at the end of the patrol, the Sopwiths landed back at their base at 1850, they were surprised to find neither sign of, nor message from, the missing pilot. Whatever were the circumstances of his disappearance, they are still unknown. Perhaps he did, indeed, break away with mechanical trouble and was subsequently picked off by the marauding Max Müller. Or, maybe he alone spotted the patrolling Albatros Scouts and dived away to engage them. Whatever the truth of the matter, his Triplane fell near Quesnoy at ten minutes after 7 pm (German time), the credit being given to the Bavarian ace.

FLIGHT SUB-LIEUTENANT
THOMAS REID SWINBURNE,
1 NAVAL SQUADRON, ROYAL NAVAL AIR SERVICE

The only son of Major Thomas Baker Swinburne and Mary H Swinburne of 'Holmwood', Beachwood Avenue, Church End, Finchley, London, he was born on 2

February 1898. He was educated at Westminster School (1913-15) and King's College, London, whence he joined the RNAS on 18 June 1916. Trained at Crystal Palace, Chingford and Cranwell. Gained his Royal Aero Club Certificate (Number 4079) on 6 January 1917. Formally qualified for his 'Wings' in April 1917 by which time he had accumulated $29\frac{1}{2}$ hours flying time. Served in Dover before crossing to France in May 1917 just a couple of weeks before he was killed in action. His remains were never found and so he is commemorated on the Arras Memorial to the Missing, France. Age 19.

VICTORY NO. 18
20 June 1917 RE8 ? 1900

Despite an exhaustive search of the surviving records, no trace can be found of an RE8 having being lost – in any circumstances – on this date. Müller put in a claim

for a machine of this type after a combat near Armentières at around 1900, going on to say that he had sent it down inside British lines. Certainly, machines under aerial attack from a superior enemy would, in their anxiety to get away, throw themselves headlong at the sheltering Allied lines – so precipitant their dives that pursuing scout pilots might think that they had crashed to their doom. Once clear of immediate danger, and often not even hit or damaged, the seemingly vanquished machine would level out and skoot for home. German front-line observers apparently could, on occasions, be persuaded to confirm the fall of the aeroplane even if land features, trees, mist or cloud, obscured their view of the final impact – the wish being the father of the thought in all human endeavours. It has also to be said that there is evidence of a sort of hysterical desperation setting in when a pilot approached the 'magic' figure of 20 victories and the prospect of the award of the Pour le Mérite loomed.

VICTORY NO. 19
28 July 1917 Sopwith 1½ Strutter (No.A8228) 45 Squadron 1810

An eight-machine sortie from 45 Squadron took off at 1700. The Distant Offensive Patrol to Comines was led by Captain R M Findlay with G W Blaiklock in the observer's seat. Shortly after crossing the lines en route for Comines, they were attacked in a pincer movement by seven Albatros scouts coming in on their left with five others converging from their right. Whilst the Strutters blazed away at the approaching machines, most of the attacking fighters disconcertingly held their fire until the very last moment – a real 'whites of their eyes' scenario. One of the enemy – almost certainly Max Müller – positioned himself below the Strutter crewed by 'Bunty' Frew and George A Brooke (A 8228) and succeeded in putting two bullets through the Sopwith's propeller as well as damaging the undercarriage. Frew, a very accomplished pilot and a future ace, threw his machine into an Immelmann turn, coming down – not on to his tormentor – but onto another Albatros that happened to be immediately below him. Frew later reported that he immediately opened fire with his front Vickers gun and continued to follow the enemy fighter down to its destruction in a crash – which event was, apparently, also witnessed by several other of his colleagues in the patrol. Frew nursed the Strutter back to their home field but because of the damage inflicted by Müller, was forced to crash-land. Although, happily, Frew and Brooke were unhurt in the crash, the same could not be said of their machine. Longerons were broken or strained, the engine damaged, the propeller smashed and the lower right wing damaged. Carted away to Number 1 AD for repair, it was estimated that it would take more than two weeks to have it serviceable again. Müller reported his victim as going down north-east of Ploegsteert – the time and circumstances broadly agreeing with the catalogue of Frew's discomfortures. 'Bunty' Frew himself was duly credited with a victory – his fourth – in this combat. He would go on to get five as a 1½ Strutter pilot and a further eighteen on the Western and Italian fronts as a Camel pilot. Frew's observer, George Brooke had, during this same combat, sent an Albatros down, apparently out of control but this machine was seen to arrest its vertical nose-dive at 500 feet, level out and fly away. Captain Findlay's observer, Lieutenant Blaiklock, also claimed one down out of control.

An observer in another of the Strutters, driver William A Fellows (Number 25988), Royal Engineers attached RFC, was badly hit in the buttocks by machine-gun fire. Although his pilot, Sergeant R A Yeomans, managed to get their machine safely back to base, Bill Fellows would die the following day as a consequence of his wounds.

SECOND LIEUTENANT
MATTHEW BROWN FREW

(LATER AIR VICE-MARSHAL SIR MATTHEW FREW, KBE, CB, DSO & BAR, MC & BAR, AFC, ITALIAN SILVER MEDAL FOR MILITARY VALOUR, COMDR ROYAL ORDER OF GEORGE I OF GREECE WITH SWORDS, BELGIAN MILITARY CROSS, 1ST CLASS)

Born on 7 April 1895, Matthew, aka 'Bunty', was the son of Harry Lorimer Frew and Annie Brown Frew of Rutherglen, Glasgow, Scotland. Educated at Hutcheson's Grammar School, Glasgow. He enlisted as a private soldier in the Highland Light Infantry in 1914, serving in the trenches in France from January 1915 until March 1916. Following a spell in the UK, he was accepted for transfer to the RFC in August 1916 and was gazetted Second Lieutenant on 26 September 1916. After gaining his 'Wings' he was sent out to join 45 Squadron in France. Serving in France and Flanders and on the Italian front, Frew achieved no less than 23 victories and a plethora of gallantry awards. Military Cross, *London Gazette* 7 March 1918, page

2915: *'For conspicuous gallantry and devotion to duty on patrol, showing a fine offensive spirit in many combats. He has shot down four enemy aeroplanes, and on one occasion leading his formation to attack twenty-two Albatros Scouts, and himself shooting one down'.* Bar to Military Cross, *London Gazette* 23 April 1918, page 4857: *'For conspicuous gallantry and devotion to duty in shooting down three enemy machines in two days. He has destroyed eight enemy machines and driven down many others out of control'.* Distinguished Service Order *London Gazette* 4 March 1918 – citation *London Gazette* 16 August 1918, page 2728: *'For conspicuous gallantry and devotion to duty. On one occasion when leader of a patrol he shot down an enemy aeroplane, two others being also accounted for in the same fight. On a later occasion he destroyed three enemy machines in one combat, all of which were seen to crash to the ground. Immediately after this combat he had to switch off his engine and make an attempt to glide towards our lines five miles away on account of his machine having received a direct hit. Owing to the great skill and courage he displayed in the handling of his damaged machine, he succeeded in bringing it safely to our lines. He has destroyed twenty-two enemy machines up to date'.* In addition to the British awards, Frew was honoured by the Italians, the Greeks and the Belgians. On 15 January 1918 his Camel was hit in the air by AA fire and he injured his neck in the subsequent forced landing. After a short period of recovery, he was transferred to a training role at the Central Flying School and it was for this work that he later received the Air Force Cross – *London Gazette* 3 June 1919, page 7033 (no citation). Frew, not surprisingly in view of his record, remained in the RAF after the war, adding a Bar to his DSO whilst serving in North Kurdistan during 1931/32, *London Gazette* 6 October 1933, page 6416 *'the King has been graciously pleased to approve of the undermentioned award in recognition of gallant and distinguished service rendered in connection with the operations in Northern Kurdistan during the period*

An immediate post-war study of Capt M B Frew wearing the ribbons of the DSO and the MC & Bar. *(Geo H Williams Jr.)*

Companion of the Order of the Bath in 1943 and Air Vice-Marshal by the war's end. Knighted in 1948 – Knight Commander of the Order of the British Empire – he retired to spend the rest of his days in Pretoria, South Africa. Sir Matthew died in South Africa on 28 May 1974. Age 79.

LIEUTENANT
GEORGE A BROOKE,
4/SOUTH STAFFORDSHIRE REGIMENT, MACHINE GUN CORPS AND 45 SQUADRON, ROYAL FLYING CORPS

A graduate of Sheffield University where he was a member of the OTC, he was a married man living in St Martins, Jersey, Channel Isles, when the war broke out. After volunteering his services, he was gazetted Second Lieutenant to the 4th (Extra Reserve) Battalion of the South Staffordshire Regiment on 27 March 1915. Served in France with the newly formed Machine Gun Corps in 1916 before successfully applying for a transfer to the RFC. Sent to the front to serve with 45 Squadron as a probationary observer in May 1917. Flying with Matthew Frew, he claimed his first victory – an Albatros DV – over Polygon Wood on 16 July 1917. Gazetted a fully fledged Flying Officer (observer) with effect from 25 July 1917 – just three days before he and his pilot, future ace Matthew Frew, were shot up by the redoubtable Max Müller. Brooke would gain four victories with 45 Squadron before being transferred to 20 Squadron with whom he would eventually achieve three further victories. Returned to the UK in 1918, to take up a training post. Brooke finally left the service in March 1919.

December 1931 to June 1932'. Prior to this, Frew had been appointed Chief Flying Instructor at the Number 1 Flying Training School, Netheravon. He went on to command both 111 Squadron and 10 Squadrons between the world wars. A Group Captain at the commencement of the Second World War in 1939, he served in various capacities being appointed a

UNCONFIRMED CLAIM
10 August 1917   Sopwith 1½ Strutter   (No.A1004)   45 Squadron am

45 Squadron's Sopwiths were up against Jasta 28 yet again during the course of a Distant OP east of Menin. Four Strutters led by Captain R M Findlay (with Second

Lieutenant J W Mullen in the back seat) had taken off shortly after 0600, making their rendezvous over Polygon Wood. Amongst the quartet was Matthew Frew – whom we have already met. Two of the Strutters were engaged by eight German fighters near Comines. Second Lieutenant Mullen's fire struck one enemy machine which went down and crashed but very shortly afterwards the observer was wounded in the leg as, at the same time, both main tanks of his Sopwith were holed. Captain Findlay headed for the lines reliant on his gravity tank, skimming to safety by less than 100 feet above the barbed wire.

In the meantime, Campbell had his observer, Peel, wounded in three places by a Müller attack which, coincidently, also perforated their fuel tanks. They just about scraped across the lines on the gravity tank before force-landing at Kemmel but, presumably, out of the sight of German front-line observers who could not confirm Müller's claim.

SECOND LIEUTENANT
ALEXANDER VICTOR CAMPBELL,
45 SQUADRON, ROYAL FLYING CORPS

From Toronto, Ontario, Canada, born 15 June 1895. Educated at Jervis School, Ontario, and having joined the RFC, was posted to 45 Squadron on 23 July 1917 with the grand total of 26 flying hours – four on Sopwith Strutters! Although he does not appear to have been wounded in this action, he went into hospital on 18 August and was struck off the strength of the squadron.

SECOND LIEUTENANT
ARTHUR ERNEST PEEL,
45 SQUADRON, ROYAL FLYING CORPS

Born on 20 July 1888 in Chislehurst, Kent, from where his family moved to South Africa, soon afterwards. Educated at the Government School for Boys, Pietermaritzberg and at the Technical Institute in the same city, there studying accountancy and business management. Spent seven years in the Natal Carabiniers, seeing active service in the Zulu uprising of 1906 (Natal Rebellion Medal and clasp). Emigrated to Canada in 1912 and there enlisted as a part-time volunteer with the 72nd Seaforth Highlanders of Canada. When the war came, he crossed the Atlantic with the CEF, serving in France and Flanders for three months until he was wounded at Ypres. After recovering from his wounds, he acted as a storekeeper for 16/Canadian Scottish in England. He was next accepted for a commission and for training as an observer with the RFC, arriving at the front shortly before his encounter with Müller. The German ace inflicted gun shot wounds on Peel in their fight on 10 August 1917 resulting in a compound facture of his femur – one bullet entering above the patella before smashing the thighbone. Unfortunately, the bone knitted badly, effectively shortening the leg length by two inches – forcing him to walk with the aid of a stick thereafter. Detained in various hospitals in France and in England, he finally saw out the war in a convalescence home in St Anne's on Sea in Lancashire. Returned to South Africa in 1919.

VICTORY NO. 20
10 August 1917 Spad VII (No. B3523) 23 Squadron 1010

A patrol of 23 Squadron over the 2nd Army Front engaged German aircraft in combat. The Spad of one of their number, flown by Douglas Collis, suddenly developed engine trouble and the pilot was forced to break off an attack and head for home. Unfortunately, however, before he could make good his escape, he was spotted by three other German machines, one flown by Max Müller. As the three attacked, Collis's faulty engine cut out completely and he was forced to make a landing inside German lines near to Wervicq – any thought of gliding his powerless Spad to the Allied lines being precluded by a strong westerly wind. Collis landed his machine in an area thickly populated by German soldiers and was consequently promptly

Above: Spad VII (B3523), 23 Squadron. This was Müller's 20th victory, forced down on 10 August 1917 – its pilot, 2Lt D P Collis, taken prisoner.
Right: Second Lieutenant Douglas P Collis, 23 Squadron RFC – in the dress! A scene from a concert in a POW Camp. The 'gentleman' is Capt GH Cock MC (POW 22 July 1917).

taken prisoner. Of course, we rely heavily upon Collis's unsupported post-war debriefing report for this version of the events surrounding his bringing down. We do know, however, that Müller claimed him as a victory, bringing his total to the magic number. Müller claimed his victim down at Wervicq, which tallies with the Collis version.

SECOND LIEUTENANT
DOUGLAS P COLLIS,
23 SQUADRON, ROYAL FLYING CORPS

Gazetted Second Lieutenant to the Special List on 15 August 1916, he was admitted for training with the RFC on 19 September 1916. He progressed through the usual courses at the CFS and at the School of Aerial Gunnery before eventually gaining his 'Wings' and being sent to join 23 Squadron at the front on 28 February 1917. Taken prisoner after his clash with Müller, he was finally repatriated on 30 December 1918, arriving in the port of Hull the following day.

VICTORY NO. 21
10 August 1917 DH4 (No.A7529) 57 Squadron 2030

An evening bombing and photo sortie by six 57 Squadron DH4s set off at 1805. The target was a dump to the north-east of Westroosebeke. Five of the aircraft carried a mixture of 112lb and 230lb bombs, the sixth carried a camera as well as bombs. Three German fighters arrived on the scene at 14,000 feet near Ledeghem and promptly attacked the bombers. In the post-war debriefing following his return from captivity in Germany, Second Lieutenant A N Barlow – who had been flying the camera machine – said that his engine and ailerons had been hit by AA fire so that when his engine cut out, he was forced to land without any lateral control. During this gliding descent he was attacked by German aircraft, his observer being hit and badly wounded in the process. Unsurprisingly in view of the considerable difficulties, Barlow's machine crashed badly near to Ingelmünster – precisely the place Müller noted in his report. Barlow helped his German captors to extricate his mortally wounded observer out of the smashed-up DH4.

SECOND LIEUTENANT
ARTHUR NORMAN BARLOW,
MID, 3/5 ROYAL FUSILIERS AND 57 SQUADRON, ROYAL FLYING CORPS

Born in 1897, he was the son of Arthur and Mrs Barlow of 'Stalheim', Westbourne Road, Birkdale, Southport, Lancashire. Educated at Terranova, Birkdale, and at Rugby (1911-14) after which he joined the management department administrating the family firms, Messrs Barlows Ltd, packers, of Manchester and Redvale's Ltd., tanners, of Bury. As soon as he was old enough, he volunteered his services and was gazetted Second Lieutenant to the 5th (Reserve) Battalion, Royal Fusiliers. His immediate application to transfer to the RFC approved, he was ordered to report to Reading for training on 3 October 1916. After qualifying for his 'Wings', he was sent to join 57 Squadron at the front on 23 July 1917, lasting little more than a fortnight before falling foul of Max Müller. Taken prisoner, he spent most of his captivity in the Heidelberg Prison Camp. Received a Mentioned in Despatches (announced in the 'Escapers' Gazette of 16 December 1919) for services performed whilst a prisoner of the Germans. It is not known

whether the award was in recognition of escape attempts on his own part or for helping others to do so – or both. Repatriated on 2 January 1919, he left the service just three weeks later, returning to civilian life and to directorships on both boards of the two family businesses.

LIEUTENANT
CECIL DUNBAR HUTCHINSON,
7/SOUTH STAFFORDSHIRE REGIMENT AND 57 SQUADRON, ROYAL FLYING CORPS

The eldest son of Arthur and Mary Ann Hutchinson of 'Mariescot', Melton Road, West Bridgford, Nottingham, he was born on 1 November 1891. He was educated at Nottingham High School and at the Technical University, Nottingham, joining the Nottingham University OTC in 1914. Soon after leaving the technical school he was made a partner in the family printing firm, A Hutchinson & Company of Nottingham. Volunteering his services, he was gazetted Second Lieutenant to the 7th Battalion South Staffordshire Regiment on 7 December 1914. Embarked at Liverpool in July 1915 bound for the Gallipoli peninsular, landing at Suvla Bay on 7 August. Following the evacuation, he served in Egypt, in Sinai and latterly in France. Promoted Lieutenant in June 1916. Returning to England, he was accepted into the RFC for observer training in June 1917. Sent out again to France in July 1917, this time joining 57 Squadron at the front. Initially reported missing, he was later declared wounded and a prisoner of war. Died of the wounds he received in aerial combat with Max Müller two days later on 12 August 1917. Buried at Harlebeke Cemetery, Belgium (Bel140). Age 26.

VICTORY NO. 22
17 August 1917 SE5 (No.A8903) 56 Squadron 0705

Captain G E Bowman led his flight of six SEs across the lines at 11,000 feet above Polygon Wood. Almost immediately they were attacked by Albatros Scouts of Jasta 28, the leading machine, it was noted, being painted red. The attackers initially went for the three lower SEs piloted by Richard Maybery, David Wilkinson and Richard Leighton.

Bowman, and the two remaining patrol members, F J Horrell and W J Potts promptly turned to help their threatened colleagues. The Flight Commander Gerald Bowman attempted to engage the red fighter but, surrounded by hostiles, he broke off and went instead for another German. He was then attacked from above and behind by yet another of the enemy and, as it zoomed over him, Bowman fired into it from close range, whereupon the Albatros began to fall away out of control. The battle continued for a while but then began to peter out, the antagonists breaking away and dispersing. The red Albatros had been prominent throughout the engagement – Richard Maybery being one who had fired at it but without effect. Maybery developed engine trouble and headed back for the British lines. En route back, he spotted an SE under attack by two Albatri and, suddenly finding his engine firing again, attempted to return

to the aid of the lone SE. By now, however, the sky was empty.

Two SE5s failed to get back – Wilkinson's and Leighton's. Both men had been shot down, badly wounded, and taken to Courtrai hospital. Leighton survived, albeit with a silver plate in his head. Wilkinson died as a consequence of his wounds and injuries ten days later. Wilkinson, who was credited to Müller, came down by the side of the canalised River Lys at Bousbeques, not far from Quesnoy. A Jasta 11 pilot accounted for Leighton.

LIEUTENANT
DAVID STANLEY WILKINSON,
6/CAMERON HIGHLANDERS AND
56 SQUADRON, ROYAL FLYING CORPS

The son of John and Martha Wilkinson of 'Linden', Malone Park, Belfast, he was born

Lieutenant David Stanley Wilkinson, 56 Squadron RFC, with SE5a (A4853), in late July 1917. Note the paintwork around the cockpit. (Via E F Cheesman)

Müller standing by the wreckage of Wilkinson's SE5a outside the town of Bousbecque, 17 August 1917.

on 20 July 1888. When war was declared, he was a student of medicine living at 2 Mount Pleasant, Belfast. He immediately enlisted into the 24th (2nd Sportsman's) Battalion, Royal Fusiliers (Number 44979). Gazetted Second Lieutenant to the 8/Cameron Highlanders on 2 November 1914 after earlier stating a preference for the Black Watch or some other Scots infantry regiment. Promoted Lieutenant on 27 September 1915 and sent out to join the 6th Battalion of his regiment in France on 5 October following. In early 1916 he had the misfortune to be kicked in the leg by a horse. As a consequence of the kick, his left leg became extremely inflamed, the wound turning septic. Evacuated home, he was forced to spend a month in hospital at Cambusbarron near Stirling, an operation having to be performed to remove some pieces of splintered bone from the leg. His health restored, he next successfully

applied for transfer to the RFC. After completing his training, he was awarded his 'Wings' and appointed Flying Officer on 13 April 1917 and, shortly afterwards, was sent out to join 56 Squadron at the front. After coming down at Bousbeques, he was taken by ambulance to Number 160 German Field Hospital, Limburg Camp, Courtrai, Belgium. Despite the best efforts of the German hospital staff, he died from the effects of gun shot wounds in the chest and spine on 26 August 1917. A German medical orderly, Eugene Scharff, who had helped to nurse the mortally wounded airman in Courtrai Hospital, afterwards sent a ring Wilkinson had been wearing to the British Embassy in Paris for onward transmission to David's parents in Belfast. He appears to be fingering that very ring in the accompanying photograph (see page 81). Buried in Courtrai Cemetery, Belgium (Bel393). Age 29.

VICTORY NO. 23
19 August 1917 Spad 0815

Another Max Müller 'victory' that cannot be verified. He claimed a Spad down into the Allied lines near Ypres during the morning of 19 August 1917. In fact, there were no Spad losses – RFC, French or Belgian – or even 'incidents' that might be linked to, or explain this claim. If, indeed, it was a Spad he attacked, then clearly it,

and its pilot, survived the encounter totally unscathed.

A 54 Squadron Sopwith Pup flown by Second Lieutenant F W Gibbes (A649), based just east of Dunkirk, was damaged on a 0500 OP by three hostile fighters. The connection seems altogether too tenuous to be offered as a feasible possibility.

VICTORY NO. 24
19 August 1917 Nieuport XVII (No.B1683) 1 Squadron 1810

There is no doubting Müller's next victory. At 1600, Captain P Fullard MC (B3459) led six Nieuport Scouts on a 1 Squadron early evening DOP and escort. The line for the patrol to follow was to be Polygon-Ledegem-

A well known shot of Müller with his Albatros Scout. He was not a tall man and his lack of stature is emphasised against the size of his fighter plane. Note markings on wheel cover.

Menin-Lille-Perenchies. At 12,000 feet over the Menin area, Fullard spotted six 'new type' enemy scouts – possibly Albatros DVas, he thought. Personally selecting one which was cruising along between him and the six FE2s they were protecting, Fullard attacked the garishly coloured yellow and black striped machine. He got in very close and fired 3/4 of a drum from his Lewis gun. The German turned to the left and hurtled down with Fullard following its descent to see it crash near Roncq (Sheet 28.x.14). The incident subsequently received confirmation from two other 1 Squadron pilots and thus became Fullard's 25th victory. Sounds clear-cut but, unfortunately, it is not. In fact, Jasta 28 suffered no losses and although their machines certainly had yellow tailplanes with varnished plywood fuselages and carried one chordwise black band on each side of the tail and elevator, neither injury nor damage to a pilot or a machine is recorded.

Turning next to the Müller victory. Either just before or during the air battle itself – depending on whose version of events you accept – Lieutenant Harold Waring's Nieuport (B1683) went missing. Fullard and the other four 1 Squadron pilots all thought that Waring took no part in the scrap. Waring, on the other hand, stated in his post-war debriefing following his return from captivity in Germany, that he and the patrol were attacked by 40 *(sic)* Albatros Scouts! After five minutes of aerial combat, his engine began to slow down and the throttle control malfunctioned. As a consequence of these difficulties, he fell below the altitude of the main dog-fight, coming down to 2,000 feet whereupon he was attacked and personally wounded, his Nieuport's engine and fuel tank hit.

The Bavarian ace claimed his victim as crashing near Menin on the German side of the line. We are left to wonder if it was, in fact, Waring's machine that was seen to crash by Fullard and his friends, who, in the heat and turmoil of the moment, mistook it for the Albatros he had attacked moments before.

The escorted FEs, from 20 Squadron, also lost one of their number to Jasta 28 – a victory credited to Leutnant Ernst Hess. The downed FE was crewed by Lieutenant C R Richards MC and Lieutenant S F Thompson, both of whom were wounded and taken prisoner. Richards was an ace with a dozen victories of his own by this date.

LIEUTENANT
HAROLD ERNEST ARTHUR WARING,
1 SQUADRON, ROYAL FLYING CORPS

Born on 20 April 1897, he was the only son of diamond setter Henry Charles Waring and Mrs Waring of Godalming, Surrey (later 63 Radlett Street, Watford, Hertfordshire). Educated at Holloway County Secondary School from where he gained the coveted Gifford Scholarship which allowed him entry into Exeter College (1911-15). Volunteered to serve with RFC in 1916, later qualifying as a pilot and being sent out to join 1 Squadron in France in the summer of 1917. Wounded in the action with Max Müller, he would remain a prisoner of the Germans until his repatriation in January 1919. Entered the Home Civil Service after leaving the RAF but continued with his academic studies. Obtained a First Class Batchelor's degree in history on 4 August 1921.

VICTORY NO. 25
21 August 1917　Martinsyde G.100 (No.7276)　27 Squadron　0820

Six single-seat Martinsyde bombers of 27 Squadron (the 'Elephants' would soon to be replaced with two-seat DH4s) took off at 0540 to mount a bombing raid. Led by Captain G K Smith (A6259), the bombers were destined to lose half of their number in this patrol. The Squadron had already suffered at the hands of Jasta 28 earlier in the month and now had the misfortune to fall foul of them again. The confrontation soon degenerated into a sprawling dog-fight across the skies east of Seclin. The Elephants flown by Captain Smith and Second Lieutenant D P Cox (A3992) were shot down, their occupants killed. Smith was claimed by Leutnant Karl Bolle of Jasta 28 whilst Oberleutnant Hans Bethge – an interloper from Jasta 30 – was credited with Cox. Sydney Thompson (Number 7276 and carrying the mark 'A6') was forced to make a

landing between Dovrin and Bouilly.

A fourth G.100 was claimed by Rudolf Berthold of Jasta 18, although, in fact, only three were lost.

SECOND LIEUTENANT
SYDNEY THOMPSON,
27 SQUADRON, ROYAL FLYING CORPS

Born in 1895, he was the son of brass-finisher Thomas Thompson and his wife, Janet Thompson of 18 Whitehall Road, Gateshead (later 157 Prince Consort Road, Gateshead). Educated at Shipcote Boys School from where he secured his first job as a shipping clerk. Enlisted into the 19th (2nd Public Schools) Battalion, Royal Fusiliers (Number 7352), with which unit he went to France for the first time on 14 November 1915 with the rank of Lance

Müller alongside Martinsyde G100 (7276) of 27 Squadron which he brought down on 21 August 1917. Its pilot, 2Lt S Thompson, was made prisoner of war. The number '6' is painted in white on the cowling; A-6 in black on undersides of lower wings.

Corporal. In early 1916, the Public Schools Battalions were brought back from France and, effectively, became officer cadet units. Sydney Thompson was gazetted to the RFC via the Special List on 26 September 1916. He eventually qualified as a pilot but was not sent to France until 21 August 1917 – the very day he was shot down and reported 'missing in action'. Taken prisoner, he would not be repatriated until 17 December 1918. Tragically, Sydney died in the 1st Northern General Hospital, Newcastle-upon-Tyne on 26 January 1919. No doubt in a weakened state after his incarceration, he fell victim to the influenza pandemic raging around the world at this time. He is buried in Gateshead East Cemetery. Age 21.

VICTORY NO. 26
21 August 1917 DH4 No. A7555 57 Squadron 1925

This was to be the third of Müller's 'double-victories-in-day' during August 1917 and like those achieved earlier on the 10th and the 19th of the month – one would be during the morning, the other in the afternoon.

At 1700, 57 Squadron sent off a six-machine bombing raid to an ammunition dump at Ledeghem – one of the DH4s being equipped with a camera as well as bombs. At 1850, between Ledeghem and Menin, the formation was engaged by an estimated 14 enemy fighters. Four of the enemy scouts were noted as being particularly persistent and aggressive – one of this quartet paying the price for his apparent recklessness by being set aflame and driven down.

Two of the RFC bombers were shot up. The first, A7555, crewed by Lieutenants W B Hutcheson and T E Godwin – was last seen at 2,000 feet over Menin, still, apparently, under control. Meanwhile the crew of A2132 – Sergeant E V Bousher and 1AM William Harmston – were both wounded and later crashed inside British lines. Harmston, who was hit in both legs, would later die of his wounds.

In his debriefing following his release from captivity in Germany, Lieutenant W B Hutcheson said that his petrol supply failed and he was forced to go below the other aircraft. Attacked by five German fighters, his observer was killed in the air before his engine finally cut out, forcing him to land. No sooner did he land than he was surrounded by German troops.

Müller recorded his victory – Hutcheson and Godwin – coming down at Ledeghem on the German side. Leutnant August Hanko, claimed the Bousher/Harmston DH4 as going down near to Hooge. This would be Hanko's fourth victory.

LIEUTENANT
W B Hutcheson,
CANADIAN ENGINEERS AND 57 SQUADRON, ROYAL FLYING CORPS

From North Bay, Ontario, Canada. Gazetted Lieutenant to the Canadian Engineers on 20 May 1916. Arriving in England, he successfully applied for transfer to the RFC and was ordered to report to Oxford for flying training on 12 August 1916. Progressed through the various stages before being awarded his 'Wings' and appointed Flying Officer on 14 December 1916. Posted to operational flying with 57 Squadron in France on 6 June 1917. Shot down by Max Müller, he would remain incarcerated until his repatriation on 14 December 1918. Anxious to return to Canada, he relinquished his commission on Christmas Eve 1918.

LIEUTENANT
Thomas Ernest Godwin,
11/CANADIAN MOUNTED RIFLES AND 57 SQUADRON, ROYAL FLYING CORPS

The son of James Thomas and Hannah Augusta Godwin of Acton, London. Thomas was living and working in Kamloops, British Columbia, Canada, in 1915 when he volunteered for service with the Canadian army. Commissioned into the 11/Canadian Mounted Rifles on 21 August 1916, he successfully applied for transfer to the RFC, completing his observer training in the summer of 1917. Killed in the air by Max Müller, he is buried in Harlebeke Cemetery, Belgium (Bel140). Age 24.

VICTORY NO. 27
9 September 1917 Sopwith Camel (No.B3916) 70 Squadron 1930

At 1645 in the late afternoon of 9 September 1917, 70 Squadron Camels took off on an Offensive Patrol to cover the area between Gheluvelt and Houthulst. Nearly three hours into the patrol, they became entangled with a formation of Albatros Scouts. Second Lieutenant Hugh Weightman in B3916 was seriously wounded in the abdomen and went down. He managed, with great difficulty, to get to the front lines but was then forced to crashland amongst the shell craters, his Camel wrecked. Two other Camels on this patrol also became casualties. Lieutenant N C Saward in B3928 was shot down and taken prisoner whilst Captain Clive Collett MC and Bar, in B2341, a Kiwi with 11 victories – including three on this very day – was personally wounded and his machine shot up and damaged.

Squadron certainly was, two of their Camels being claimed by Werner Voss — although the Nachrichtenblatt, confusingly, suggests that they may have fallen to Hess and Ray.

SECOND LIEUTENANT
HUGH WEIGHTMAN,
(LATER SIR HUGH WEIGHTMAN, KT BACHELOR 1947, COMPANION OF THE MOST EXALTED ORDER OF THE STAR OF INDIA 1946, KAISAR-I-HIND MEDAL (GOLD) 1936), 70 SQUADRON, ROYAL FLYING CORPS

Born on 29 November 1898, he was the son of Mr and Mrs Weightman of 98 Lancaster Gate West, London and of 76 Broadmead Road, Folkestone. Educated at Hymer's College and, post-war, at Corpus Christi College, Cambridge from where he eventually graduated BA. Whilst still considerably underage, he was gazetted Second Lieutenant to 15th (Reserve) Battalion of the Middlesex Regiment on 5 October 1914. Promoted to Lieutenant on 25 March 1915. Took a reduction in rank to be transferred as a Second Lieutenant to the RFC via the General List on 13 April 1917. Awarded his 'Wings' and posted to 70 Squadron at the front on 22 August 1917. Quite badly wounded in the abdomen, Hugh Weightman would, upon recovery, be appointed to a number of training posts, never to fly operationally again. Left the RAF with the rank of Captain on 20 January 1919, returning to his studies at Cambridge. After securing his degree and passing the necessary civil service examinations, he entered the Indian Civil Service in 1922. Married Margaret Elizabeth Agnes Deans in 1924. Transferred to the Indian Political Service in 1929, subsequently serving with distinction in Assam, Central India, Baluchistan, the Persian Gulf and in Dehli, where he was Secretary to the Government of India, External Affairs Department. Awarded the Kaisar-i-Hind Medal in Gold (1st Class) in 1936 for the performance of outstanding public service in India. Appointed CSI in 1946 and created Knight Bachelor upon his retirement in 1947. Died on 28 October 1949 in his fifty-first year.

Confusion over this patrol action is largely due to the fact that some accounts have it occurring on the 10th of September. The formal confirmation of Müller's victory — Hugh Weightman — was later than was usual, not appearing in the Nachrichtenblatt (the German equivalent of RFC Communiqués) until quite some time after the event (see page 417, late confirmations for August and September 1917). Perhaps the fact that the Camel came down on the British side of the front-line trenches inhibited and delayed confirmation. In fact, Jasta 28 was not in action on 10th September although 70

VICTORY NOS. 28 & 29
22 October 1917 Sopwith Pups (Nos.B1782 & B1834) 54 Squadron 1625

As we have seen, Müller had scored double victories in a single day before but this was his first double claim in a single action.

54 Squadron took off from its base near Dunkirk to fly an Offensive Patrol to Roulers. En route, battle was joined with a group of German fighters, during which two of the Pups collided – not an uncommon occurrence in the whirling confusion of dog-fighting above the Western Front. The report of the collision found its way into the formal records courtesy of the surviving pilot – Percy Goodbehere – during his post-war debriefing following his return from captivity in Germany.

Did Müller force the collision and therefore feel justified in seizing upon the opportunity of improving his victory tally by two in one fell swoop? Or, as was often the case, did the returning pilot put a better 'spin' on the event than it deserved? Better to admit to an accidental collision than to a defeat in combat? Whatever the truth of the matter, the Bavarian claimed both Pups and was duly credited accordingly. Both came down west of Beerst, inside German lines.

(NO. 28)
SECOND LIEUTENANT
GEORGE COWIE,
54 SQUADRON, ROYAL FLYING CORPS

The only son of Captain Alexander Mitchell Cowie and Sylvia Margaret Cowie of Dulland Brae, Dufftown, Banffshire, Scotland, he was born on 26 February 1899. Educated at Rugby School (1912-16), representing the school in the 1916 XV. Receiving his commission in May 1917, he had completed his pilot training by 11 October of the same year when he was sent to France and Flanders and 54 Squadron. Less than a fortnight later he had the misfortune to run into Max Müller. Anecdotal evidence tells us that Cowie's father never recovered from the news of his son's early death – he was still only eighteen – his own health and the family's fortunes (there were four daughters as well as Mrs Cowie) suffering irredeemably. George Cowie's grave is one of the more than 11,000 in Tyne Cot Cemetery, Passchendaele, Belgium (Bel 125).

(NO.29)
LIEUTENANT
PERCY GOODBEHERE,
5/MANCHESTER REGIMENT (TF) AND 54
SQUADRON, ROYAL FLYING CORPS

The son of Mr and Mrs F G Goodbehere of 'Fern Bank', Plymouth Grove, Manchester, he was born on 10 March 1892. Educated at King William College, Isle of Man (1904-08). He enlisted into a Public Schools Battalion of the Royal Fusiliers in September 1914.

Gazetted Second Lieutenant into the 5th Battalion (TF) of the Manchester Regiment on 2 October 1915. After a period in the UK with a provisional battalion, he served in the trenches from June to October 1916. Percy sought a transfer to the RFC, which was eventually granted in December 1916. Subsequently, he gained the Royal Aero Club Certificate (Number 4419) at the Military School, Birmingham, on 20 March 1917 before qualifying for his official 'Wings' two months later. Posted to 54 Squadron at the front on 2 June 1917. Wounded and taken

prisoner on 22 October 1917, he would be incarcerated in Germany until his repatriation on 17 December 1918. Relinquished his commission due to ill health on 22 August 1919. Lived, post-war, at 'Kinleith', Styal Road, Wilmslow, Cheshire. Died on Christmas Day 1967 at the age of 75.

These were the final victories credited to Müller with Jasta 28. It has been said that Müller had not got on too well with the newly appointed Staffelführer, Edmund Thuy, who had arrived on 26 September 1917. Thuy's 15 victories were unlikely to impress Müller with his 29. Müller already had the Pour le Mérite – Thuy would not receive his until June 1918. No doubt Müller thought that he should have been given command of Jasta 28. Although a former NCO himself, Thuy had, nonetheless, been commissioned since early 1916 – considerably longer than Müller. In some respects, Müller's outstanding record was an embarrassment to the hierarchy of the Imperial German Air Service. He had been an NCO for a long time and a commissioned officer for a relatively short period. Müller took his leave of Jasta 28 on 29 October 1917.

Despite his impressive record and the plethora of awards that had been showered upon him by this time, he would take up his duties with Jasta Boelcke as just another Jasta pilot – there would be no advancement or additional responsibilities for the former NCO. His new Commanding Officer was an old acquaintance, Erwin Böhme.

VICTORY NO. 30
6 November 1917 Spad 19 Squadron 0930?

Another instance of an unsustainable claim. Perhaps in his anxiety to make an impression on his new comrades and environment, he submitted a flimsily based claim which was, surprisingly, allowed to stand. Certainly there is no corresponding record of Allied loss or damage. Initially, the problem was thought to be one of date as, in some records, the claim is listed as having

arisen as a consequence of an action on 7 November 1917. The Nachrichtenblatt, however, is insistent that it occurred on 6 November. Müller claimed that he engaged a Spad south-west of St Julien and saw it go down into Allied lines. To add to the uncertainty, the time is given variously as 0930, 1610 and 2130.

There are no Allied Spad losses during

the afternoon or evening of 6 November (nor 7 November, come to that). The 6 November was certainly a busy day in terms of aerial combat but virtually all of the fighting took place during the earlier morning hours – the weather turning severe from mid-morning.

A 19 Squadron Spad was lost on a low OP near Passchendaele at 0740 on the morning of the 6th, the pilot – Second Lieutenant Francis Gartside-Tippinge – killed. In trying to match this casualty with Müller's claim, it has to be said that the timing is wrong as is the location – not dramatically but neverthe-

less significantly. Furthermore, Paul Bäumer claimed a Spad at 0825 German time east of Zonnebeke (in between Passchendaele and St Julien) which came down in the front lines – surely more likely to be the 19 Squadron Spad in question.

Müller, in a letter home, stated that Jasta 2 shot down seven English planes during the mornings of 6th and 7th of November. Six, either lost or shot-up, can be accounted for – one Spad, three Camels, an SE5 and an RE8. The seventh, still unidentified, is the Bavarian's phantom Spad.

VICTORY NO. 31
11 November 1917 DH5 (No.A9439) 32 Squadron 1220

Max Müller in flight gear in front of his Albatros DV.

Three 32 Squadron DH5s, flown by Second Lieutenants C J Howson, W A Tyrrell and Lieutenant A Claydon, were engaged on an Inner OP. At 1000 over Westroosbeke, Claydon and Tyrrell first intercepted an Albatros with a yellow and green fuselage and yellow nose. Claydon was forced to pull out of the fight with a gun jam, but Tyrrell carried on the attack. The German began a staggering flutter in a downwards direction. As the pilot attempted to pull the stricken Albatros out of the dive, Tyrrell fired again, his bullets striking the pilot's head and the instrument panel in front of him. The Albatros reared upwards before spinning down again. Tyrrell lost sight of his quarry at 300 feet as it fell through and below other circling German aircraft – it was obviously too dangerous to follow it down any further. Despite Tyrrell's strong claim, there were, in fact, no German fighter pilot fatalities this day. Nevertheless, Tyrrell added this 'out of control' claim to his score – a score which eventually reached 17 before his own death in action on 9 June 1918.

Continuing the patrol, the 32 Squadron trio next spotted six more Albatros Scouts above them at 11,000 feet and began climbing towards them. The Albatri, perhaps surprised at the audacity of the outnumbered DH5s, dived on the impudent British scouts, both sides manoeuvring for

the most advantageous attacking positions.

Despite the initial posturing, the actual confrontation was brief. One Albatros was seen to get on Claydon's tail before both machines disappeared into cloud at about 1,500 feet. Howson got away a few short bursts at another Albatros before the rest of the German machines turned and flew away east.

Claydon had his fuel tank shot through by the chasing Albatros and was forced to make a landing inside Allied lines, the DH5 turning over on the uneven ground. Müller reported his victim as having fallen near to Wieltje, between Ypres and Zonnebeke, on the British side. Front-line observers confirmed Müller's claim albeit wrongly identifying the downed machine as an SE5a. Both side's timing of Claydon's descent reasonably coincide and, furthermore, this was the only British casualty of the day.

LIEUTENANT
ARTHUR CLAYDON,
DFC, CANADIAN FIELD ARTILLERY AND 32 SQUADRON, ROYAL FLYING CORPS

Born in Deeping St James, Lincolnshire on 25 September 1895, Arthur was the son of Mr and Mrs B M Claydon. The family emigrated to Winnipeg, Canada, where, after completing his education, Arthur (pictured above) joined his father in the family building firm, living with his parents at 442 Balmoral Road. Claydon, who had already served in the local Militia Artillery, volunteered for active service and was gazetted Lieutenant to the Canadian Field Artillery on 26 February 1916. Following service at the front, he successfully sought transfer to the RFC in 1917 and after qualifying as a pilot, was posted to 32 Squadron. Subsequent to his close encounter with Max Müller, Claydon went on to become an ace, gaining no less than seven victories of his own – the first in a DH5 (A9300), the remaining six in an SE5A (C1089). Claydon met his own nemesis over Carvin on 8 July 1918 in the form of Leutnant Paul Billik of Jasta 52, becoming the 24th of the German ace's eventual 31 victories. The recently introduced Distinguished Flying Cross was conferred

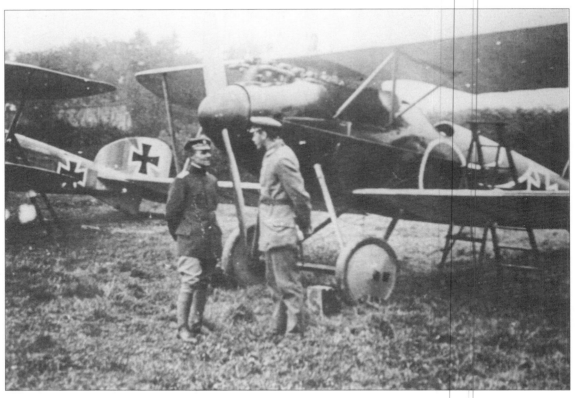

Müller (left) with his Albatros DV. *(Greg VanWyngarden)*

upon Arthur Claydon – the announcement, unfortunately, being made after his death, *London Gazette* 3 August 1918, page 9199: *'Recently this officer, single-handed, went to the assistance of another pilot, attacked by eleven Fokker bi-planes and six scouts. By his gallant conduct and skilful manoeuvring he not only extricated the pilot, but drove down several of the enemy aeroplanes. He has shown great initiative and gallantry in locating, bombing and attacking troops on the ground from low altitudes'.* Claydon is buried in Cabaret-Rouge Cemetery, France (Fr924). Age 22.

VICTORY NO. 32
29 November 1917 DH 1610

This day saw the end of Jasta Boelcke's leader, Erwin Böhme.

Two victories were also claimed on the day, one by Böhme, the other by Müller – neither of which can be attributed to British or Belgian losses. Böhme, the Staffelführer, supposedly downed a Camel during his last fight at 1255. Müller later claimed a Rumpf DD (distinctively a fuselaged biplane – as opposed to a lattice-tail pusher). Subsequent speculation has this as being, more probably, a DH4 or perhaps even a single-seat DH5.

To add to the confusion, this machine – whatever type it may have been – supposedly came down at 1610 inside the German lines south of Shaep Baillie. In practice and in theory, therefore, there should not have been a problem in establishing its identity. In fact, however, the only DH5 shot up on the day was in action further south near Bourlon, and, despite the damage it sustained, managed to return to its base. Two DH4s of 49 Squadron were also in action – one falling to a combination of fighter attack and hostile AA fire, eventually coming down in flames at 1010 near Thun St Martin on the Cambrai front. Another returned safely home after being damaged by AA fire. The only other vague possibilities were two Bristol Fighters, but,

here again, a feasible connection cannot be made – one getting down safely onto the British side of the lines, the other being credited to Jasta 36.

Victory Number 32 has therefore to be counted as another of the phantom variety.

VICTORY NO. 33
2 December 1917 DH4 (No.A7422) 57 Squadron 0945

Whatever the doubts and uncertainties surrounding the events of 29 November 1917, the next Müller victory appears clear cut. 57 Squadron's 'Fours' took part in a bombing and reconnaissance sortie, departing their base in dribs-and-drabs commencing at 0700. They were sent out to 'seek targets of opportunity' in the areas of Houthulst Forest, Clercken and Westroosbeke. Müller's victims were in a machine that had taken off at 0800. Following his ferocious assault, they fell north-west of Menin at 0840 (0940 German time).

SECOND LIEUTENANT
DAVID MILLER,
57 SQUADRON, ROYAL FLYING CORPS

Born in 1898, he was the son of Mr and Mrs Miller of Hill Farm, Hadleigh, Suffolk. Joined the Inns of Court OTC (Number B/11042) on 9 April 1917 and was gazetted to the RFC via the General List on 4 July 1917. Appointed a Flying Officer, he was sent out to Flanders to join 57 Squadron on 29 September 1917. Wounded and taken prisoner on 2 December 1917, he was repatriated a little more than a year later on 17 December 1918. Employed in administration until his eventual transfer to the Unemployed List on 21 June 1919.

SECOND LIEUTENANT
ARTHUR HARRY CHILD HOYLES,
5/HIGHLAND LIGHT INFANTRY AND
57 SQUADRON, ROYAL FLYING CORPS

Born in London on 8 November 1894, Arthur (above) was the son of Henry Child Hoyles and Grace Gertrude Hoyles. The family moved to Glasgow in August 1905, living at 57 Kirsland Street, in the West End of that city. Harry, who had been privately educated in London, now entered Glasgow High School (1905-10). After leaving school, he went into the offices of grain merchants John Jackson & Company Ltd., of Hope Street, Glasgow. Harry enlisted as a private soldier (Number 343) in the Royal Army Medical Corps in the first weeks of the war. Selected for officer training, he was gazetted Second Lieutenant to the 5th (City of Glasgow) Battalion, Highland Light Infantry on 16 June 1915. An application for transfer to the RFC was granted on 11 September 1916 when he was accepted for pilot training. He crashed at 60 mph during a training flight and whilst the machine was badly smashed up, he sustained only slight injury – nothing more than a grazed face, in fact. His nerve had gone, however, and he was obliged to return to his regiment, serving in the trenches for seven months with the combined 10/11th battalions of the Highland Light Infantry in France. After a month or two in the trenches, he had begun again to agitate for a transfer to the RFC and, surprisingly perhaps, in August 1917 he was accepted for training as an observer. Successfully completing his training at Hythe, he was posted to 57 Squadron in France on 8 October 1917. Initially posted as missing, the Germans confirmed his death in a note dropped onto a British airfield on Christmas Day 1917. His burial place was subsequently lost and hence he is commemorated on the Arras Memorial to the Missing, France. Age 23.

VICTORY NO. 34
5 December 1917 SE5a ? 1440

Yet more problems of identification and connection with this so-called 'victory'. Müller requested confirmation of a British SE5 shot down into the British lines south-west of Poelcapelle. There were, in fact, no SE5s lost this day nor, indeed, any that appeared to have suffered even minor damage. Other single-seaters in action are all satisfactorily attributed to other claimants.

The great ace, Ernst Udet, of Jasta 4 was also guilty of claiming a 'phantom' SE5 on this day. German pilots were notorious for their apparent inability to correctly identify Allied types of aeroplanes.

VICTORY NO. 35
7 December 1917 Spad VII (No.B3559) 19 Squadron 1155

19 Squadron Spads took off at 0950 on a designated Northern Offensive Patrol. Forty minutes later they engaged an enemy two-seater but, as they did so, six German fighters came down on them like avenging angels. Thick cloud prevented a wholesale dog-fight but somewhere along the line, Lieutenant Yeo fell to the guns of Max Müller.

Coming back from Germany at the war's end, Yeo confirmed in his debriefing report that his aircraft had been badly hit in the engine. He managed to land the Spad reasonably well in the circumstances but found himself smack in the middle of a German rest camp area. He was taken prisoner before he could attempt to set his Spad alight.

In fact, Jasta 2 claimed two Spads this day. The downing of the second of the pair into Allied lines near Zonnebeke, giving Paul Bäumer his 14th victory.

LIEUTENANT
HERBERT ALLAN YEO,
19 SQUADRON, ROYAL FLYING CORPS

Born in Brock Weir, Gloucestershire, on 10 December 1897, he was the son of Thomas and Mrs Yeo of 'The Cot', Portishead, Bristol. Educated at the Merchant Venturers School and at Bristol University where he was a member of the OTC. A pupil teacher in November 1915, he freely volunteered for service with the Somerset Light Infantry (Number 35815) before compulsory conscription was introduced. Indeed, in the weeks before the legislation was to be enacted in January 1916, recruiting stations all over Britain were besieged and overwhelmed by men anxious to avoid the 'stigma' of conscription. So many volunteers, in fact, that the system could not cope. Most were told to return to civilian life

Müller with his Albatros – its black comet insignia and white rudder highlighted against the 'yellow' varnished plywood fuselage. The spinner was red, the wheel covers white.

for the time being and, to single them out as volunteers, were given a distinctive khaki armband bearing a red crown which could be worn with their civilian clothes until such time as their turn came. Probably because he was a teacher – of which there was a shortage – Herbert was not called up until 31 January 1917. After a short period of service with the Somerset Light Infantry, he was gazetted to the RFC via the General List on 10 May 1917. Qualified for his 'Wings' in the summer of 1917 and was sent out to join

19 Squadron at the front on 3 November following. Initially reported as missing in action, his parents were greatly relieved subsequently to learn that he was safe – albeit a prisoner of war. He spent most of his enforced incarceration at Karlsruhe before his repatriation on 17 December 1918. Transferred to the Unemployed List on 18 April 1919, he returned to teaching, taking up a post in Newport, Monmouthshire and living at 16 Linden Road, in that town.

VICTORY NO. 36
16 December 1917 Camel (No.B2450) 70 Squadron 1410

The Camels of 70 Squadron took off on an Offensive Patrol at 1250. In a subsequent clash with Albatros Scouts, Lieutenant K G Seth-Smith in B2450 was severely shot up and forced to make a bee-line for the deck. He skimmed his damaged machine over the lines and managed to put it down just beyond the trench lines, the Camel ending up in a shell hole just east of St Julien (Sheet 28.D.10.c.9). Seth-Smith scrambled clear of

the wrecked machine which had its wings and centre section smashed, all longerons broken, wheels ripped off, engine bearers broken and engine damaged. Beyond salvage, B2450 was 'struck off charge'.

Müller's formal claim stated that his victim had fallen west of Passchendaele, into the British lines (St Julien is just to the west of Passchendaele). He duly received confirmation from front-line observers.

Lieutenant Kenneth Gordon Seth-Smith, (front row, seated right) 70 Squadron RFC, with a group of colleagues. Back, standing: Crang, Gribben, Jones, Thompson, Matthews. Front, sitting: Allen, Webb, Smyth, McKenzie, Seth-Smith *(E F Cheesman)*

LIEUTENANT
Kenneth Gordon Seth-Smith,
1/NORTHUMBERLAND FUSILIERS AND
70 SQUADRON, ROYAL FLYING CORPS

Born on 19 October 1897, he was the son of Mr and Mrs Seth-Smith of 'Colwood', Bolney, Sussex. Gazetted to the 1/Northumberland Fusiliers on 24 March 1915. Eventually sought transfer to the RFC and was ordered to report for observer training at Reading on 15 March 1917. Completing his training at Hythe, he was sent to France as a probationary observer on 5 April 1917. Three months later, he returned home for pilot training, again reporting to Reading, this time on 27 July 1917. Evidently a pilot of some marked ability, he was posted for further tuition to the School of Special Flying on 2 September 1917. Sent out to join 70 Squadron in France on 10 November 1917 but ordered first to report to Number 1 Aeroplane Supply Depot en route. Actually joined 70 Squadron on 19 November 1917. Unscathed in the action with Max Müller on 16 December 1917, he was not so lucky on 23 March 1918 when he was wounded in action. By this time he had seven victories of his own. Yet another ace who received no overt award for his skill and courage. After recovering from his wounds, he took up a training role – never again flying operationally. Finally relinquished his RAF commission to return to the army on 17 November 1919. By the time of the Second World War, Seth-Smith was a test pilot for Hawker Aircraft Ltd, living at 'Whitedown', Thorndown Lane, Windlesham. Killed on 11 August 1942 at Egham, Surrey, whilst testing a prototype Typhoon. Age 45.

Max Ritter von Müller, Pour le Mérite.

This was to be Müller's last victory. Even after Böhme's death on 29 November, Müller had still not been given command of the Jasta, nor even given temporary command until such time that a replacement could be found. It was two weeks after Bohme's death before the new Staffelführer arrived. Leutnant Walter von Bülow-Bothkamp had achieved 28 victories with Jasta 36, receiving the Pour le Mérite on 8 October 1917, a month after Müller had received his. If Müller had not been dissatisfied before, he most certainly was by now. His new Commanding Officer was seven years younger than the Bavarian and a 'von' to boot.

On 6 January 1918 von Bülow fell in combat without adding to his score, but then, neither had Müller added to his tally since his 36th victory on 16 December 1917. He was, however, finally given his due and appointed to command the Jasta in von Bülow's stead. A long-awaited appointment that would last for just three days.

Captain George Zimmer and Second Lieutenant H A Somerville MC, 21 Squadron RFC, the RE8 crew that brought down Müller on 9 January 1918.

Right: A memorial plaque on the wall of the house where Max Müller was born. It translates as follows: *'In this house was born, on 1 January 1887, the German hero Leutnant Ritter von Müller the most successful battle flyer of Bavaria. Honorary Citizen of the market town of Rottenburg. He fell after 39 victories on 9 January 1918'.* (Dr. -Ing. Niedermeyer)

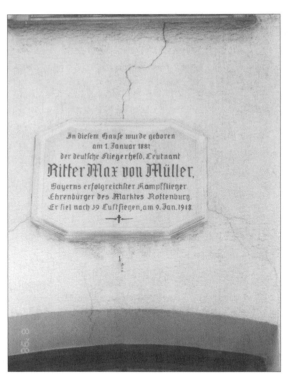

In diesem Hause wurde geboren
am 1. Januar 1881
der deutsche Fliegerheld, Leutnant
Ritter Max von Müller.
Bayerns erfolgreichster Kampfflieger.
Ehrenbürger des Marktes Rottenburg.
Er fiel nach 39 Luftsiegen, am 9. Jan. 1918.
✝

Below: A Guard of Honour flanks the coffin of Max Ritter von Müller at St Joseph's Church, Courtrai, France.

On 9 January 1918, whilst attacking an RE8 of 21 Squadron (B5045) at 1250, he apparently did not pay sufficient attention to his angle of approach, thus allowing the two-seater's observer to get in a good burst of fire. Machine-gun bullets streamed into his engine and fuel tank, the Albatros catching fire. His Jasta 2 subordinates watched in horror as he either leapt or fell from his burning fighter. His British conquerors were Captain G F W Zimmer and Second Lieutenant H A Somerville, flying a photographic sortie over the Corps counter-battery area.

The Bavarian's body was taken to St Joseph's Church in Courtrai on a dismal January day, for the first of several ceremonies. Finally, Max Müller's coffin was carried by train to his home town of Rottenburg ob der Tauber for ceremonial burial. He was 31.

CHAPTER 3

OBERLEUTNANT ADOLF VON TUTSCHEK

Von Tutschek with his observer, Leutnant von Stein, on 26 December 1916, when serving with FA6. Note the wire caught around the propeller boss – picked up while low flying. (Trevor Henshaw)

Bavarian-born Adolf von Tutschek hailed from Ingolstadt, about fifty miles north of Munich, coming into the world on 16 May 1891. His father Karl was the Chief Medical Officer to the Royal Bavarian Military

Academy, and indeed his family had a strong military background. An uncle was a Lieutenant-General, and his mother was the daughter of Hauptmann Schmidbauer who, after serving with distinction in the Franco-Prussian war, died from wounds received in that war five years later in 1875.

His father died when he was eight, his mother afterwards moving the family to Augsburg where she had spent her childhood. His military service commenced in 1910 when he entered the Royal Bavarian Cadet School. Completing his training on 28 October 1912, he received a commission in his grandfather's old regiment, the 3rd Bavarian Infantry. Two years later in 1914, he transferred to the 40th Infantry Regiment. He saw action on the Western Front in the first months of the war, and then on the Eastern Front in 1915.

He was wounded by an exploding hand grenade on 2 May 1915, having already distinguished himself sufficiently to merit the Iron Cross 2nd Class on 26 November 1914 and the Bavarian Military Merit Order 4th Class with Swords on 10 December 1914. After recovering from his wounds and returning again to the front, he next won the Knight's Cross of the Military Max-Joseph Order, a distinction which enabled him to add the title 'Ritter' to his name. He received this prestigious award for a seventeen-day stand against a superior force of Russians. On 25 July 1915 he had volunteered to lead an assault on an important Russian position south of the village of Petrolow. Capturing the objective

Adolf von Tutschek, Jasta 2.

after some bitter hand-to-hand fighting, von Tutschek and his rapidly dwindling number of survivors held the position despite repeated Russian counter-attacks until finally relieved on 10 August. The award was formally announced on 31 January 1916, just two weeks after his promotion to Oberleutnant and appointment as battalion adjutant. Other awards showered upon him during this period had been the Iron Cross 1st Class on 30 July 1915, and the Austrian Military Merit Cross, 3rd Class, with War Decoration, on 28 October of the same year.

Returning again to the Western Front, he took part in the mighty assault on the French at Verdun. He was wounded for a second time, this time suffering gassing. No doubt having had his fill of life in the trenches, he asked for a transfer to aviation. In July 1916 he trained first with FEA1 at Schleissheim, followed by a posting to Feldflieger-Abteilung 6b, where he stayed until October. This period of service as a 'two-seater' pilot yielded him the Bavarian Military Merit Order with Crown and Swords on 17 January 1917. Just over a week later he was assigned to single-seaters and ordered to report to Jasta 2 (Boelcke) on the 27th of the same month.

VICTORY NO. 1
6 March 1917 DH2 (No. 7882) 32 Squadron 1630

It was well over a month before von Tutschek was able to claim his first confirmed victory but it was a distinguished one. Whilst the DH2 was rapidly becoming obsolete by the early spring of 1917, when handled by a competent pilot, the machine was still potentially more than a match for any embryonic opponent. And the British pilot on this occasion was more than competent.

Lieutenant Maximilian John Jules Gabriel Mare-Montembault was already an ace air fighter with five combat successes by this date. A seasoned campaigner, he had been flying with 32 Squadron since August 1916, when von Tutschek was still under pilot training. On this day, six of the Squadron's DH2s mounted an escort to four FE2b machines flying a photographic sortie. In his debriefing following his post-war return from a POW camp, Mare-Montembault reported: *'Having been attacked by 15 hostile aircraft at 12,000 feet, my main petrol tank was pierced by machine-gun fire. I spun down to about 100 feet and was set on fire by a rocket on my way home. Crashed in*

Second Lieutenant Maximilian John Jules Gabriel Mare-Montembault, MC, MID, 32 Squadron RFC (Centre of the group, light trousers).

SECOND LIEUTENANT
MAXIMILIAN JOHN JULES GABRIEL MARE-MONTEMBAULT,
MC, MID, NORTH SOMERSET YEOMANRY AND 32 SQUADRON, ROYAL FLYING CORPS

The ward of the Honourable Mrs Cook of 'Baynords', Cranleigh, Surrey, he joined the Inns of Court OTC (Number Sq/3054) on 15 March 1915 and was gazetted Second Lieutenant to the North Somerset Yeomanry just over three months later on 25 June 1915. Transferring to the Royal Flying Corps in the early summer of 1916, he was awarded his 'Wings' and appointed Flying Officer on 3 August 1916. Joined 32 Squadron at the front just one week later on 10 August 1916 and rapidly made a name for himself as an outstanding scout pilot. Claimed his first victory on 15 September 1916 and was, on 10 October 1916, himself shot down by the legendary Oswald Boelcke – the ace's 34th victory. Boelcke had sat on 'Monte's' tail for almost the whole length of the Bapaume-Albert road before sending him down into the British lines, thankfully relatively unharmed. That the experience did not affect his nerve is evidenced by the fact that he had five more victories before falling foul of yet another great German fighter ace to be on 6 March 1917 – this time Adolf von Tutschek. Mare-Montembault's gallantry and effectiveness was recognised by the award of a Military Cross, the announcement of which appeared in the King's Birthday Honours List of 4 June 1917, although, in fact, he had actually been recommended for the higher award of the Distinguished Service Order. Wounded in the von Tutschek engagement, he spent the remainder of the war in German prison camps before being repatriated in January 1919. He appears to have been a less than model POW from the German point of view as he received a Mention in Despatches for gallant services in the 'Escaper's Gazette' of 16 December 1919.

flames – OK.' A contradictory witness report stated that the airman, before he was taken prisoner, had succeeded in setting fire to his machine after the forced landing. Just to confuse the issue further, von Tutschek later wrote that he had cut the serial number and a cockade from the machine and nailed them to the wall of his room! The DH2 had fallen near Mory, north of Beugnatre on the Somme.

Von Tutschek had been flying Albatros DII 1994/16. On 26 March, he received his *Ehrenbecher* (Honour Cup) for his first victory together with a congratulatory letter from General Ernst von Hoeppner, leader of Kofl 1.

VICTORY NO. 2
31 March 1917 Nieuport (?) 0900

There is no obvious candidate for this second victory. It was a quiet day as far as air fighting was concerned with just one RFC aircraft – an FE2b – listed as a casualty. A Nieuport Scout was in combat early in the morning, its pilot claiming a victory south of Gavrelle at 07.30 hours. The pilot of the Nieuport, Canadian Second Lieutenant W A Bishop (later VC), had taken off just after 0600 and so, if the times are accurate, it is unlikely he was still in the air three hours later at the time of the von Tutschek action. Furthermore, the fight was north-west of Loos and von Tutschek's opponent was said to have gone down inside Allied lines; again, these disparate locations would also

eliminate Bishop's Nieuport.

Despite this, von Tutschek, flying Albatros DII 2004/16, later wrote that the Nieuport he shot down could be seen lying on the western edge of Loos. It was silver-grey in colour, carried pennants on its wings and the pilot was dead, although how he could determine this for certain is unclear and frankly unlikely. He also stated that the Nieuport had been close behind an Albatros two-seater when he engaged it but quickly it broke off and headed down vertically being seen to crash with flying debris also being observed. Bishop was a patrol leader and may well have carried pennants on his wing struts but he most certainly was NOT shot down.

VICTORY NO. 3
6 April 1917 FE2b (No. A22) 57 Squadron 0830

The 'Fees' of 57 Squadron were flying a five-machine Offensive Patrol between Somain and Beauvais during this early part of a month which would later become known as 'Bloody April'. The Flight had taken off at 0700 led by Captain A C Wright, originally with six machines, but one had aborted with engine trouble. They were engaged by a number of fighters, perhaps as many as 15, over Solesmes. In the attack, A22 was hit in the oil and petrol tanks. The pilot fought to reach his own lines but the engine soon seized up and he was forced to put down at Anneux, near Cambrai. The machine's observer, however, reported a different version of A22's last flight when he was de-briefed following his post-war return from captivity. He said that they had already been hit in the oil tank by anti-aircraft fire prior to being attacked by nine (not fifteen) German fighters. He confirmed that the engine had failed and that his pilot had withdrawn from the scrap before eventually dropping at Anneux, to the south-west of Cambrai.

In fact, all five of the two-seaters were brought down by pilots of Jastas 2, 5 and 12 – although von Tutschek's was the only claim by Jasta Boelcke. AvT later drove over to the crash-site, noting about 60 hits in the engine and fuselage. As Werner Voss had also been attacking this machine, and the German system did not allow for 'shared' victories, the two men flipped a coin for the victory. Voss lost.

LIEUTENANT
RAYMOND TERRANCE BRYMER SCHREIBER,
6/SUFFOLK REGIMENT AND 57 SQUADRON, ROYAL FLYING CORPS

Born on 29 January 1894, he was the son of tobacco manufacturer, William A Schreiber and Annie Amelia Schreiber of Greenhill Road, Allerton, Surrey. Educated at the Royal Grammar School, Guildford, Surrey, he was training as an accountant when he decided to enlist in the 2/6th Battalion, Suffolk Regiment (Cyclist Reserve) on 31 December 1914. Selected as officer material, he was gazetted Second Lieutenant to his own regiment on 23 April 1915. Sought transfer to the RFC for which he was interviewed on 8 July 1916 but was obliged to wait until 9 January 1917 before his secondment to the flying service came through. Quickly qualifying as a pilot, he had been at the front for a matter of days when he was downed by the German ace. Taken prisoner but otherwise unharmed, he remained incarcerated until December 1918 when he was at last repatriated. Left the service after being placed on the Unemployed List on 14 January 1919.

SECOND LIEUTENANT
MARTIN LEWIS,
57 SQUADRON, ROYAL FLYING CORPS

The son of Lewis Lewis and Mary Lewis of 'Swangrove', Chalfont St Peter's, Bucking-hamshire. Born in 1891, he was studying engineering at Liverpool University when, on 18 February 1915, he decided to volunteer. Accepted into the Royal Engineers as a Sapper (Number 78787), he trained as a motor cycle despatch rider. Promoted to Corporal, he was sent to a signals unit in France on 6 May 1915. Suffered a severe bout of rheumatism in July 1915 which initially hospitalised him in France (Number 2 Canadian Stationary Hospital) before he was sent home for further treatment. After he recovered his health he was selected for officer training and sent to the Cadet School, Pembroke College, Cambridge in March 1916. An application to join the RFC accepted, he was gazetted to the General List on 10 January 1917 and sent for training as an observer. Joined 57 Squadron in France on probation shortly before his encounter with von Tutschek. Taken prisoner, he was detained at various camps but mainly at Strohim before finally being repatriated on 17 December 1918.

VICTORY NO. 4
30 April 1917 FE2d (No. A6352) 57 Squadron 0755

Despite the scale and intensity of the air actions during April, von Tutschek did not score again until the last day of the month – another machine from 57 Squadron and by then commanding a new Jasta. On the 28th von Tutschek had heard that he was to leave Jasta 2 to take command of Jasta 12. On the face of it, incredibly swift promotion for a still relatively new and untried pilot. It has to be remembered, however, that he already had extensive combat and command experience in the trenches prior to his aviation career. He was, indeed, a seasoned soldier and a commander of men. Von Tutschek took over Jasta 12 at Epinoy on the German 6th Army Front on 30 April 1917.

His victory actually began on the ground, the attacking FEs having the temerity to be bombing the Jasta 12 airfield! Von Tutschek raced to the hangars in his car, bombs falling all around him.

The 57 Squadron Line Patrol had taken off at 0600, led by Captain Harker, to cover the area Lieven to Noreuil. Harker later reported an engagement with 20 German scouts (from Jastas 11, 12 and 33) near L'Ecluse at 0700. A6352 was last seen by other members of the patrol near to Douai, surrounded by a number of German fighters.

Fortunately both of the FE crewmen survived von Tutschek's onslaught and so we have their post-war debriefing reports to help us understand what actually happened. Lingard, the observer, said that they had been dived upon by a formation of enemy machines and in the subsequent fight, two fighters had got behind them. At a height of 5,000 feet, their engine had been knocked out with machine-gun fire. His pilot wrestled them down to a forced landing without injury whereupon they were immediately surrounded by German soldiers and taken prisoner. They had come down near Izel, which coincides with von Tutschek's record of events. The remaining 57 Squadron FEs fared little better, with Lothar von Richthofen of Jasta 11 claiming one as his 16th victory, whilst two others crash-landed inside Allied lines – one with its crew wounded, the pilot mortally so.

The only contradiction in the accounts is that von Tutschek later wrote that his bullets had struck the observer who was seen to drop into his cockpit. Furthermore, after the two-seater landed four or five kilometres behind the German lines, he said he watched as the pilot helped the wounded observer from the machine. However, so far as is known, neither of the captured airmen was wounded. On his way home von Tutschek's Albatros developed engine trouble and he had to force land it in a field near Izel.

SECOND LIEUTENANT
EDWARD DUDLEY JENNINGS,
57 SQUADRON, ROYAL FLYING CORPS

Born on 25 March 1896, the son of solicitor Edward Jennings and Mrs Jennings of 67 Dartmouth Park Hill, St Pancras, London NW. Educated at Owens School, subsequently qualifying as a draughtsman. He was working as a clerk in the War Office when war came. In May 1915, as soon as he was old enough, he unsuccessfully applied for entry into the Royal Naval Air Service. Next he enlisted into the 28/London Regiment – Artist's Rifles – and was eventually gazetted Second Lieutenant to the RFC via the General List on 6 September 1916. Admitted for pilot training on 11 November 1916, he qualified for his

'Wings' shortly before joining 57 Squadron at the front on 28 March 1917. Repatriated on 30 December 1918 and placed on the Unemployed List on 4 June 1919.

SECOND LIEUTENANT
JOHN ROBINSON LINGARD,
16/CHESHIRE REGIMENT AND
57 SQUADRON, ROYAL FLYING CORPS

The son of wadding manufacturer John Lingard and Mrs Lingard of 'Oak Bank', Fairfield, Audenshaw, Manchester, he was born on 19 June 1893. A pre-war volunteer, he was a Sergeant (Number 2502) in the 1/6th (Territorial Force) Battalion of the Manchester Regiment when war broke out in August 1914. He was immediately mobilised with the rest of the Territorial Force and obliged to leave his job as works manager in his father's company. Accompanied his regiment to Gallipoli, landing on the peninsular on 5 May 1915. Invalided home in November 1915, it was some months before he regained his health. Gazetted Second Lieutenant to the 16/Cheshires (2nd Birkenhead) on 7 July 1916 and married his wife, Catherine, at this time, setting up home at 67 Manchester Road, Fairfield, Manchester. Having had enough of trench warfare, Lingard applied for transfer to the RFC and was eventually admitted for training as an observer on 12 March 1917. On 5 April 1917, Lingard found himself in France, a probationary with 57 Squadron. He was still very much a tyro when he and his equally 'green' pilot had the misfortune to meet AvT on 30 April. Repatriated on the last day of 1918, finally leaving the service on 2 March 1919.

VICTORY NO. 5
1 May 1917 Sopwith Pup (No. N6186) 3 Naval Squadron 1140

No. 3 Naval Squadron was destined to suffer badly at the hands of von Tutschek in the early weeks of May. The squadron's misfortunes began on the very first morning of the month as Flight Sub-Lieutenant F C Armstrong led B

Flight on a 1030 take-off escort sortie. At 18,000 feet above Epinoy, six German fighters came in behind the Pups as they headed east. Armstrong later reported that he waited until they 'looked dangerous' (!), before turning to

Flight Sub-Lieutenant Arthur Stuart Mather, 3/Naval Sqd, RNAS, surrounded by his German captors. *(E F Cheesman)*

Albatros pilot and he disengaged. On the credit side, Flight Sub-Lieutenant J S T Fall had accounted for one Albatros, sending it down 'out of control' but, in the debit column, one of the Pups failed to get home.

Von Tutschek claimed his victim as down north of Cantaing, inside German lines. The pilot was taken prisoner. Jasta 12 lost one pilot, Leutnant Gerhard Streahl, killed at Epinoy – obviously Joe Fall's 'OOC' victim.

FLIGHT SUB-LIEUTENANT
ARTHUR STUART MATHER,
3 NAVAL SQUADRON, ROYAL NAVAL AIR SERVICE

Born on 26 February 1895, he was twenty years old when, on 18 June 1916, he was accepted into the RNAS and posted to Crystal Palace. His pilot training followed the usual progression with transfers to Eastbourne, Eastchurch and East Fortune until, fully fledged, he was sent to Dover on 7 March 1917. Transfer to France and 3 Naval Squadron followed. With only $41\frac{1}{2}$ flying hours in his log book, he was still relatively inexperienced when he was taken prisoner on 1 May 1917. Mather served as an officer in the Merchant Navy after the Great War. He applied for a commission in the RAFVR in June 1940 shortly after the Dunkirk evacuation.

Mather's crash-landed Sopwith Pup attracts great interest. *(E F Cheesman)*

engage them. Two of the enemy were directly above him and started to dive, one turning underneath his Pup, the second carrying on with its dive. As the turning EA pulled up towards him, Armstrong manoeuvred into a circling match with it, firing 20 rounds at the very moment his colleague, Flight Sub-Lieutenant L H Rochford, came to his help. The combination was too much for the

VICTORY NO. 6
4 May 1917   Sopwith Pup (No. N6207)   3 Naval Squadron   2040

The naval pilots had taken off at 1800 hours to fly an Offensive Patrol. They were engaged near Vitry by German fighters, and N6207 was last seen flying west over Ecourt St Quentin at 12,000 feet at 1940 (British time). Von Tutschek claimed his victim down near Barelle, between Fresnes and Vitry. Again, the pilot was taken prisoner.

FLIGHT SUB-LIEUTENANT
HARRY STEPHEN MURTON,
3 NAVAL SQUADRON, ROYAL NAVAL AIR SERVICE

Born on 22 October 1888, Harry was living at 8 Normont Avenue, Toronto, Canada, when war was declared. He volunteered for service and was enlisted into the Canadian Engineers (Number 5438). Murton accompanied the Canadian Expeditionary Force to England and then to France as a member of the 2nd Field Company, Canadian Engineers. His subsequent application to join the flying service was approved and he was ordered to report to White City on 17 April 1916. He progressed through the training establishments at Crystal Palace, Chingford and Cranwell before he finally qualified as a Flying Officer at 3 Wing, RNAS on 4 December 1916. Sent to France on 22 April 1917, his operational service was cut short less than two weeks later by von Tutschek. Taken prisoner, he was incarcerated mainly at Freiburg and Holzminden before finally being repatriated on 14 December 1918.

Murton stayed on in the service after the war was over, joining 47 Squadron, Royal Air Force on 13 June 1919. Exactly one month later he was sent with the rank of Captain – via Port Said and Constantinople – to take part in the unsuccessful Allied intervention in South Russia. Murton finally left the service on 18 June 1920.

UNCONFIRMED VICTORY
10 May 1917   Sopwith Pup (?)   1320

Von Tutschek and his pilots were in a fight with a number of Pups this afternoon. Although not definitely identified, they were almost certainly aircraft from 3 Naval Squadron. That Squadron later reported engaging in action a number of Albatros and Halberstadt Scouts over Bourlon Wood at 1230, whilst escorting FEs to Cambrai.

Flight Sub-Lieutenant Armstrong was engaged by two EAs near the lines and dived his Pup away to the east. Was this the Pup von Tutschek thought he had sent down into the British front lines? The German believed his victim had gone down near Monchy but, in fact, 3 Naval suffered no losses.

54 Squadron, on the other hand, did have a Pup (A668) shot up in a fight. The pilot, Captain R G H Pixley, was forced down near the front lines. At 50 feet above the ground, almost at the end of his descent, his port lower wing buckled, the effect of which was to flip him upside down – his machine finally ending up in a shell hole, a write-off. Pixley took off at 1355 British time (1455 German time) so unless von Tutschek's recorded victory time of *1320* was, in fact,

1520, there is an unreconcilable disparity.

There is also a faint chance that the aeroplane was a Sopwith two-seater. The Jasta records merely state a 'Sopwith', so it could have been either a Pup or a Strutter. 70 Squadron did lose a Strutter (A8174) on a recce between Caudry and Neuvilly, to the south-east of Cambrai. Not too far from Jasta 12's base at Epinoy.

The very word, 'Monchy', is less than definitive as there are several Monchy or Monchy prefaced towns and villages in the area. Furthermore 'Monchy' was sometimes confused in reports with 'Inchy' – just to add to the uncertainty! All of this speculation is academic as the supposed victory still remains unconfirmed and unknown despite our efforts to identify it all these many years later!

VICTORY NO. 7
11 May 1917 Sopwith Pup (No. N6162) 3 Naval Squadron 1540

Once again 3 Naval Squadron ran into Jasta 12 this afternoon, losing one of their Pups shot down in the vicinity of Bourlon Wood. Jasta 12, however, claimed two Pups. Vizefeldwebel Robert Riessinger reported his victim going down to land south-east of Hayencourt (NE of Bourlon Wood) at 1535, on the German side. This then has to be

Flight Sub-Lieutenant J Bampfylde-Daniell, 3/Naval Squadron, RNAS, in POW Camp – shot down in the same fight as Hubert Broad.

Flight Sub-Lieutenant J Bampfylde-Daniell, from Canada, in N6464, who was taken prisoner. Only the previous month Bampfylde-Daniell had the seat of his aircraft shot away from under him during a combat. He managed to keep flying despite his precarious position but, understandably in the circumstances, got himself lost, before eventually gratefully landing at an RFC airfield north of Marieux. His hosts, of course, wined and dined him that evening but demanded that he 'sang for his supper' by recounting his experiences in an after dinner speech. He confided that he had avoided trouble by '... *hopping lightly from cloud to cloud*', recommending the tactic to all present.

Von Tutschek's Pup appeared to go down inside British lines near Croisilles some five minutes after Bampfylde-Daniell's. On this occasion AvT could perhaps be forgiven for thinking this to be an absolutely certain victory, for undoubtedly the Pup would have been hurtling down at speed, imparting the impression to onlookers that the pilot was dead or unconscious. In fact the pilot had suffered a nasty wound but, happily, not a fatal one. Hubert Broad was heading for the lines as the attack came. Alerted by either a signal from the Flight leader or on hearing the rattle of Spandau machine guns, he turned his head, his mouth inexplicably open. An Albatros was firing at him from extreme range. A single bullet entered his open mouth and exited under his chin.

The sheer shock of the impact to his face, the resultant agony, the panic-inducing uncertainty as to the extent of the damage, all contrived – unsurprisingly – to make him lose control for several minutes and, as a consequence, the Pup lost height very rapidly. Adjusting to the pain and realising that the wound was probably not life-threatening, the instinct for survival reasserted itself and he dragged the plunging machine back under control, crossed the lines at low level and force-landed near to Bapaume.

Just to muddy the waters even further, von Tutschek wrote in a letter to a friend that he had shot down a Sopwith *two-seater* on the 11th. However, we are certain that it was this Pup.

FLIGHT SUB-LIEUTENANT
HUBERT STANFORD BROAD,
LATER MBE, AFC, 3 NAVAL SQUADRON, ROYAL NAVAL AIR SERVICE

Born on 20 May 1897, he was the son of solicitor Thomas John Broad and Mrs Broad of 'Langlea', Langley Way, Watford, Hertfordshire. Educated at Aldenham (1911-15). Learnt to fly at the Hall School of Flight, Hendon, gaining his Royal Aero Club Certificate (Number 2044) on 15 November 1915. In 1916 he joined the Royal Naval Air Service, reporting to Eastchurch in Kent where he was obliged to learn to fly again, this time to service standards! His early attempts were not without mishaps as, for instance, the time when he crashed a Curtis JN-4 (Number 3437), *'while playing the fool near the aerodrome'*. Following further training and with 57 hours and 5 minutes flying time in his log, he crossed to France

on 28 February 1917. He recorded two victories in the following April; the first on 21st of the month – an Albatros DIII destroyed (shared with Flight Sub-Lieutenant E Casey), the second eight days later, yet another Albatros DIII – OOC/Smoking. The career of an outstanding airman could so easily have ended on 11 May 1917 when a von Tutschek bullet missed its mark by a fraction. Amazingly, he was in the air again by the 14th day of the following month, *'flying joyflips – first time after being hit'*, according to his diary. Service as an instructor was followed in December 1917 by a course at the RFC's School of Special Flying at Gosport, where he became one of the first aviators to learn the previously unknown art of sideslipping – a further addition to his considerable portfolio of aerobatic 'stunts'. He returned to the front in the summer of 1918, this time as a Flight Commander with the Camel-equipped 46 Squadron, claiming two further OOC victims. Awarded an Air Force Cross before being demobilised in June 1919, he had spells as a joyride pilot and

Hubert Broad's Sopwith Pup (N6162) 3 Naval Squadron, shot down by von Tutschek on 11 May 1917 – the German ace's 7th victory.

1925 Schneider Trophy flying a Gloster III. He won the King's Cup in a Cirrus 1 Moth in 1926 and the 1929 Zenith Cup in a Gypsy Moth DH60G. In between – in 1927 – he broke the 100 km closed circuit record at a speed of 186.47 mph in a DH71 Tiger Moth monoplane. In August 1928 he stayed in the air for twenty-four hours to test the new 100hp DH Gipsy engine fitted in a Moth, travelling 1,500 miles in the process as well as, reputedly, reading three novels. Freelanced for other aircraft companies including Handley Page. Joined the Air Registration Board in 1935 and was with the Royal Aircraft Establishment at Farnborough in 1939 as the Second World War came. Joined Hawkers as chief production test pilot in 1940, testing many subsequently famous machines from their earliest development such as Typhoons and Tempests as well as the constantly evolving and improving Hurricanes and Sea Furies. Retired in 1947, he became a representative for Dowty Equipment Ltd whilst also working as a patent broker. Later accepted directorships with Wynstruments Ltd and with Chilton Engineering Products Ltd, his home by then being in Basingstoke, Hampshire. Died on 30 July 1975 at the age of seventy-eight having been deservedly regarded as one of the outstanding aviators of his time.

working for the International Airways Corporation. Became chief test pilot for Welsh Aviation in early 1921 and later – in the same year – was taken on in the same capacity by the De Havilland Company. Competed in various air races in the 'twenties, achieving second place in the

VICTORY NO. 8
12 May 1917 Sopwith Pup (No. A664) 66 Squadron 1050

On the morning of the 12th von Tutschek and Unteroffizier Friedrich Gille combined to shoot down a Nieuport Scout from 29 Squadron, but, as Gille had fired first, von Tutschek graciously gave full credit to him.

Despite this act of generosity, von Tutschek still made it five Pups in a row – four confirmed, one unconfirmed. On this occasion it was an RFC rather than an RNAS machine. Captain J O Andrews MC, led a six-strong Offensive Patrol away at 0800, although one returned with engine trouble at 0920. They were patrolling ten miles east of

Boiry-Lens just an hour after take-off when an aerial combat began. The patrol engaged an Albatros two-seater but soon enemy fighters appeared on the scene. After the ensuing mêlée and the general action had broken up, Lieutenant J R Robertson was missing. AvT claimed his victim had gone down in flames between Barelle and Marquion. He had also attacked another Pup but his guns failed because of a jammed loading chamber. On the next day, the exasperated von Tutschek had entirely new guns fitted to his Albatros DIII (2274/16).

LIEUTENANT
JOHN ROSS ROBERTSON,
FIFE AND FORFAR YEOMANRY AND
66 SQUADRON, ROYAL FLYING CORPS

Born in 1893, John was the son of Sir William and Lady Robertson of Benachie, Dunfermline, Scotland, and was educated at Dunfermline High School. A pre-war volunteer into the Fife and Forfar Yeomanry, he was mobilised with the rest of his regiment as soon as war was declared on 4 August 1914. He served with the Yeomanry detachment in the Gallipoli campaign and subsequently in the Sudan before his application to transfer to the RFC was approved in 1916. Said to have actually been killed in the air, his machine crashing behind the German lines at Marquion near Cambrai. In November 1918, shortly after the signing of the Armistice, John's brother, Major William Berry Robertson MC, 16/Royal Scots, set out to search for the grave in the reported vicinity of the crash site. He was successful, finding that the Germans had erected a *'handsome wooden cross'* over his brother's resting place which bore the inscription, *'He died the death of a hero'*. The grave was subsequently relocated and John Robertson is now buried in the Commonwealth War Graves Commission cemetery at Quarry Marquion, France (Fr272). He was 23 years old.

VICTORY NO. 9
19 May 1917 Sopwith Triplane (No. N5461) 1 Naval Squadron 0905

Five Triplanes took off at 0715, led by Flight Lieutenant C A Eyre, the other pilots being Flight Sub-Lieutenants R P Minifie, H LeR Wallace, O B Ellis and G G Bowman. Forty-five minutes later, a formation of between five and eight hostile aircraft came up from Marquion and were engaged by three of the naval Triplanes. Eyre drove one off. Wallace, attacking a two-seater, had his engine hit and damaged by the enemy observer's fire and was forced to beat a hasty retreat to his own lines, force landing safely near Boiry St Martin.

Bowman was seen to be engaged by no less than three of the German fighters. He put up a very fine and plucky fight for over ten minutes, this despite apparently not having the full potential of his engine – he had previously lagged and laboured behind the main formation. The inevitable happened and his machine fell away from the fight vertically, caught fire and crashed burning east of Eterpigny from 5,000 feet.

During a second patrol between 1130 and 1200 on the same day, von Tutschek's machine was so badly shot about that he was forced to crash-land his Albatros DIII (2274/16), the wheels being ripped off in the process. He was unhurt but his favourite aeroplane was smashed beyond repair.

On the same evening, another survivor of the morning dogfight was killed. 1 Naval's Flight Sub-Lieutenant Oliver Ellis from Leicester was seen to leap from his burning machine following an attack by Leutnant Gisbert-Wilhelm Groos of Jasta 4 – the first of the German pilot's eventual seven victories.

FLIGHT SUB-LIEUTENANT
GEOFFREY GLENDINNING BOWMAN,
1 NAVAL SQUADRON, ROYAL NAVAL AIR SERVICE

The second son of William Powell Bowman and Mary Grace Bowman of 16 North Grange Road, Headingley, Leeds, he was born on 11 March 1898. Educated at Filey Preparatory School and at Repton (1913-16) where he was a member of the shooting VIII. Accepted as a Sub-Lieutenant into the Royal Navy on 28 June 1916 with the intention of joining the flying arm of the Senior Service. His introduction into the RNAS got off to an inauspicious start, being injured during flight training on 20 October 1916. His Maurice Farman (Number 146) landed 'heavily' resulting in him receiving slight abrasions to both shins, a slight facial

wound and, of course, shock. Recovering quickly, he gained the Royal Aero Club Certificate, Number 3934, at Chingford, Essex, on 7 December 1916 and was appointed Flight Sub-Lieutenant at Cranwell in February 1917. Spent a short period in Dover before being sent to France and 1 Naval Squadron with just 28 flying hours in April 1917. Geoffrey Bowman's remains were never found and hence he is commemorated on the Arras Memorial to the Missing, France. Age 19.

VICTORY NO. 10
20 May 1917 Spad VII (No.B1587) 23 Squadron 1110

---

23 Squadron's home field was at Baizieux, between Amiens and Albert, but, like a number of other units, they sometimes used an 'Advanced Landing Ground' (ALG). These ALGs were usually occupied when the Squadron was alerted by RFC HQ's Intelligence service to expect more than the normal quota of German two-seater photo-reconnaissance machines over the front. Movements of troops on the ground – by

either side – invariably attracted increased surveillance. 23 Squadron were standing-by on their ALG this morning when Second Lieutenant H T Garrett was detailed to intercept a German intruder which was reported at 0950.

Whether Garrett had found the interloper before he himself engaged two Albatros Scouts behind the Geman lines, is not known. Von Tutschek and one of his pilots had just finished a routine patrol and were heading for home. The two were in the process of letting down towards their airfield at Epinoy, when they were suddenly attacked by a Spad – von Tutchek's companion receiving the main brunt of the assault. Von Tutschek immediately counter-attacked in order to protect his colleague but the Spad pilot, nothing daunted, reared up towards him, putting several shots through his Albatros, before turning to dash for the lines. Von Tutschek chased the Spad, the RFC pilot managing to protect himself quite successfully throughout most of the pursuit. As they approached the lines, one of the German ace's guns jammed. This would for most have been good reason to desist from further pursuit, but not for AvT. Closing in even more and firing with just his left-hand gun, his fire finally hit home and the Spad caught fire. Falling burning from 700 metres, it came to earth near Riencourt, four kilometres inside German lines.

Von Tutschek acknowledged that he had certainly been in a fight – and then some. Metaphorically tipping his hat to his worthy opponent, he later concluded, wrongly, that he must have been up against, '... a big shot.'

SECOND LIEUTENANT
HYDE TREGALLAS GARRETT,
23 SQUADRON, ROYAL FLYING CORPS

The son of Mark and Kate Garrett of 'Retreat', Cape Province, South Africa, Hyde was born in 1894. Came to England at his own expense and was accepted into the Inns of Court Officer Training Corps (Number 6/4/8168) on 6 December 1915. Gazetted Second Lieutenant and accepted for entry to the Royal Flying Corps on 4 September 1916. Following the usual training, he was awarded his 'Wings' and sent to France to join 23 Squadron in early 1917. His remains were never found and hence he is commemorated on the Arras Memorial to the Missing, France. Age 22.

21 May 1917 found von Tutschek flying alone. He wrote later that he had attacked a formation of Spads he found sniffing around the German balloon lines during the morning. The Spads, he related disparagingly, once attacked by this lone all-black Albatros, quickly turned tail and headed for their own lines. In hot pursuit, he shot the wings off the rearmost of the retreating Spads before attacking another which he sent down diving vertically and smoking heavily. Closing in on the remainder, his guns jammed yet again and he was obliged to break off the action.

We are presented here with something of an embarrassing quandary – the explanation of which can hardly be flattering to Adolf von Tutschek. For, in fact, there were no British Spads lost on 21 May 1917. The RFC lost only one machine during the entire day and that was a FE2b. Nor were there any French or Belgian losses matching von Tutschek's vividly described but unwitnessed action. It appears, therefore, that AvT might have felt the need to 'accelerate' his claim for the award of the Blue Max at this time.

On 26 May von Tutschek left for a period of leave, which extended to 24 June. Two days later, following a visit to Jasta Boelcke's airfield, von Tutschek was returning to his own field when he spotted four Sopwith two-seaters. He attacked without hesitation, his fire appearing to cripple one of the Sopwiths so that it began to glide down. Hoping for a neat capitulation, he flew beside the stricken machine, shepherding it down like a lost sheep. Apparently, however, hidden beneath the sheep's clothing was a veritable wolf. Suddenly the Sopwith's observer opened fire, hitting the Albatros in the petrol tank and radiator. Streaming white vapour behind him, von Tutschek's stricken Albatros lost height. Fortunately AvT was unhurt and able to make a good forced landing. Looking up from the cockpit of his stationary Albatros, von Tutschek was amazed to see his supposed victim making for the lines with no sign of the difficulties he had apparently been labouring under.

Three days later on 29 June, he was in a fight with British fighters. His motor damaged in the scrap, he was forced to make an emergency landing near Cantin, his Albatros being destroyed in the process. His opponents on this occasion were Nieuport Scouts from 60 Squadron. Two of that squadron's pilots made claims, Captain W E Molesworth (B1652) for an Albatros crashed and Lieutenant W S Jenkins (B 1629) for another, 'out of control'. Molesworth reported his claimed crashed Albatros down at 1800 hours between Douai and Estrées. Cantin – where von Tutschek came to ground – is slightly to the east but between these two locations. Jenkins's claim, timed as half an hour later to the east of Lens, is sometimes noted as being von Tutschek but Molesworth's claim, time and location-wise, looks the more likely.

Both British pilots recorded their third individual victory in this action. Irishman 'Moley' Molesworth went on to score 18 victories by March 1918 when he returned to England. Bill Jenkins from Cambridgeshire scored ten before being killed in a collision with Second Lieutenant M West-Thompson over Poperinghe on 23 November 1917.

VICTORY NO. 11
3 July 1917 Sopwith (?) 1030

What with his month's leave intervening and his recent set-backs, it was hardly surprising that some seven weeks had elapsed since his last victory. He did claim a Sopwith two-seater on this day, which, he said, went down into the British lines. Unfortunately, there is no corresponding loss on the Allied side. One has to conclude therefore that either the machine got down safe and sound or was flying so low that it deluded German observers into the false assumption that it must have crashed. 43 Squadron did have a man wounded on this date but in a combat that had absolutely nothing to do with this incident. Von Tutschek gave the location of his combat as north of Vaulx and that was quite close to a fight over Quéant involving 48 Squadron's Bristol Fighters. But the Brisfits suffered no losses, although they did claim one Albatros shot down. It was not unknown for German pilots to misidentify British aeroplane types but once again, there is no corresponding evidence to support even the possibility of any sort of mis-identification.

Von Tutschek himself wrote that the Sopwith was forced down to 400 metres whereupon it flipped over and went down vertically to the ground – although he did not actually say it had crashed. What he did say, however, was that he had procured solidly indisputable witness statements!

VICTORY NO. 12
11 July 1917 RE8/BE2 (?) 1815

Again we have a problem with this claim. The British aeroplane was said to go down into the Allied side of the lines, near to Thelus, but there is no corresponding RE8/BE2 losses on this day. One 5 Squadron RE8 machine was shot up before noon but it returned otherwise safely to its aerodrome.

VICTORY NO. 13
11 July 1917 FE2d (No.A6370) 25 Squadron 1845

At least the second of von Tutschek's first 'double' can be reasonably identified. 25 Squadron took off at 1630 on a Line Patrol between La Bassée and the Scarpe, the FE2ds carrying bombs in case 'targets of opportunity' presented themselves. Over the front-line area they were attacked. Three enemy fighters shot up 'A6370', forcing its pilot to crash 800 yards west of the front-line trenches near Monchy Foss Farm. Second Lieutenant Sargant was wounded in the attack, but he and his observer managed to scramble from the wreck of the crashed machine and dive into the nearest British trenches. What remained of the FE2d was promptly blown into matchwood by German shell fire.

With these two (?) victories came the award of the Knight's Cross, with Swords, of the Royal Hohenzollern House Order, the usual precursor for the subsequent recommendation for the Blue Max – the Pour le Mérite – providing, of course, that the pilot achieved at least twenty victories.

SECOND LIEUTENANT
FREDERICK HUBERT ST CLAIR SARGANT,
DFC, MID, 25 SQUADRON, ROYAL FLYING CORPS

Born in 1897, the son of Mr and Mrs Sargant of 'Bank House', Sevenoaks, Kent. In the late summer of 1916 he was working as a bank clerk in his employer's Durham branch. As soon as he attained the acceptable age, he volunteered for service, joining the 28th Battalion, London Regiment (Artist's Rifles) on 6 September 1916. Picked out immediately as officer material, he completed his training and was gazetted Second Lieutenant (General List) on 26 January 1917. His application to enter the RFC approved, he trained as a pilot and, duly qualified, was sent to join 22 Squadron in France on 29 June 1917. Less than two weeks later he was bested in a duel with AvT – hit by a machine-gun bullet which entered and lodged in his right gluteal (buttock). Despite their best efforts, surgeons were unable to extract the bullet and the wound was allowed to heal over it. Subsequently pronounced fit for light duties but still not allowed to fly, he was posted to 51 Home Defence Squadron based at Tydd St Mary, Lincolnshire. A period of ill health followed, probably brought about as a consequence of his brush with death. He was diagnosed as 'slightly tremulous' with 'poor balance', his 'sleeping affected'. Despite these problems, he was still thought sufficiently recovered to be sent back to France in 1918 to join 38 Squadron at the front, subsequently taking part in no less than 26 night raids. His outstanding services were recognised by a Mention in Despatches and by the award of the Distinguished Flying Cross in the New Year's Honours List of 1 January 1919.

LIEUTENANT
JAMES HERBERT KIRK,
13/CANADIAN RESERVE BATTALION AND 25 SQUADRON, ROYAL FLYING CORPS

Born in 1897, James was the son of James J and Helen Kirk of Sussex, New Brunswick, Canada. Commissioned Lieutenant on 16 September 1916, seeking transfer to the Royal Flying Corps shortly afterwards. Joined 25 Squadron as a probationary observer at the front on 31 May 1917. Survived both Adolf von Tutschek and the war.

VICTORY NO. 14
12 July 1917 Kite Balloon 1 Balloon Wing 1800

Not many of the big aces on the German side sought out Allied balloons for destruction – this was rather wise of them for they were extremely dangerous targets. They may have looked easy, hanging large and docile in the sky just behind the lines, but they were very heavily defended by numerous anti-aircraft guns and concentrations of machine guns. Furthermore, in order to attack the balloons the German airmen were also obliged to fly into Allied airspace, something they did not contemplate too often and never lightly.

Some pilots, of course, German and Allied both, including aces, seemed almost mesmerised by these targets and appeared to take delight in attacking them. Many hopeful attacks succumbed to the defensive ground fire – thick and heavy as it was. No doubt the likes of the von Richthofen brothers, Voss, Wolff, Göring, et al, thought the game too dangerous and the targets too tawdry to tempt perfidious fate with the destruction of mere balloons. Others, such as Heinrich Gontermann and Friedrich von Röth, could not keep away from the gaseous rotunds.

Von Tutschek did attack balloons and quite successfully, too – achieving three successes. He had admitted having contemplated a balloon assault for some time and today decided to implement the intention.

Prevailing ground mist and low cloud aided his decision. In the event that he might be brought down and captured, he donned a freshly pressed uniform!

The balloon, tethered north-west of Lens, stuck up above the mist at a height of about 1,500 metres. Closely escorted by one of his men, whilst others of his Jasta circled just inside the German lines to protect the attacking pair from predatory Allied fighters, von Tutschek headed for the 'gas-bag'. After firing ten to 20 rounds of phosphorus ammunition, he climbed away, looking over his shoulder to see the results of his work. Nothing. He turned and started to dive for a second strafe just as the balloon erupted in a ball of fire and fell burning through the mist to the ground. His second dive had took him down to below 600 metres and he found himself surrounded on all sides by curtains of ground fire. Bullets struck the undersides of his machine and even his seat was hit but, miraculously, he came out of the maelstrom unscathed.

The balloon was British, belonging to the 36th Section, 16th Company, 1st Balloon Wing – usually identified by just the three sets of numbers 36-16-1. The individual balloon was numbered FM80.

VICTORY NO. 15
13 July 1917 Martinsyde G102 (No.7123) 27 Squadron 0800

Another doubt exists about this claim in that it is recorded in the Nachtrichtenblatt as occurring on 12 July, against as a 'Nieuport Einf' – ie: Nieuport Scout or single-seater, brought down near to Lens. However, the Jasta's own records have it as being on 13 July, the location noted as Noeux-les-Mines on the British side, some seven kilometres west of Lens. Von Tutschek himself reported

the crash as occurring three kilometres north of Lens and 20 kilometres south of the road running between Lens and Béthune.

As confirmations were sometimes slow in coming, a German pilot might have earlier victories actually confirmed *after* later claims. Confusingly, these later confirmations would be numbered in the chronology of the confirmation, rather than of the event.

For example, the late confirmation of a claim on, say, 1 May, would be numbered *after* an already confirmed claim of, say, 5 May. So it is that the 5 May victory may be No.10, whilst the earlier 1 May victory would then be No.11. In the recent series of Grub Street books on aces, the authors ignored this for reasons of clarity and invariably listed the victory number in strict chronological order. We mention this only to explain the reason why the Nachrichtenblatt notes the balloon of 12 July as AvT's victory number 14 and the Nieuport as number 15, despite the disparities in the timing. We again face an identification problem with yet another of von Tutschek's claims. It seems reasonable to assume that von Tutschek would, by this stage of the war, be able to clearly distinguish between a rotary-engined Nieuport and an in-line-engined Martinsyde. Some of those with an interest in this subject and who think the 13th date is correct, choose Captain H O D Wilkins's 27 Squadron G.102 as the victim, despite that gentleman's statement that he had been hit by AA fire before crashing into the British side of the lines. Wilkins came down in a forced landing near Noeux-les-Mines, his machine wrecked. He had been a member of a bomb raiding party on Ath which took off at 0440 hours.

It is interesting to note at this point that after Wilkins was subsequently brought down and captured on 28 July 1917, he reported that he had engine failure and he had been forced to land, whereupon his machine ran into a ditch and was wrecked. He was, however, shot down by a German two-seater aeroplane and, furthermore, whilst subsequent photographs of his crashed machine appear to indicate a heavy crash-landing which smashed his undercarriage, there is no sign of a ditch and the Martinsyde is far from wrecked.

There are no Nieuport losses this early – 0700 British time. Nor is there anything comparable on the 12th, not with time, type or location.

CAPTAIN
HAROLD OSWALD DAY WILKINS,
BEDFORDSHIRE REGIMENT AND 27 SQUADRON, ROYAL FLYING CORPS

A Regular Army officer with the Bedfordshire Regiment when the war came in August 1914, Wilkins came originally from Norwood, Ontario, Canada. After serving in the trenches in France, Wilkins sought transfer to the RFC, being admitted for pilot training to the CFS in late 1916. Joined 27 Squadron at the front on 23 April 1917. On 4 June 1917, an Albatros he fired upon, *'flicked over on to its back, hesitated, then fell away upside down'*. Unable to be sure of its fate, Wilkins was obliged to claim it as 'out of control'. Forced down and wounded on 28 July 1917 by Leutnant Horauf and Offizierstellvertreter Sattler of Flieger-Abteilung 45. Taken prisoner after his enforced landing, Wilkins would remain so until his repatriation on 14 December 1918. Resigned his commission and left the service on 11 October 1919.

VICTORY NO. 16
15 July 1917 Nieuport XXIII (No.B1575) 60 Squadron 2025

A patrol of 60 Squadron Nieuports took off at 1900 hours and headed towards Douai. One of the Nieuports lagged behind the others and von Tutschek's wolves closed for the kill.

According to von Tutschek's account, he, as it were, stepped aside to allow the men in his Staffel the honour of shooting down the Nieuport which had got itself cut off from its companions, none of whom seemed disposed to come to its aid. A number of other Albatros Scouts also joined in the denouement but none of them seemed able to despatch the silver-grey British scout.

The Nieuport flown by 2Lt G A H Parkes of 60 Squadron – shot down by von Tutschek on 15 July 1917.

Finally von Tutschek came down from his watching height and administered the *coup de grâce.*

After his repatriation via Switzerland, the pilot of the downed Nieuport, Lieutenant Gerard Parkes, reported that the 60 Squadron patrol had been in a fight with 11 Albatros Scouts. He was hit in the left forearm by a machine-gun bullet and his safety belt was shot through and severed. Without the restraining belt, he fell upwards and outwards onto the top wing as his machine fell out of control. Just to add to the jollity, his engine shuddered to a stop, thanks to a pierced fuel tank having leaked away his fuel. Inexplicably, the machine righted itself at about 1,000 feet above the ground and he was able to scramble back into the cockpit. By now the Nieuport was too low to glide him back to his own lines but still he was immensely relieved to be able to make a good landing about one mile west of Douai, whereupon he was taken prisoner.

Meanwhile, in the air just a few score feet above Parkes and his Nieuport, von Tutschek said he could see the downed pilot scrabbling at the pockets of his flying suit trying to locate a match or a lighter to burn the machine. To deter him, or so he said, von Tutschek dived and fired, his bullets kicking up the ground along one side of the aeroplane. Unsurprisingly, the pilot immediately leapt out of his cockpit and ran some 150 metres before throwing himself flat on to the ground. Understandably, Parkes later complained to his German interrogator about the pilot who had tried to shoot him up on the ground. The downed but largely intact Nieuport was later brought to Jasta 12's own airfield and repaired by the Staffel's own engineers.

SECOND LIEUTENANT
GERARD ALLPORT
HICKLING PARKES,
60 SQUADRON, ROYAL FLYING CORPS

Born on 16 September 1898, the son of Mr and Mrs Parkes of 498 City Road, Edgbaston, near Birmingham. Educated at Shrewsbury School (1912-15). Volunteering for service as soon as he was old enough, he was accepted into the Officer Cadet School, Oxford, on 20 December 1916. A pilot of promise, he was awarded his 'Wings' in the spring of 1917 and sent out to France as a scout pilot with 60 Squadron. Still a relative tyro when he ran into von Tutschek just over a month into his operational career. Taken prisoner by German ground troops, it would be the last day of 1918 before he was repatriated via neutral Switzerland. Remained in the RAF after the war's end and was sent to Russia as part of the Allied Intervention Force on 14 July 1919. Taken ill and hospitalised on 30 August 1919, he was eventually sent home for treatment and finally left the service on 16 December 1919. Died in Melbourne, Australia, in 1937.

VICTORY NO. 17
21 July 1917 Nieuport XXVII (No.B1694) 40 Squadron 2130

A 40 Squadron Offensive Patrol took off in the late afternoon. It was led by Captain J B Quested MC, a former 11 Squadron FE2b pilot who had shot down the ace Gustav Leffers back in December 1916. His four companions were Second Lieutenants A E Godfrey, J E Barlow, F W Rook and Sergeant L A Herbert. The 40 Squadron quintet was engaged by elements of von Tutschek's Jasta and a monumental scrap ensued. Von Tutschek would later describe this fight as the toughest he had ever been in. He started by picking out a Nieuport and was convinced he had registered hits. However, before he could finish off this first Nieuport, another engaged him full on. The two antagonists circled and fought for a full twenty minutes – a veritable marathon of a dogfight. Despite the ferocity of the fight, neither could get in a telling burst – although AvT would later

discover twenty bullet holes in his machine. Suddenly two further Nieuports joined in the mêlée seeking to extricate their comrade. After holding von Tutschek off for such a long time, the intervention of his colleagues encouraged the relieved Nieuport to make a break for home. Unfortunately, in pointing the Nieuport towards the lines, he exposed himself to a final burst from AvT's machine guns. The young Canadian pilot was hit in the head and he and his Nieuport plummeted down to crash behind the German wire by the Cambrai to Bapaume road.

Von Tutschek regarded this as his 20th victory although only 17 had been formally recognised. He was still desperately anxious to achieve enough victories to merit the coveted award of the Ordre Pour le Mérite.

SECOND LIEUTENANT
FREDERICK WILLIAM ROOK,
40 SQUADRON, ROYAL FLYING CORPS

Born in Toronto on 3 December 1894, Fred was one of the six children of English immigrants, Samuel and Martha Ann Rook of 7 Scarborough Road, Balmy Beach, Toronto. He was educated in his native city at Ogden Public School (1904-09) and at Oakwood Collegiate (1909-11). After leaving school he was employed in the customs brokerage business in Toronto. Joined the Canadian army in 1915 and, on 1 April 1916, was posted to the CEF in France with the rank of Corporal. An application for a transfer to the RFC was granted and he was gazetted a probationary Second Lieutenant to the Military Wing on 17 November 1916. After qualifying as a pilot, he was again sent out to France, arriving at 40 Squadron shortly before his fateful meeting with Adolf von Tutschek. A small leather case containing some of his belongings was recovered from his crashed Nieuport and sent home by the German army – via the Red Cross – to his family in Toronto, arriving some six months after his death. Buried by the Germans near to Boursies, the site of his grave was subsequently lost in the fighting over the area and hence he is commemorated on the Arras Memorial to the Missing, France. Age 23.

VICTORY NO. 18
23 July 1917 Kite Balloon 20th Section, Kite Balloon Wing 1755

Still anxious to rachet up sufficient victories to get that Blue Max, von Tutschek decided to have a go at another balloon. According to the 20th Kite Balloon Section, RFC, one of their balloons was attacked at 1655 British time by four Albatros Scouts – three coming in from the west and one from the east. The 'balloonatics' were caught napping and the German fighters were spotted only one minute before the balloon was hit and ignited. Even so, in the minute available to them, they had managed to haul the balloon down from 2,000 feet to 1,100 by the time the German fighters laced it with phosphorous bullets.

As it happened, the lorry engine, which doubled as a winch, had already been started, the driver about to move the balloon into the wind when von Tutschek and company arrived. Fortunately, the driver was sufficiently alert to stop the winch pulling the blazing debris down onto the Officers' Mess. Hopefully, there would be enough time for the balloon's observer to parachute to safety, although the falling, burning wreckage being dragged down behind the unfortunate man would present yet another danger. Happily, the records show no balloonatic casualties on this day. Von Tutschek's balloon victory – his second – was numbered BMS 91 D.

Earlier in the day, at around noon, von Tutschek had a narrow squeak in an aerial combat, his gloves and leather jacket being shot through! The 'casualty' on this occasion was his prized 'yellow' RFC leather flying coat which he had taken from one of his downed adversaries and worn in preference to the standard German flying gear.

Right: Hockstetter's Jasta 12 Albatros DV as reported seen in the combat of 28 July 1917. Black rear fuselage and three black circles, described, incorrectly, in 40 Squadron reports as 'Clubs' (as in the card suit). *(Greg VanWyngarden)*

Below: Von Tutschek in his 'liberated' RFC flying coat alongside his all-black Albatros DIII of Jasta 12; the propeller boss is white. *(Greg VanWyngarden)*

Opposite: Adolf von Tutschek was in action with Sopwith Triplanes of 8 Naval Squadron on 28 July 1917. The British pilot, FSL E D Crundall, survived the fight despite his machine suffering numerous hits and although he appeared to dive to the ground, in fact he survived and got back to base. Nevertheless, von Tutschek was credited with his 19th victory.

Opposite: Von Tutschek was hit a glancing blow to the temple in a surprise attack by an SE5a of 24 Squadron on 15 March 1918. The pilot who fired the fatal burst was Lieutenant H B Redler, a South African.

VICTORY NO. 19
28 July 1917   Sopwith Triplane (No.N5493)   8 Naval Squadron   0730

German fighter pilots in the Great War were very aware of the high honours and fame that awaited their success in combat. In the early years of aerial fighting, it took eight victories to secure the Pour le Mérite. Later the threshold was raised to 16 as more and more aviators began to amass 'kills'. The most successful of them all, Manfred von Richthofen, narrowly missed the eight mark and had to wait until reaching 16 victories before receiving the Blue Max. Even then, he only just made it before the mark was again raised, this time to 20.

Through the mid-war years, the mark was, generally, 20. By 1918 – and especially in late 1918 – the paperwork took longer and longer to process and, as a consequence, several pilots with 20 or more kills were denied Germany's highest gallantry award. Certainly the Kaiser and his court had more to concern themselves with during the last weeks of the war and, once he had abdicated, all chance was lost.

The thought that the 'magic' figure of 20 might also be suddenly edged upwards – perhaps to 25 or even 30 – was never far from the minds of men like Adolf von Tutschek who were desperately keen to clear the twentieth hurdle before the stakes were raised. This, inevitably, led to some deliberate over-claiming, or at the very least, hopeful and wishful thinking. Von Richthofen had been guilty of this with his 15th victory back in December 1916 (see *Under the Guns of the Red Baron*, by Franks, Giblin and McCrery, Grub Street, 1995), and now – probably not for the first time – von Tutschek was to be guilty of it, twice in one day.

Reflecting on his combat claims of the last two days, he wrote: '*Yesterday at 0750 hours I downed a triplane near Méricourt. At 1000 a Nieuport fighter near Lieven, and today at 0800 a new SE5 at Henin-Lietard. They went down burning on this side. With that one I personally scored the 100th air*

victory of the Staffel in my black Albatros. Verified through Kogenluft as the 19th, 20th and 21st victorious air combats.' Translation problems aside, it is quite certain that he did not see the first two aircraft fall inside German lines, nor were they 'in flames'.

The first was one of 8 Naval's Sopwith Triplanes, piloted by Flight Sub-Lieutenant E D Crundall [a man I once met and spoke to – NF]. The Squadron had mounted a three-machine Offensive Patrol at 0620 – the pilots being C D Booker, S H McCrudden and Crundall. Not long into the patrol they were engaged and greatly out-numbered by a large formation of Albatros Scouts. Ed Crundall, later an RAF Wing Commander with the DSC and the AFC, wrote of his experiences (*Fighter Pilot on the Western Front*, Wm. Kimber & Co, 1975): '*Booker, McCrudden and I went on an offensive patrol. When we were in the vicinity of Douai we were attacked by about ten Albatros Scouts and two-seaters. Booker attacked an Albatros Scout at close range and another Albatros got on his tail. I attacked the Albatros on Booker's tail and it dived away. I fired at another which climbed and I got fairly close to its tail. It turned left into a steep climbing turn. I did likewise trying to get my gun to bear on him when, suddenly, there was a terrific racket of machine gun firing behind me. I looked round and saw five or six Albatros Scouts attacking me. In the excitement of the moment, my glove accidentally pressed the engine blip switch, causing the engine to stop. At that moment I was in a steep climbing turn, almost at stalling point, and the sudden lack of engine thrust caused the Triplane to fall into a spinning nose dive. I was absolutely scared stiff for two reasons: firstly the Huns and secondly the spin. I was at 10,000 feet when this happened. I had never been in a spinning nose dive before and I was not at all sure whether I should be able to regain control.*

'*However, the Huns were the immediate and most pressing danger so I allowed the*

Line-up of Jasta 12 aircraft. Black tails and various fuselage markings feature - including Hockstetter's 'Clubs' and another marked with a double cross.

Triplane to continue its spin, hoping the Huns would think they had got me and leave me alone. I did not attempt to get out of the spin until I was getting fairly close to the ground. Then I centralised the controls, the spinning ceased and became a straight vertical dive, and I eased the machine out of it to a level position.

'Steering towards the west I went straight down to ground level, hopping over any obstruction which happened to be in the way. This method of hedge-hopping my way home served me well because I was passing and out of sight before the Germans on the ground could shoot at me. I crossed the lines at this low altitude and got back to Mont St. Eloi without further incident. Booker and McCrudden arrived at the same time. On inspection my machine was found to be riddled with bullet holes but no vital part had been hit.'

There is no doubt that this was the combat for which AvT made his first claim of the day. Furthermore, no Triplanes at all were lost at this time and in this area (10 Naval did lose one near Armentières that evening, probably to AA fire). To be fair, German front-line observers, when asked if they had seen a Triplane go down, might well have confirmed one falling in a spinning nose dive from 10,000 feet. It might have appeared to have been a victory for one of their airmen and, at first flush, one that had fallen inside the German lines. What they obviously did not see was the pilot regaining control of the Tripe and hedge-hopping it home.

Although Crundall's machine was badly shot about it was far from a write-off. Indeed, after the mechanics had worked on it for a day, he air tested it during the following afternoon.

FLIGHT SUB-LIEUTENANT
EDWARD DUNCAN CRUNDALL,
DFC, AFC, 8 NAVAL SQUADRON, ROYAL NAVAL AIR SERVICE

Born on 9 December 1896, the son of Edward and Mrs Crundall of Westfield, near Dover, Kent. After leaving school he worked as a clerk in the Dover branch of the National Provincial Bank of England from November 1914 until July 1916. Joined the RNAS, gaining his Royal Aero Club Certificate (Number 3543) on 5 September 1916. By 10 May 1917, when he was shot down by OffStellv Alois Heldman, Crundall had three victories of his own. He had only just returned to operational flying again when he ran into AvT on 28 July 1917. In 1918 Crundall was posted to 210 Squadron as a Flight Commander, gaining four more victories. Awarded the Distinguished Flying Cross – *London Gazette* 10 October 1919 (no citation) – shortly after he left the RAF on 28 August 1919. After his demobilisation Crundall turned to civil aviation, mainly piloting charter flights of one sort or another. Re-joined the RAF again in 1939, commanding 116 Calibration Squadron (Acting Wing Commander) until 1945, receiving the Air Force Cross for the valuable services he had rendered – *London Gazette* 1 January 1945, page 58. After the end of the Second World War he opened charter routes to South Africa and to French Equatorial Africa, bringing his total flying time to over 8,500 hours.

VICTORY NO. 20
28 July 1917 Nieuport XVII (No.B1558) 40 Squadron 1040

At 0930, 40 Squadron sent out a three-machine patrol to the area north-east of Lens. The men piloting the Nieuport scout planes were Lieutenants E Mannock, H A Kennedy and J H Tudhope. No sooner had the trio crossed the invisible frontier into German air space than they were challenged by seven Albatri. The German planes were all light in colour with patches of yellow and green. One distinctively sported a purple club – a club of the playing card variety, that is!

A bitter, intensive dogfight ensued. The British, heavily outnumbered, fought a brilliant defensive battle before eventually disentangling themselves, 'to fight another day'.

When a shocked Mannock landed, he related the details of the recent fight to Lieutenant W 'Mac' MacLanachan and confessed that he had never been so frightened. When, a few minutes later, the two other members of the patrol touched down, Mannock audibly offered thanks to God, observing, *'Poor old Tud must be shot to hell.'* MacLanachan relates the aftermath of the von Tutschek encounter in his book *Fighter Pilot*, originally published in 1936, and more recently by Greenhill Books in 1985:

'Tud's machine was in such a condition that it might have been sent to a flying school to act as an inspiration and a warning to budding fighters. An explosive bullet had burnt through his main spar a few inches from the 'V' strut, one of the top planes had been cut to ribbons by bullets, every one of his instruments was smashed, and a bullet had passed through his coat collar. Tud's face was a study, it depicted a combination of cynicism and amusement. He had certainly been very close to death that morning.

'It transpired that on crossing the lines towards Douai they had encountered nine (sic) enemy scouts flying in formation. Mick, intent on 'showing 'em' had waded right into the Germans, only to be met with a vigorous resistance, from which he had been only too glad to escape. The Germans also, finding they could not destroy the three Nieuports, considered that their victory was not assured.'

There can be no doubt that Tud and Co's opponents were Jasta 12. In their combat reports, the 40 Squadron pilots described various characteristics of their adversary's machines and whilst these may have been fleetingly glimpsed, they seemed to have imprinted themselves onto their conscious-ness. Mannock mentions a purple-coloured Albatros. Although, in fact, von Tutschek actually flew an Albatros with black fuselage and tail, the upper surfaces of his wings were the standard mauve and dark green. This combination, blending with the black, would appear to be overall purple in the midst of a hectic air fight. Furthermore, the black paint on these aircraft tended to fade slightly and what had been black often took on a purplish hue.

Kennedy particularly noted an Albatros with a purple club. This was the distin-guishing logo on the aircraft usually flown

by Jasta 12's Friedrich Hochstetter. There was also mention of an Albatros with a cross on the fuselage – by that is meant a cross in addition to the standard German national marking. This was a large lattice-type cross or 'XX' marking, and there exists a photograph of a Jasta 12 machine with just this marking on the fuselage. Von Tutschek had two machines of his own and photographs indicate that neither was totally black, each having a lightish band along the side of the fuselage.

So, this supposed second von Tutschek 'victory' of the morning also actually got home, albeit more than a little 'shot about'. With the exception of a 1 Squadron machine shot down in the vicinity of Polygon Wood at 1025 German time – thought to have been downed by a German two-seater crew – there were no other Nieuport losses during this morning.

SECOND LIEUTENANT
JOHN HENRY TUDHOPE,
MC & BAR, 40 SQUADRON, ROYAL FLYING CORPS

Born on 17 April 1891 in Johannesburg, South Africa, he was the only son of chartered accountant turned farmer, Francis Selwyn Tudhope and Mrs Tudhope. Educated at the Dioecian College, Capetown, at St John's College, Johannesburg and at Tonbridge, Kent (1906-10), representing that school at rugby football and rowing. Returned to South Africa and spent two years as a fitter in the gold mines in the Transvaal. As soon as the war started in August 1914, he immediately enlisted as a trooper/machine gunner into the Imperial Light Horse, South African Defence Force. Served in the SA Rebellion and in the German South West Africa campaign. Came to England in 1916, married Jessie Graham Elizabeth Jackson from Hinton St Mary, Dorset and enlisted as a private soldier into the Dorset Regiment (Number 27400). Accepted as a RFC officer cadet on 1 February 1917 and commissioned to the

Squadron on 14 June 1917, fighting in and above the great land battles of the last two years of the war as a Flight Commander and Captain. Awarded the Military Cross and Bar – MC, *London Gazette* 26 March 1918, page 3746 (Citation 24 August 1918): *'For conspicuous gallantry and devotion to duty. He showed a splendid offensive spirit continually attacking enemy aeroplanes. He has destroyed three enemy machines and has driven others down out of control and always set a splendid example of courage and initiative'*. Bar to the MC, *London Gazette* 26 July 1918, page 8767: *'For conspicuous gallantry and devotion to duty in fighting with exceptional dash and skill over a period of nine months, when he carried out numerous reconnaissances, flying low and engaging with bombs and machine-gun fire enemy troops, guns and transport. He obtained many direct hits and inflicted heavy casualties, often flying under very difficult weather conditions. He has crashed three enemy aeroplanes and shot down two others out of control. His determination and courage have been a brilliant example to the other pilots of the flight he has been leading'*. Credited with ten victories before returning to the Home Establishment in 1918. Finally left the RAF on 13 November 1919. Crossed over to Canada in 1920 and joined the Royal Canadian Air Force. Died in London, Ontario, Canada, on 12 October 1956. At his direction, his ashes were scattered from the air over the Rocky Mountains.

General List on 13 April 1917. Awarded his 'Wings' and appointed a Flying Officer on 29 May 1917. First sent to France and 40

VICTORY NO. 21
29 July 1917 SE5a (No.A8937) 60 Squadron 0805

This was to be Jasta 12's 100th recorded victim.

60 Squadron had now exchanged its Nieuport Scouts for SE5s. Von Tutschek records the SE5 as being a new machine over the front, whereas, in fact, it was not that new. 56 Squadron had first brought this scout to France back in April 1917. But by now it had

begun arriving in greater numbers, superceding the long established Nieuports.

On this morning a 60 Squadron patrol got into a fight with Jasta 12 and one of its members, Second Lieutenant Gunner, was last seen up above the German fighter formation near Douai. Shortly afterwards, he came down near to Henin-Lietard on the German side of the lines.

SECOND LIEUTENANT

WILLIAM HENRY GUNNER,

MC, 60 SQUADRON, ROYAL FLYING CORPS

The son of bank manager William Henry Gunner and his wife, Louise Jane Gunner of 'Winfold', Maltravers Street, Arundel, Sussex, William was born on 19 April 1891 and educated at Elmsdale School, Redhill. Before the war he worked in London as a clerk with cigarette manufacturers W D & H O Wills, in their offices at Holborn Viaduct, lodging with relatives at 'Ravenscroft', Stanley Road, Sutton, Surrey. A pre-war volunteer, he joined the London Rifle Brigade as a private soldier (Number 8916) on 25 March 1909. At the end of his five-year engagement with the LRB he decided to change his commitment to the 3rd County of London Yeomanry – Trooper, Number 1037 – with effect from 6 March 1914. Mobilised in August 1914, he embarked at Avonmouth on 14 April 1915 bound for Alexandria and the Middle East. From Egypt, he and the Yeomanry Brigade landed in Gallipoli on 14 August 1915. Six weeks later on 24 September 1915, he was admitted first to Field Hospital A3 and from there on to a military hospital in Alexandria, suffering from dysentery. Failing to respond to treatment, he was sent home on the hospital ship, *Ebani*, arriving in Cardiff on 13 November 1915. His health restored, he was gazetted Second Lieutenant to the General List on 5 September 1916, following which he successfully applied for a transfer to the RFC. Obtained his Royal Aero Club Certificate (Number 4565) on 3 February 1917. After his formal training was completed, he was awarded his 'Wings' and, before proceeding to France and 60 Squadron, married his fiancée, Mary Stevens of Radlett, Hertfordshire. Gunner enjoyed considerable success with 60 Squadron, being quickly elevated to Acting Flight Commander and awarded the Military Cross. In a letter home, one of Gunner's contemporaries, Captain W E Molesworth, compliments his efforts: '......*every cloud has a silver lining. This time it is in the shape of an MC for one of our flight commanders (sic) who thoroughly deserves it. He hasn't managed to get a big bag yet, but there is lots of 'good stuff' in him, in both senses of the word. We are going to have a great 'bust' tonight to commemorate it, and to cheer things up a bit'*. The Military Cross was announced in the *London Gazette* of 18 July 1917, page 7230: '*For conspicuous gallantry and devotion to duty. While on Offensive Patrol he engaged and attacked 9 hostile aircraft, two of which were attacking the rear machine of our patrol. Having convoyed the other machine back to the aerodrome, he again returned with his patrol in response to an urgent call for aeroplanes to drive off hostile aircraft. He had been wounded in his previous encounter, but insisted on carrying on, and on numerous other occasions he has shown great skill and courage in offensive work'*. (Although the authors may be accused of pedantry, it has to be said that Gunner was not actually a fully fledged

Flight Commander, although he did, occasionally, lead patrols from time to time). His death on 29 July 1917 was announced in the *Nord Deutche Allgemeine Zeitung*, viz: '*BE one-seater, Motor Wolesey 700/2233. Occupant burnt*'. Buried by the German army with honour. Cabaret-Rouge Cemetery (Fr924). Age 26.

On the afternoon of his two phantom victories, Adolf von Tutschek was invited to lunch with General von Moser of the XIV Reserve Corps and in the evening, to dine with General von Bülow. He was advised of the award of the Blue Max – the Pour le Mérite – on 3 August although the official announcement was delayed until the 7th. The actual decoration was hung around his neck on 15 August 1917 by General von Bülow.

Jasta 12 had moved their base to Roucourt on 27 July, still though part of the 6th Army. The squadron was now almost completely equipped with Albatros DV fighters. However, the Jasta pilots had begun to be aware that the 'edge' they had enjoyed for so long was becoming somewhat blunted. They were increasingly impressed – and concerned – by the high standards of the new breed of fighters they were coming up against. The SE5s, the Sopwith Camels, the Bristol F2B two-seat fighters and the improved 200 hp French Spad XIII now presented a new set of problems for the German airmen.

VICTORY NO. 22
11 August 1918 Bristol F2B (No.A7169) 22 Squadron 0910

A poor morning with rain and low cloud seemed to indicate a non-flying day but at 0740 a telephone call informed the Jasta that a flight of Bristol Fighters were heading for Monchy. Von Tutschek was still in bed but was soon running for his machine, taking off after most of the others had already left. He soon caught up with his five colleagues and settled into the formation. Within minutes, at 0750 over Arleux, they spotted the British two-seaters above them. The leading Brisfit, streaming pennants from his wing struts, led an attacking dive down onto the Albatros fighters. Von Tutschek pulled up the nose of his machine to lead a head-on pass. The inevitable dog-fight ensued and von Tutschek clinically took out 'A7169', wounding the pilot and forcing him to crash-land in a shell hole just behind the lines.

An hour later von Tutschek travelled to the crash site – which he recorded as being east of Biache – and had his photograph taken alongside the wreckage before visiting the two British crewmen in hospital. Captain Chambers had been badly wounded and the German ace promised to send a note to his mother in Canada, expressing the hope that he would be able to visit him after the war. Chambers, however, was very seriously injured, having been hit in the throat and stomach in the air and, in the ensuing crash, had broken both arms and both legs.

The Brisfit's observer, Yorkshireman Walter Richman, had sustained a cut on the forehead as well as breaking a few ribs. He was cursing himself for shooting so poorly and glared belligerently at his erstwhile opponent and bedside visitor.

CAPTAIN
PERCY WILMOT CHAMBERS,
22 SQUADRON, ROYAL FLYING CORPS

Of Irish descent, Percy was born on 22 May 1887, the son of Mr and Ann Jane Chambers of 570 Runnymede Road, Toronto, Canada. He was educated at Albert College, Belleville, from where he went into farming in Pontypool, Ontario. Volunteering immediately the war broke out, he enlisted into the 4th Battalion, Canadian Infantry (Service Number 11214) on 10 August 1914.

Capt Percy Wilmot Chambers.

his stated preference he should be transferred to the British army as a private soldier. Chambers undertook to learn to fly at his own expense and subsequently qualified at the Ruffy-Bauman Flying School on 3 October 1915 (Royal Aero Club Certificate Number 1813). Gazetted Second Lieutenant (General List) on 15 March 1916, he was invited to report to Oxford on 6 April 1916 for preliminary training. Chamber's rapid advance to the rank of Captain was evidence of his competence as a pilot. Shot in the neck in the engagement with von Tutschek, he died three days later – just three days short of his thirtieth birthday – in the Feldlaz. at Douai and was buried there with full military honours accorded by the Imperial German Air Service. Details of his death and interment were published in the *Nord Deutche Allgemeine Zeitung* on 15 September 1917. Subsequently re-buried in the British Military Cemetery, Douai, France (Fr1276). More than a year after his death, his mother and two sisters (all resident in the Ontario area) were still trying to recover back-pay owed to their son and brother.

SERGEANT
WALTER RICHMAN,
22 SQUADRON, ROYAL FLYING CORPS

Born in 1883, Walter was the son of Mr and Mrs Richman of Howsham, York. A chauffeur in civilian life, he volunteered very early on in the war, joining the Army Service Corps (Number M/Z/182688). Shortly after the completion of his basic training, he was transferred as an ambulance driver to the Royal Army Medical Corps (Number 31480) and was sent to France in that capacity on 11 May 1915. Qualified drivers of motor vehicles were relatively scarce in the early days of the war and he was reclaimed by the ASC on 29 June 1916 although continuing to serve in France (with 399th Company) until 27 January 1917, when he returned to England to train as an observer with the RFC. His training success-fully completed, he was off to France yet again, this time as a probationary

Proceeded to England and subsequently to France with the first contingent of the Canadian Expeditionary Force. Invalided from the front with a gunshot wound received during the first ever gas attack in April 1915, when the Canadians stood firm and undoubtedly saved the Ypres Salient from falling to the German army. In July 1915, he had recovered his health and fitness and was attached to the 12th Battalion, Canadian Infantry, then based at Shorncliff Camp, Kent. It was at this time that he requested a transfer to the RFC. The Canadian army, who were about to commission him, decided that in view of gunner/observer with 22 Squadron. On 17 March 1917, flying with Second Lieutenant F R Hudson in FE2b Number 4900, he and his pilot were wounded in action – Walter receiving a gun shot in the right foot. Their opponent on this occasion was almost certainly Leutnant Heinrich Gontermann of Jasta 5 – the fourth of the ace's eventual 39 victory claims. On 28 June 1917, Walter married his fiancée, Elizabeth, at Egton-cum-Newland. Elizabeth continued to live with her parents at 'The High Farm', Greenodd, Ulverston, Lancashire, when Walter returned to France and the Bristol Fighters of 22 Squadron. Had reached the acting rank of Sergeant when he was shot down by von Tutschek. After being taken prisoner, he was incarcerated mainly at Langensalya before his eventual repatriation on 20 December 1918.

VICTORY NO. 23
11 August 1917   Bristol F2B (No.A7179)   22 Squadron   1830

Rain had continued for much of the day but at around 1800 another call came, reporting more British interlopers, this time spotting for artillery near Lens. Von Tutschek and two of his pilots immediately took off to intercept. Their approach was spotted from a distance and the artillery observing BEs dived away to the safety of their own lines. The three Albatros Scouts continued to patrol, looking for trouble. This was soon forthcoming in the shape of five 22 Squadron Bristol Fighters – the same squadron they had scrapped with that morning. The Bristols had taken off at 1715 on a Distant Offensive Patrol.

Soon after the inevitable fight began, von Tutschek briefly glimpsed one of his companions under fierce attack by a Brisfit but was himself too heavily engaged with another to effect any help. His Albatros was

One of the two BF2Bs shot down by von Tutschek on 11 August 1917. The victor stands astride the wreck.

hit several times but then they were both suddenly swallowed up by dense cloud. Emerging in clear sky von Tutschek found himself plumb behind yet another Bristol whose crew was completely oblivious of the impending menace. His machine-gun fire set the British machine alight, von Tutschek was so close he could feel the heat. Following the burning machine down, von Tutschek saw – just before it hit the ground – the wings rip off and the observer leap out in a vain attempt to save his life. The incinerated Bristol Fighter hit the ground west of Courcelles, between Douai and Henin-Lietard.

LIEUTENANT
ARTHUR EDWARD HUNTER WARD,
6/WEST YORKSHIRE REGIMENT AND 22 SQUADRON, ROYAL FLYING CORPS

The son of accountant John Henry Ward and Mrs Ward of 14, Lichfield Avenue, Waterloo, Liverpool, Edward was born in 1897. Graduated Bachelor of Arts from Hertford College, Oxford. Gazetted Second Lieutenant to the West Yorkshire Regiment on 22 October 1915. The German Air Service accorded him full honour and he is buried in Noyelles-Godault Cemetery, France (Fr1314). Age 20.

LIEUTENANT
KENNETH WOODFULL HOLMES,
4/AUSTRALIAN PIONEERS AND 22 SQUADRON, ROYAL FLYING CORPS

Born on 30 June 1890 in Praham, Victoria, Australia, Ken Holmes (above right) was educated at Caulfield Grammar School and at Trinity College, Melbourne University from where he graduated in engineering in 1911. Subsequently held a position as a civil engineer with Victoria Railways of Armadale, Victoria. Enlisted as a Sapper in the 5th Field Company, Royal Australian Engineers on 7 June 1915. Transferred to the 4th Pioneer Battalion with whom he went to Egypt on 16 March 1916. Gazetted Second Lieutenant to his own unit on 24 March 1916. Accompanied the Pioneers to France on 4 June 1916, landing in Marseilles exactly one week later. A series of transfers followed, including temporary postings to the Salvage Company and to the Anzac Light Railways. On 19 April 1917, his long held wish to join the Australian Flying Corps was granted and hence he was posted to Reading for observer training at the Number 1 School of Instruction. Just under two months later, on 17 June 1917, he was sent to join 22 Squadron in France as a probationary observer. Died from wounds, burns and injuries as a prisoner of the Germans later on the same day he was shot down by Adolf von Tutschek. Buried in Noyelles-Godault Cemetery, France (Fr1314). He was 27 years old.

Shot down – or the biter bit!

The weather had cleared by 2100 at which time von Tutschek led yet another six-machine counter-offensive against a reported British incursion, this time comprising 12 SE5s. The two formations converged between Arras and Lens. The SE5s attacked first and von Tutschek soon got into a fight with one of them but he also saw a Sopwith Triplane bearing down on him from above. At that crucial moment his guns jammed and his machine was hit in the radiator, hot water spurting over him. He dived away, streaming white vapour. The Triplane followed his dive, sending machine-gun bullets whistling past his ears. The Albatros abruptly flicked into a spin as von Tutschek was hit in the shoulder and blacked out.

He came round at a low altitude, slowly becoming aware that the Triplane was still

Flight Commander C D Booker, 8/Naval Squadron, who shot down and wounded von Tutschek on the evening of 11 August 1917.

attacking, his machine still in a spin. Fortunately one of his colleagues arrived to drive off the persistent attacker. Gasping with relief, von Tutschek managed to get his engine re-started. Covered in blood from the wound in his shoulder, he turned for home. Feeling himself slipping into unconsciousness again, he hurriedly force-landed his Albatros near Douai.

The lower part of his right shoulder blade had been shattered. At first he thought he had been wounded in the lung as he was bringing up blood – a particularly serious life-threatening condition at that time. Fortunately this was not the case – his lungs were intact. He wrote a breezily cheerful letter to his mother, telling her he had been wounded in the shoulder but that he would be back in action within four weeks. He knew it would take longer than this, but he did not want to worry her unduly.

Adolf von Tutschek was out of action until December. On the 6th of that month he was promoted to Hauptmann. During his recuperation in Münster, von Tutschek learnt that his uncle, Generalmajor (later Generalleutnant) Ludwig Ritter von Tutschek had also been awarded the Pour le Mérite. The General commanded the Austro-German Alpine Corps and was given the decoration for his leadership during the Battle of Isonso.

Von Tutschek was given a job flying a desk at Kogenluft (Headquarters) in December 1917 but, by February 1918, he was fit again and appointed Commander of Jagdgeschwader Nr.II. His new Group, comprising Jastas 12, 13, 15 and 19, operated in the German 7th Army area. Oberleutnant Paul Blumenbach had been appointed to the command of Jasta 12 in his stead.

JGII operated in an area where the French and British fronts conjoined and so were just as likely to encounter French as well as British aeroplanes. Their old airfield at Toulis is situated on the road which runs between Autremencourt and Vesles.

Above: Von Tutschek, now with the Blue Max at his neck, recovering from wounds he received on 11 August 1917. *(Greg VanWyngarden)*

Right: Von Tutschek and his Jasta 12 pilots outside the Château at Toulis in early 1918. The top three on the stairs are Ulrich Neckel, Paul Blumenbach and Hermann Becker.

VICTORY NO. 24
26 February 1918 Spad XIII (No.B6732) 23 Squadron 1120

The Spads of 23 Squadron flew a morning Offensive Patrol from Cambrai to Laon. Second Lieutenant Doyle's machine suffered engine trouble and began to cut out over the German lines and so he left the formation and headed back. Doyle then contrived not only to get himself lost but also to have the misfortune to run into von Tutschek. The Spad's already malfunctioning engine was hit by von Tutschek's bullets and now, not being in any position to defend himself, Doyle had no option but to land. In his post-war debriefing, he complained that he had been shot at from the air after he had landed. But let us be charitable and assume that this was just von Tutschek's way of dissuading Doyle from setting fire to his Spad before German troops reached him. Minutes after he landed, German cavalry arrived at the scene and took him captive.

Von Tutschek later wrote that at noon he was standing on the airfield when AA bursts in the sky indicated the presence of an intruding hostile aeroplane and he immediately took off. Finding the lost and lonely Spad, he quickly despatched it, the machine trailing white smoke as if radiator or fuel tank had been punctured.

The German ace also indicated that he had later driven to where the machine had landed to inspect his handiwork. He said he spoke to the Irish *(sic)* pilot, the son of a Colonel in the British army. Von Tutschek said the pilot had one slight graze to one of his little toes, otherwise he was unharmed. The strange thing is that there are several photos of von Tutschek with the Spad, with his Fokker Triplane in the immediate background. This would seem to indicate that the Spad had been taken to Toulis aerodrome and the Fokker afterwards wheeled up to look as though the victor had alighted alongside his victim. What we now call a photo-opportunity!

The next day von Tutschek and Paul Blumenbach combined to shoot down a British two-seater but, on this occasion, JGII's commander magnanimously awarded the kill to the Staffelführer as the latter had smashed the machine's fuel tank, effectively administering the *coup de grâce*. The machine is noted as being a Spad two-seater – presumably a French machine – sent down at Essigny le Grand on the Allied side of the line (the time not given but possibly in the morning). Possibly a Nieuport 24 from GDE. What von Tutschek did not mention was that he and Blumenbach collided in the air – fortunately with both men surviving.

SECOND LIEUTENANT
DAVID COLQUHOUN DOYLE,
23 SQUADRON, ROYAL FLYING CORPS

Born on 22 June 1898, David was the son of architect and surveyor Colonel S W Doyle and Mrs Doyle of 'Rye Moor', 57 Broadgreen

Road, Page Moss, Liverpool. Educated at Greenbank School, Liverpool (1907-12) and at Shrewsbury (1912-15). After leaving school, he secured a position with Andrew Yule and Company, Calcutta, India, before returning to England to volunteer for the Royal Flying Corps in the spring of 1917. Gazetted Second Lieutenant, General List, on 21 June 1917, he completed his pilot training in October 1917 and was sent overseas to join 23 Squadron on 15 December 1917. Taken prisoner after his encounter with von Tutschek, he was incarcerated at Landschut Holzminden until 14 December 1918 when he was repatriated at last. Shortly afterwards, on 16 February 1919, he left the service, consigned to the Unemployed List. In later life, Doyle became a director of Insurance and Re-insurance Limited of New Bond Street, London.

Above: Von Tutschek examines his 24th victory – David Doyle's Spad XIII (B6732).

Right: POW group, Holzminden 1918: Back row: 2Lt W G Ivamy (54 Sqd), C H S Ackers (KRRC/25 Sqd), —?—, 2Lt D C Doyle (23 Sqd), Lt C H Crosbee (24 Sqd), Lt J M Allen (57 Sqd), Lt R E Duke (84 Sqd). Centre: Lt G G Jackson (Essex R/RFC), Lt J R Law (CASC/54 Sqd), —?—, Lt W H Taylor (83 Sqd) Front: 2Lt C G Logan (2 AFC), *(Via Jeff Taylor)*

Right: Von Tutschek in front of the Spad XIII (B6732).

Below right: Holzminden menu cover depicting the camp cookhouse drawn by J M Allen, 20 October 1918. *(Via Jeff Taylor)*

Below: Birthday celebration menu. *(Via Jeff Taylor)*

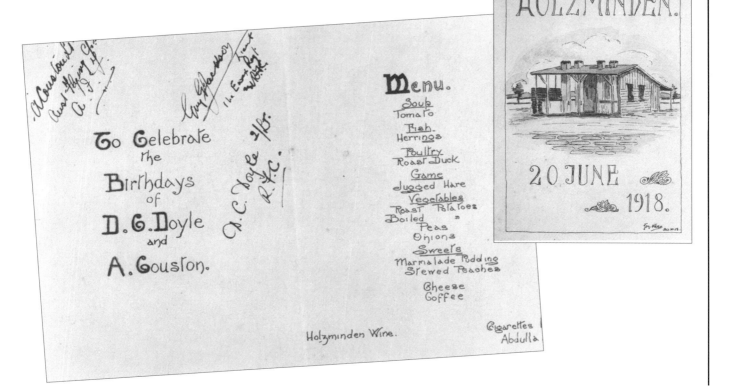

To Celebrate the Birthdays of D. G. Doyle and A. Couston.

HOLZMINDEN.

20 JUNE 1918.

Menu.

Soup
Tomato

Fish.
Herrings

Poultry
Roast Duck

Game
Jugged Hare

Vegetables
Roast Potatoes
Boiled   "
Peas
Onions

Sweets
Marmalade Pudding
Stewed Peaches

Cheese
Coffee

Holzminden Wine.

Cigarettes
Abdulla

VICTORY NO. 25
1 March 1918 Kite Balloon French 0845

Flying his black-tailed Fokker Dr1 Nr.404/17 von Tutschek – accompanied by Blumenbach and Offizierstellvertreter Dobberahn – dived from 3,000 metres onto a kite balloon near Terny. After only ten shots the balloon burst into flames and von Tutschek watched as the camera and both observers went over the side of the basket and descended in parachutes. The occupants were probably Lieutenant P Bacalou and Second Lieutenant F Morgan, US Balloon Company. Von Tutschek attacked another balloon on 5 March 1917, but this one did not burn.

Von Tutschek and SE5a Number C1057. Forced down by the German ace on 6 March 1918, its former occupant, 2Lt A P C Wigan, had been escorted away to captivity. (Via Greg VanWyngarden)

VICTORY NO.26
6 March 1918 SE5a No.C1057 24 Squadron 1445

24 Squadron, based at Matigny, near Ham, sent out a four-man Offensive Patrol at 1320. Just over an hour later they were engaged by several Fokker Triplanes, which were soon joined by others of the same ilk. Lieutenant Wigan, one of the 24 Squadron

pilots, said in his debriefing after returning from Germany that he had been cut out of the pack by four Triplanes, his engine had been hit and he was forced to make a landing behind German lines, near St Gobien.

Von Tutschek's version of the events was that he had been flying with three other Triplanes and four Albatros DVs of Jasta 12 when they encountered seven *(sic)* SE5s above the woods at Groupy. He said he attacked the leader, who sported red pennants streaming from his struts, and forced him into a smooth landing near Bertaucourt, eight kilometres south-east of La Fère, whereupon the downed pilot was immediately taken prisoner.

Several photographs exist of von Tutschek posing with the intact SE5a, with captions to the effect that Wigan was the Staffel leader. One assumes that Wigan was merely leading the patrol – or perhaps acting as deputy leader – hence the red pennants, certainly he was too junior to be a Staffel leader or its British equivalent.

SECOND LIEUTENANT
ARTHUR PENWARNE CLEVELAND WIGAN,
24 SQUADRON, ROYAL FLYING CORPS

The son of brewery manager Basil Penwarne Wigan and Mrs Wigan of 'Penair', Church Road, Whitchurch, Glamorgan, Arthur was born on 11 October 1898. He was educated at St Peter's School, Weston-super-Mare and at Clifton College (1913-16). Arthur left Clifton in Easter 1916 and immediately enlisted into the motor transport branch of the Army Service Corps (Number 285911), training as a motor-cycle despatch rider at 20th Company, ASC, based at Penge. Following an interview he was accepted for the RFC in November 1916 but was obliged to await a call-up vacancy which eventually arrived in February 1917. Pilot training successfully completed, he was gazetted Second Lieutenant to the General List on 10 August 1917. Taken prisoner after his fight with AvT, he remained in captivity until his repatriation on 14 December 1918.

VICTORY NO.27
10 March 1918 Spad XIII Spa 86 1745

All we know of this action with this French Escadrille is that von Tutschek, flying 404/17, was on his second patrol of the day in company with Blumenbach and Leutnant Paul Hoffmann, They flew beneath five Spads at 3,000 metres which immediately dived upon the German trio. In the ensuing fight, von Tutschek got behind one of the Spads, who he thought was the leader. After a burst of 50 rounds at close range, the French scout plane nosed over trailing fire and smoke. The Spad went straight down just north-west of Fort Malmaison, not far from Chavigon, and smashed into a French trench, the wreckage burning to ashes.

ADJUTANT
EUGÈNE VOLLOD,
SPA 86

Born in Lyon on 25 March 1888. Qualified for his pilot's brevet (Number 2595) on 12 November 1915. Killed in combat with three enemy machines on 10 March 1918. Cited in Orders 16 March 1918.

Von Tutschek flew his final sortie on the morning of 15 March 1918. In company with several others of his command – flying a mixture of Triplanes and Albatros DVs – he took off shortly after 1000, again in '404/17'.

Over the years there has been some controversy as to who actually shot AvT down. The evidence now currently available points to his last combat being with 24 Squadron's SE5s near Prémontré at 1030 hours (British and German times

coinciding during this period). The five RFC pilots involved were led by Captain B P G Beanlands MC, with Lieutenants A K Cowper, R T Mark, Richardson and H B Redler (in SE5a B79) – the latter a seasoned veteran who had fought with 40 Squadron in 1917.

Redler spotted three Triplanes and three Albatros Scouts heading west some 1,000 feet below him and without hesitation, dived to attack. He fired 40 rounds at the highest of the Triplanes at almost point-blank range, so close, in fact, that he almost collided with the enemy machine. The Dr1 stalled to the right and began to spin down, apparently out of control. Redler could not follow his victim down as he had to deal with the falling Triplane's comrades who, by now, were reacting to his surprise attack and responding appropriately.

And surprise attack it undoubtedly was. None of the German pilots had seen it coming and the first they knew of any impending danger was the sight of von Tutschek's Triplane spinning and falling away. At least two of the Jasta pilots anxiously followed the Triplane down and were relieved to see it finally pull out and make what they later described as a good landing. Some accounts said that von Tutschek climbed out of the Dr1, waved and then fell dead, whilst other versions say that he was found slumped dead in the cockpit. His uncle Ludwig was advised of his nephew's death the same day.

Von Tutschek it seems was hit a severe glancing blow to the temple which knocked him out momentarily. He must have regained consciousness near the ground and instinctively managed a good landing

Right: Lieutenant H B Redler MC, 24 Squadron, claimed a Fokker Dr I shot down on 15 March 1918 which proved to be, in the event, von Tutchek's.

before he died. The precise causes of his death – internal haemorrhaging or perhaps even a heart attack – have never been established.

The ace had come down near Brancourt-en-Laonnois, which is just a mile or so from Prémontré, the reported scene of Redler's attack action. Redler was credited with an 'out of control' victory, his first with 24 Squadron and his fourth success to date. He would go on to achieve ten victories and receive the Military Cross before he left for England at the end of April. He was killed in a flying accident at Turnberry on 21 June 1918, flying in a DH9 along with another successful fighter pilot, Captain I H D Henderson MC, late of 19 and 56 Squadrons, and the son of General Sir David Henderson who commanded the RFC.

LIEUTENANT
HAROLD BOLTON REDLER,
MC, 24 SQUADRON, ROYAL FLYING CORPS

The son of Daniel Bolton Redler and Annie Pethick Redler of Boschbeek, Newlands, Cape Town, South Africa, he was born in West Moncton, Somerset, in 1897. Flew Nieuports with 40 Squadron in 1917, claiming three victories, before transferring in early 1918 to 24 Squadron and its SE5As. Gained a further seven victories before the end of April 1918, including, on 15 March 1918, Adolf von Tutschek. Awarded the Military Cross, *London Gazette* 22 June 1918, page 7421: *'For conspicuous gallantry and devotion to duty. He encountered four enemy two-seater machines and attacking the lowest drove it to the ground with its engine damaged. Later, he attacked one of five enemy two-seater machines and drove it down out of control. He has destroyed in all three enemy machines and driven three others down out of control. He continually attacked enemy troops and transport from a low altitude during operations, and showed splendid qualities of courage and determi-*

nation throughout'. Harold Redler, who had returned to the UK for a well deserved rest was, as has already been mentioned, subsequently killed in a flying accident. He is buried in West Monckton (St Augustine) Churchyard, Somerset. Age 21.

Hauptmann Adolf Ritter von Tutschek, Pour le Mérite .

Adolf von Tutschek's body was recovered and laid in state in the church at Marle, Laon, where a memorial service were held on 17 March 1918. From here his remains were returned to Munich for burial. His final resting place was at the Waldfriedhof. Age 26.

Not for the first time, the authors of the 'Under the Guns' series of books have thrown doubts on the veracity of certain victory claims of a leading ace. In this case it appears that at least three so-called 'victories' have no foundation in fact (numbers 2, 11 and 12) and that the circumstances surrounding others – in particular numbers 4, 15, 19 and 20 – are, to say the least, evidentially inconclusive.

Armed with the doubtful gift of hindsight and from the supine comfort of armchairs, we are acutely conscious of falling into the trap of making shabbily portentous pronouncements regarding life and death events of decades ago. In our own defence, we must stress that we do not set out to *disprove* these claims but rather the diametric opposite. In no way do we wish to denigrate these brave men, fighting with supreme skill, for their country and for their lives.

However, human nature being what it is, when widespread fame and the acclamation of one's peers beckons, 'performance enhancement', to a lesser or greater degree, is often an irresistible temptation.

CHAPTER 4

OBERLEUTNANT KURT WOLFF

The popular perception of a 'fighter pilot' as a keen-eyed, dashingly handsome young man could hardly be applied to Kurt Wolff – even his best friends could not describe him thus. And yet this diminutive, almost Chaplinesque figure was, without doubt, one of the very best exponents of the art.

Leutnant Kurt Wolff, Jasta 11. *(Greg VanWyngarden)*

Born on 6 February 1895, in the north-eastern German town of Greifswald, on the fringe of the Pomeranian Bay and orphaned whilst still a youngster, he was brought up by relatives living in Memel. He began his military service with the Eisenbahn (Railway) Regiment Nr.4, at Schoesberg, with which unit he was commissioned on 17 April 1915. A transfer to the Air Service followed in July 1916.

During his very first flight he was involved in a crash which killed his instructor. The experience would have destroyed the nerve and resolve of many men but not Wolff's. Small in statue but a veritable giant in spirit, he continued his flight training and soon received his pilot's badge. Some sources mistakenly have him going directly to Jasta 11 at this point, but that was not the case. Along with the majority of fighter pilots of the period, Wolff was initially assigned to a two-seater unit. First a pilot with Kasta 26 of Kagohl 5, he next went on to Kagohl 7 and finally to KG40, before his posting to Jasta 11 on 12 October 1916.

His arrival at Jasta 11, then based at Douai on the German 6th Army Front, was some weeks before Manfred von Richthofen took over as Staffelführer. The Staffel, currently commanded by Oberleutnant Rudolf Lang, was destined not to achieve a single victory until the coming of the Red Baron in January 1917. Wolff and a number of other novices blossomed under the expert tutelage of Manfred von Richtofen, soon becoming highly proficient air fighters. The

Wolff stands by his Albatros DIII (632/17) in Spring 1917. He favoured a 'plum purple' Albatros although, like most Jasta 11 machines, red was the predominant colour. He added a personally distinctive touch by having the tailplane and elevators painted green.
(Greg VanWyngarden)

commencement of the Allied spring offensive in early April would give the young tyros, equipped with nimble Albatros Scouts, ample opportunity to hone their skills. Amongst Jasta 11's embryonic 'aces' at this time were Karl Allmenröder, Emil Schäfer, Sebastian Festner, Wolff and the Red Baron's younger brother, Lothar. During March and on into the following month – destined to become sanguinarily but aptly dubbed, 'Bloody April' by the Royal Flying Corps – these men cut a veritable swathe through the ranks and machines of their opponents.

No doubt emulating his mentor, Kurt Wolff became an avid collector of souvenirs and 'relics' from the aircraft he had shot down. His room on the airfield was soon 'decorated' with numbers, guns and parts looted from the machines of his vanquished foes.

Wolff's person was also to become highly decorated! He received the coveted Pour le Mérite on 4 May 1917 and, at other times, the Royal Hohenzollern House Order, Knight's Cross with Swords, the Iron Cross 1st and 2nd Classes and the Bavarian Military Merit Order, 4th Class with Swords.

His scoring began as the German army, strung out along the Somme front, started to withdraw to previously prepared positions known as the Hindenburg Line. To the north, along the front opposing Jasta 11's sector, the RFC began their preparations for the Battle of Arras. The British Staff's demands for photographic and other intelligence, forced the lumbering RFC reconnaissance machines into the air over and behind the German front lines. Easy prey, as it turned out, for the fast and manoeuvrable German scouts.

VICTORY NO. 1
6 March 1917 BE2d (No. 5856) 16 Squadron 1230

Winter's beastly weather had severely curtailed much operational flying over recent months. Now, as the first tentative signs of spring began to appear, the Jasta pilots on the Western Front ached to test their new tactics and aircraft against the enemy. There were a number of British aircraft operating over the sector on this day and Jasta 11 would be destined to see some hard fighting before darkness came. A BE two-seater from 16 Squadron had taken off at 1015 am on a photographic mission. Wolff, scouting the sector, engaged this particular BE above Givenchy; his attack quickly wiped out the crew in the air, their machine falling first into an uncontrolled spin which, oddly, changed to a rough glide before falling to the ground at 1130 British time. German ground troops found both the machine's occupants dead, carefully noting the machine number as 5856.

SECOND LIEUTENANT
GEORGE MILNE UNDERWOOD,
16 SQUADRON, ROYAL FLYING CORPS

The son of Dr G R and Mrs Joanna Underwood of 50 Morningside Park, Edinburgh, Scotland and of Kiukiang, China, he was born on 17 March 1897. Educated at Merchiston Castle School (1911-15) and at Edinburgh University, where he studied medicine and was a member of the OTC. Curtailing his studies on 17 January 1916, he joined the Inns of Court Officers Training Corps (Number 6/8977). Following the usual training, he was gazetted Second Lieutenant to the RFC via the General List on 6 July 1916. Soon after being awarded his 'Wings' in early 1917, he was sent to join 16 Squadron in France. Destined to become the first of Kurt Wolff's many victories on 6 March 1917, his grave was subsequently lost and he is commemorated on the Arras Memorial to the Missing, France. He was 19 years old.

SECOND LIEUTENANT
ALBERT EDWARD WATTS,
16 SQUADRON, ROYAL FLYING CORPS

From Thedford, Ontario, Canada, Watts was a customs officer in Port Frances, Roaring River, prior to volunteering (Number 7199) to join the first contingent of the Canadian Expeditionary Force to cross to England and, eventually, to France. An application to transfer to the RFC was approved and he was gazetted to the Special Reserve on 19 October 1916. Following the usual training at Oxford and at Brooklands, he was sent to 16 Squadron as a probationary observer on 20 February 1917. His body was recovered by the Germans in the Givenchy-en-Gohell area, his identity discs collected and returned home via the Red Cross. Apparently, however, his grave was lost in the heavy fighting over the area and hence he is commemorated on the Arras Memorial to the Missing, France.

VICTORY NO. 2
9 March 1917 FE8 (No. 6456) 40 Squadron 1020

40 Squadron were up on an Offensive Patrol when they met and engaged Jasta 11 near Douai with disastrous results. On his return from captivity in Germany in January 1919, Tom Shepard reported that he had been a member of the OP along

with seven other FEs and confirmed that the formation was over Vimy Ridge when they ran into Richthofen's squadron. Shepard witnessed five machines from his patrol driven down before he himself was forced to land, his controls shot away. He crashed heavily alongside the Lens-Carvin road, the FE8 turning completely over. German ground troops led him away to captivity.

Two of the other 40 Squadron machines were shot down by Schäfer and another by Allmenröder, whilst two more – both very badly shot about – somehow managed to limp back across the lines. One of these would make a forced landing at 2 Squadron's base at Hesdigneul, the other wrecked as it came into land. Fortunately both pilots survived. As, indeed, did Wolff's second victim:

SECOND LIEUTENANT
THOMAS ALOYIMS SHEPARD,
ROYAL WARWICKSHIRE REGIMENT AND 40 SQUADRON, ROYAL FLYING CORPS

The son of Major and Mrs J Shepard of 'Linden Lodge', Trewsbury Road, Sydenham, London, SE. He was admitted to the Central Flying School on the same day – 28 December 1916 – as he was gazetted Second Lieutenant to the Royal Warwickshire Regiment. Completing his training in exceptionally quick time, he was posted to 40 Squadron in France on 13 February 1917. Less than a month later he was shot down and taken prisoner. Repatriated and placed on the Unemployed List in January 1919, he returned to the new Shepard family home at 9 Altingworth Street, Kemptown, Brighton.

66.   Bei Meurchin am 9.8.17. abgeschos. engl. Jagdflugs

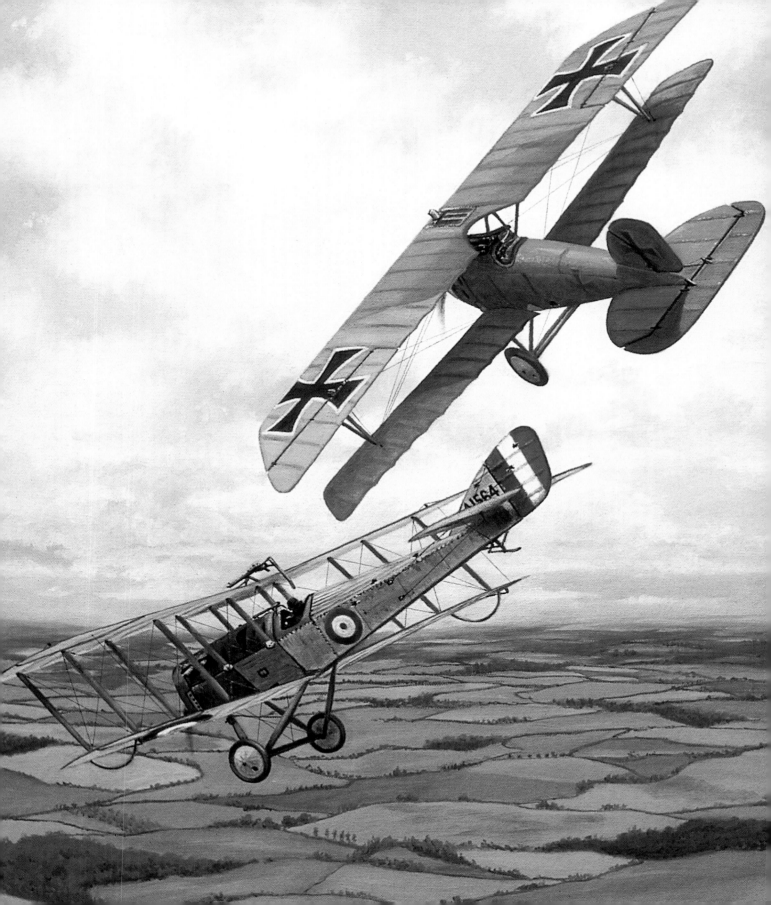

Opposite: Having returned from a period of sick leave, Kurt Wolff began to try out the new Fokker Triplanes that had been given to Jasta 11. He fought an action against 10 Naval Squadron on 15 September 1917 and was shot down and killed by Flight Lieutenant N M MacGregor RNAS.

VICTORY NO.3
17 March 1917   Sopwith 1½ Strutter (No. A1097)   43 Squadron   1145

43 Squadron put up nine of its Strutters on OP at 0910 hours, the formation led by Captain Donald Campbell Rutter (later MC, kia 7 June 1917). One aircraft had to abort due to mechanical problems and staggered off back to base. Among the pilots was the unit's CO, Major A S W Dore, but in a subordinate role for the purpose of this mission. Beyond the front line, the formation was engaged by Jasta 11's fighters and two Sopwiths were brought down, one near Pont du Jour (south-west of Athies), the other – by Allmenröder – between Athies and Oppy. Both machines were timed as falling at around 1045 (British time). In retaliation, Lt F M Kitto and 2/Lt H E Ward claimed one German fighter down out of control. Soon after this Ward was wounded and Kitto broke off the action to land back with his injured observer at 1120. The five remaining Strutters landed more than an hour later at 1225.

SECOND LIEUTENANT
ARTHUR LESLIE CONSTABLE,
43 SQUADRON, ROYAL FLYING CORPS

Born on 21 April 1891, he was the only son of Alfred Kirby Constable and Rosa Constable of 2 Terrace, Arthog, Merioneth. Arthur (left) was brought up mainly in Liverpool where his father was the manager of Copes Bonded Tobacco Factory. After completing his education, he obtained a position as a pupil manager at the British American Tobacco works in Liverpool. Having – at his own expense – gained the Royal Aero Club Certificate (Number 3446) on 25 August 1916, he was accepted directly into the RFC in the same month. The Strutter fell behind the German lines – its pilot, Arthur Leslie Constable is buried in Cabaret-Rouge Cemetery, Souchez, France (Fr924). Age 25.

SECOND LIEUTENANT
CHARLES DUNCAN KNOX,
10/SUFFOLK REGIMENT AND 43 SQUADRON, ROYAL FLYING CORPS

Born in Manchester in 1895, he was the son of Mr and Mrs James Knox of 'Norne Villa', 27 Grosvenor Road, Westcliffe-on-Sea, Essex. He enlisted into the 10/Cameron Highlanders in September 1914 and served

'Buried Near This Spot', the CWGC headstone commemorating 2Lt Charles Duncan Knox.

in the trenches with his regiment, taking part in the Battle of Neuve Chapelle in March 1915. Returned to England for officer training and was subsequently gazetted Second Lieutenant to the Suffolk Regiment on 7 April 1915, before eventually accompanying the first battalion of his new regiment to Egypt in the following October. With an application to join the RFC successful, he returned to England in the summer of 1916. After completing his training as an observer, he accompanied 43 Squadron to France in January 1917. Said to have been responsible for bringing down an enemy machine on 7 March 1917. Buried in Cabaret-Rouge Cemetery, Souchez, France (Fr924). Age 21.

VICTORY NO. 4
30 March 1917 Nieuport XVII (No. A273) 60 Squadron 1145

A 60 Squadron patrol led by the Australian acting flight commander, Lieutenant Alan Binnie, took off at 1055 hours. Their intended patrol line was Arras-Vitry-Douai. A very strong west wind was blowing, a perennial problem for Allied airmen. Later in the morning, British AA gunners reported seeing six Nieuports crossing the lines but only four returned. A fight had begun as Jasta 11 struck at the Nieuports east of Douai. Second Lieutenant F Bower suddenly found himself being chased by no fewer than six Albatros Scouts. He and his machine were badly hit, one bullet passing through his stomach. Astonishingly, he shook his pursuers off and flew back across the lines to land four miles east of Chipilly with a part of his bowel exposed and protruding. Tragically, he died the following day.

Lieutenant Garnett, in another of the Nieuports, was making his first serious combat sortie – so far he had only been involved in training flights behind the British lines. Last seen over Fampoux, his machine fell to the ground near to Fresnoy, north-west of Arras. Despite subsequent reports to the contrary, he was not brought down by Manfred von Richthofen but by the maestro's protegée, Kurt Wolff. It appears

that Garnett remained alive for a short time after his crash and was able to talk to his captors.

LIEUTENANT
WILLIAM PATRICK GARNETT,
ROYAL BERKSHIRE REGIMENT AND 60 SQUADRON, ROYAL FLYING CORPS

Born on 18 October 1894, he was the son of corn merchant William and Jane Russell Garnett of Backwell Hill House, Flax Bourton, West Town, Bristol. Educated at Glenalmond (1908-12) and at Pembroke College, Cambridge, where he was a member of the OTC. Successfully applied for a commission with the Royal Berkshire Regiment, being gazetted to the 3/Battalion on 12 September 1914. Served with the 2nd Battalion of his regiment in France in 1915. Accepted into the RFC on 1 January 1916, he gained his Royal Aero Club 'ticket' (Number 2415) on 31 January 1916. His formal pilot training was interrupted in April 1916 as he crashed his machine, fractured a collar bone and suffered severe shock as a consequence. So it was not until

Right: Lieutenant W M Garnett. *(Via Mac Hawkins)*

Far right: 'Pat' Garnett (22) marries Mary Whiddan Oatley (18) on 15 January 1917. Mary pinned a piece of the material from this dress to the inside of her husband's tunic, 'For Luck'..... *(Via Mac Hawkins)*

Below right: The mangled wreckage of Garnett's Nieuport XVII (A273). *(Via Greg VanWyngarden)*

16 December 1916 that he was finally awarded his 'Wings' and appointed a Flying Officer. On 15 January 1917, 'Pat' married his 18-year-old fiancée, Mary Whiddan Oatley, from nearby Clifton. After a brief honeymoon at Minehead, Pat bade his bride good-bye and left to join 60 Squadron in France. Mary had pinned a piece of material from her wedding dress to the inside of his tunic as a sort of talisman. The 'charm', however, proved no defence against Wolff's machine guns. Pat was lifted from his smashed Nieuport, wounded and burnt, and taken to the nearest aid station, dying shortly afterwards. In a generous gesture, Kurt Wolff's commanding officer, Manfred von Richthofen, collected some of Garnett's personal effects – including the fragment of wedding dress and Pat's gold cufflinks and binoculars – and returned them via the Red Cross to the newly created widow. A letter commending her husband's bravery and offering the Red Baron's sympathy, accompanied the relics. This action led the family to believe, erroneously, that it was von Richthofen himself who had been responsible for their loss and it would be many years before the truth was unearthed by Mary's grandson, Mac Hawkins from Bridgwater, Somerset. Mary had married

again after Pat's death and Mac was a grandson from that union. In the course of his research, Mac Hawkins discovered that a 12-foot crucifix had been erected in Pat's memory at St Andrew's Church in Blackwell, near Bristol. The cross had become overgrown and was somewhat neglected. Mac galvanised the present-day family members into action and they paid

for the necessary restoration. The memorial was rededicated on Easter Saturday 1997, on the 80th anniversary of Pat Garnett's death. A bugler from the Royal Gloucestershire, Berkshire and Wiltshire Regiment – the modern equivalent of his old regiment – played the Last Post. William Patrick Garnett is buried in Villers Station Cemetery, France (Fr81). Age 22.

VICTORY NO. 5
31 March 1917 FE2b No.7691 11 Squadron 0750

Only one RFC machine is recorded as having been lost on this day and that was brought down by Kurt Wolff. A formation from 11 Squadron lifted off from Le Hameau at 0620, on a photo-reconnaissance sortie. Lt L A T Strange in FE2b number 7691, bringing up the rear of the patrol, was blithely unaware of the flock of Albatri closing on his tail. Jasta 11's attack came, literally, out of the blue. Leslie Strange suddenly found himself in the centre of a maelstrom of machine-gun fire. A stream of bullets hit the engine and fuel tank; his observer, Will Clifton, fell mortally wounded to the floor of the front cockpit. Strange, wrestling with the controls as his engine faltered and spluttered, looked for somewhere to put down. He eventually got the FE down near Gavrelle behind German lines. He could not, as was expected of him, set fire to his machine as Clifton was still in the front cockpit and there was not sufficient time to lift him down before German ground troops arrived.

LIEUTENANT
LESLIE ARTHUR TREW STRANGE,
3/4 THE BUFFS (TF) (EAST KENT REGIMENT) AND 11 SQUADRON, ROYAL FLYING CORPS

Born on 11 October 1894, he was the son of A M and Mrs Strange of 'Casila', West Byfleet, Surrey. Educated at Lancing College (1910-11) as was his brother, B L S Strange, who would also serve in the Great War with

the Honourable Artillery Company and later with the British South African Mounted Police. Leslie himself was gazetted to the 3/4 Buffs on 5 October 1915 but soon afterwards sought a transfer to the RFC. He was awarded the Royal Aero Club Certificate (Number 3488) on 6 September 1916, going on through the various processes of pilot training until joining 11 Squadron in France on 9 February 1917. Relatively unscathed in the confrontation with Wolff, he remained a prisoner until his joyful repatriation on the last day of 1918. Left the service and placed on the Unemployed List on 2 March 1919.

SECOND LIEUTENANT
WILLIAM GERARD TALBOT CLIFTON,
3/OXFORDSHIRE AND BUCKINGHAMSHIRE LIGHT INFANTRY AND 11 SQUADRON, ROYAL FLYING CORPS

Born on 27 November 1893, he was the son of William Charles and Agnes M Clifton of 'The Bungalow', Stoke Poges, Buckinghamshire and 21 Elm Park Gardens, London.

Educated at Marlborough (1907-11). Gazetted Second Lieutenant to the Oxs and Bucks Light Infantry on 27 November 1915. Sent out to join the 5th Battalion of his regiment on the Somme on 12 September 1916, just in time to take part in an attack on the dreaded Delville Wood just three days later. His long standing request for a transfer to the flying service at last came through on 12 December 1916 and he returned to England for observer training. He had been flying operationally for only a matter of days when he had the misfortune to run into Wolff. Badly wounded by the opening burst, he was pulled out of the FE2b by his pilot and taken by his German captors to a field hospital at Corbehem where he died within hours. Buried in Corbehem Cemetery, France (Fr1311). Age 23.

VICTORY NO. 6
6 April 1917 RE8 (No. A3421) 59 Squadron 1015

The Battle of Arras would begin in three days time on 9 April. One of the main objectives of the campaign was to be the capture of the strategically important Vimy Ridge. Much of the air fighting was over and around this high ground with its commanding views across vast expanses of the surrounding countryside. The Staff needed to know every move the enemy made if the British and Canadian troops were successfully to dislodge him from this natural citadel. Amongst the many sorties flown on this day was a photo-recce patrol of RE8s from 59 Squadron, led by Captain G B Hodgson (who would be killed one week later). Most two-seater patrols at this time did not merit a direct escort, instead single-seater RFC fighter planes patrolled corridors or zones in the hope of engaging and diverting the marauding German scout planes. Unsurprisingly in the circumstances, two-seater units contrived their own protection as best they could. Which is why, of the six aircraft on this particular photographic patrol, only one was equipped with a camera – the remaining five were

there to look after it!

The formation was engaged by fighters from Jasta 2, 3 and 11 – a veritable circus, indeed. Each Jasta claimed one RE8 each. Wolff's victim was first hit by AA fire which damaged the left-hand planes, then, as if that was not enough, was attacked by three Albatros Scouts. Almost at once, Lieutenant Day in the observer's cockpit, was hit and killed. Then the universal joint at the bottom of the control column was damaged, making it difficult to use. Next the engine itself was hit, forcing the wounded pilot, Clay Pepper, to make a hurried crash-landing in the area of Bois Bernard. Of the two other RE8s which were brought down, one was credited to Karl Menckhoff of Jasta 3, the other to Otto Bernert of Jasta 2.

LIEUTENANT
A CLAYTON PEPPER,
59 SQUADRON, ROYAL FLYING CORPS

The son of Mr and Mrs Arthur J Pepper of 54 Frederick Street, Birmingham, earlier of Warwick Hall, Bromsgrove. Educated at

Bromsgrove School, Pepper was commissioned into the New Armies on 16 February 1915. A transfer to the RFC in the summer of 1916 culminated in qualification as a pilot and an appointment as a Flying Officer on 16 December 1916. He accompanied 59 Squadron to France on 23 February 1917 and was still relatively 'green' operationally when he met Kurt Wolff some six weeks later. The Germans appeared to have treated Pepper shabbily from the moment he was captured. The wound in his arm – apart from a cursory dressing by a medical orderly – was neglected for five days as he lay in solitude and isolation in a prison cell. His suspicion that he was being 'softened up' for interrogation was confirmed when a smooth-talking German officer arrived to apologise profusely for the neglect, promising him better treatment if he would just answer a few questions. Pepper declined and was sent on his way to Karlsruhe. From Karlsruhe he was transferred to Treves where an energetic escape committee was beavering away on a large tunnel. Unfortunately, the tunnel was discovered virtually at the moment it was finished, leaving those concerned with the suspicion that the Germans had known about it for some time and had allowed the prisoners to expend their energy and ingenuity to no purpose – a massive blow to morale. In July 1918, Pepper was sent to the dreaded Holzminden camp with its equally despised commandant, Hauptmann Niemeyer. Pepper was high on the escape list for the famous Holzminden tunnel from which it was hoped 150 to 200 prisoners would escape. The first batch reached the tunnel mouth and set off on their pre-planned routes but then the breakout was beset with problems including a man getting stuck in the narrow passage. By the time it was all sorted out, daylight stopped any further departures. Niemeyer, who had considered his camp escape-proof, was furious and made life extremely unpleasant for the remaining prisoners. Understandably, Clayton Pepper was relieved and delighted to be finally repatriated on 14 December 1918.

LIEUTENANT
WILLIAM LEONARD DAY,
BORDER REGIMENT AND 59 SQUADRON, ROYAL FLYING CORPS

Born at Walpole St Peters, Norfolk, on 28 April 1884, the son of William and Louise Day. When war came in August 1914, William was working in a bank in London and living at Beverley House, Barnes. His mother had re-married and now, as Mrs Forlong, lived at 35 St George's Street, Ipswich. In addition to his blood brother, Cecil, William had acquired a step-brother and two step-sisters. He enlisted (Number 2494) into the 28/County of London Battalion (TF) – The Artist's Rifles – on 7 September 1914. Sent to France with a re-enforcing draft on 22 January 1915, he fought in the trenches until being gazetted Second Lieutenant to the Border Regiment on 14 August 1915. Transferring almost immediately, he joined the 2/Borders at the front on 1 September 1915. On 23 September 1915 he wrote to his mother with various instructions to be carried out in the event of his death, *'You need not worry, Mother, because I mention these things but one never knows....'*. Two days later he was wounded on the first day of the Battle of Loos during the 2/Borders' assault on the German positions at Hulluch. Served again at

Pepper and Day's crashed RE8 (A3421). *(Via Greg VanWyngarden)*

the front until February 1917 when his application for transfer to the RFC was approved. Actually, at almost 33 years of age, he was too old to be considered for the flying service. However, as he informed his mother in another letter, *'I told a fib about my age!'*. He trained at Reading and at Weybridge – *'There are wonderful devices here for teaching one to spot the flash of hostile batteries when we fly over the Hun land'*. Great emphasis was placed on the proficient sending and receiving of Morse; *'we have to know Morse because we have to signal by* *wireless from the aeroplane to the battery. My head is buzzing......'* The financial incentive was a factor and an added incentive to pass the course, *'I am getting three shillings a day more now and when I qualify I get 25 shillings a day, that is over £450 a year!'*. Day did, of course, qualify for his 'Wing' at the end of March 1917, joining 59 Squadron as a probationary soon afterwards. His flying career was, however, short-lived. His remains were never traced and he is commemorated on the Arras Memorial to the Missing, France. Age 32.

VICTORY NO. 7
7 April 1917 Nieuport (XVII No. A6766) 60 Squadron 1745

So far, all six of Wolff's victories had fallen behind German lines but today's victim would fall smack bang onto the front lines. 60 Squadron was ordered into the air on a 'Special Mission' at 1640. It was special because, most unusually, one of the Nieuports carried a camera. The Intelligence people had charged the Squadron with obtaining photographs – preferably at low level – of a particularly pivotal German entrenchment. This, obviously, was the reason the fight took place directly above the front lines rather than, more usually, inside German territory. Jasta 11 claimed three victories, one each to Manfred von Richthofen, Schäfer and Wolff. 60 Squadron, however, only lost two machines, with another – Schäfer's claim – shot up and seen heading down into British lines. Wolff's Nieuport came down northeast of Mercatel.

(60 Squadron *did* lose a third Nieuport on this day – credited to Jasta 4 – but it was later in the evening.)

Constantin Krefft, Wolff and Karl Allenröder of Jasta 11 – the latter plays with Wolff's 'lucky' stocking cap. *(Via Greg VanWyngarden)*

SECOND LIEUTENANT
CHARLES SIDNEY HALL,
60 SQUADRON, ROYAL FLYING CORPS

Born on 9 April 1898, he was the son of mining engineer Joseph John Hall and Emily Eleanor 'Nellie' Hall of 'Westfield', Ashington, Northumberland. He was educated at the North Eastern County School, Barnard Castle and at Armstrong College, University of Durham, where he had begun training as a mining engineer. Hall was a member of the OTC both at school and at the university. An outstanding swimmer, he held an honorary Instructor's Certificate and the medallion of the Royal Life Saving Society. Charles's eldest brother, Captain L W Hall, 1/Border Regiment and RFC, had served in an operational squadron at the front for a year before becoming a flying instructor. His other brother had been in France for two years with the Royal Engineers (50th Division) before being taken prisoner by the Germans on 27 May 1918. Charles was gazetted Second Lieutenant directly into the Royal Flying Corps on 28 June 1916, just a few weeks after his eighteenth birthday. A pilot of some promise, he was sent to the crack 60 Squadron. The Squadron history mentions the good work Hall was doing during March and April, 'adding to the Squadron's laurels'. Declared missing just two days before his nineteenth birthday, his parents received a letter from his Squadron commander, *'He was leading a fighting patrol of six machines on the evening of the 7th. They most gallantly attacked a formation of hostile aeroplanes of much superior number, and two machines were brought down. They got at least one Hun. Of the four who returned, three were very badly shot about. Both our machines were observed to land behind the lines quite close to the German line. One hopes they are unhurt. We all liked your son immensely and miss him sorely'*. In fact, Charles's body was found by an officer of the Royal Field Artillery as the British advance forced back the German line two days later on the first day of the Battle of Arras. He is buried in Tilloy Cemetery, France (Fr581). Age 18.

Charles Sidney Hall.

VICTORY NO. 8
8 April 1917 DH4 (No.A2141) 55 Squadron 1430

The DH4 bombers of 55 Squadron had only recently arrived in France, being based at Fienvillers, south-west of Doullens. They had begun bombing raids for the first time on 3 April and would, today, suffer their first loss. A raid was mounted upon a château at Hardenpont, near Mons, which was the HQ of Crown Prince Rupprecht's Army Group. On their return journey, they were intercepted by Jasta 11 north of Cambrai at 1425 German time. Two were shot down, one by Schäfer, the other by Wolff, whilst a third, hit by AA fire, came down near Amigny. Wolff's DH4 came down near Blécourt, the machine's serial number being identified in the action report.

LIEUTENANT
BERNARD EVANS,
17/MIDDLESEX REGIMENT AND
55 SQUADRON, ROYAL FLYING CORPS

Born on 19 December 1887, he was the son of Sir Edwin and Lady Evans of 9 Ashley

Gardens, Victoria, London. Educated at Marlborough (1901-06) and at Trinity College, Cambridge, where he graduated BA and LLB in 1909. Admitted a solicitor in October 1912, practising at Stangate House, 235 Westminster Bridge Road, London SE. Married Bessie Murray and set up home at 86 Emmanuel Road, Streatham Hill, London. Enlisted in the Royal Naval Division in 1914 from where he was gazetted Second Lieutenant to 17/Middlesex Regiment (Footballers Battalion) in early 1915. Promoted to Lieutenant on 27 July 1915. Sought transfer to the RFC in the summer of 1916 and after successfully completing his pilot training was appointed a Flying Officer on 15 December 1916. Bernard Evans joined 55 Squadron – the first to receive the DH4 – and accompanied that unit to France on 6 March 1917. Buried in Ontario Cemetery, Sains-les-Marquion, France (Fr481). Age 29.

SECOND LIEUTENANT
BASIL WALWYN WHITE,
KING'S LIVERPOOL REGIMENT AND
55 SQUADRON, ROYAL FLYING CORPS

The only son of railway engineer Joseph Walwyn White and Nancy White of 'Strathdene', Woolton, Liverpool. Born in 1897, he was educated at Mr Glover's School, Rhos-on-Sea, at Sedbergh and at the Royal Military College, Sandhurst, from where he was commissioned to 1/King's Liverpool Regiment on 27 October 1916. Immediately and successfully sought transfer to the RFC, being posted to observer training. Awarded his 'Wing', he crossed to France with 55 Squadron in March 1917. Buried in Ontario Cemetery, Sains-les-Marquion, France (Fr481). Age 19.

VICTORY NO.9
11 April 1917   Bristol F2a(No.A3338)   48 Squadron   0910

Another newly arrived aeroplane in France at around this time was the BF2a two-seat fighter. 48 Squadron had brought out this new type to France on 8 March. On 5 April it was ready for action but on its very first sortie ran into Jasta 11 and lost four machines. Now, six days later, they met Jasta 11 again, this time losing yet another three – one each being shared between Lothar von Richthofen, Schäfer and Wolff. Wolff's 'Brisfit' came down near Mouville Farm, its pilot a veteran air fighter who had earlier made a name for himself on single-seaters. Upon his return from captivity, Captain Tidmarsh related how his patrol of three machines was attacked by seven German scouts, one of which was brought down. The first attack beaten off, the German machines regrouped. During the second attack, Tidmarsh's observer was wounded and his engine, also hit by machine-gun fire, cut out. Tidmarsh had no choice but to glide the BF2a down into enemy territory. The captured Bristol, intact as it was, was no doubt of great interest to the Germans.

These early encounters with the Bristol Fighters gave the Germans a false sense of security, whilst the British seriously wondered if this new machine was yet another dead loss – literally! However, 48 Squadron was, perhaps understandably, using the aeroplane far too defensively – their tactics were simply wrong. Once the crews began to realise the true potential of their craft and to fly and fight as a team, the Bristol Fighter became a more than worthy opponent for the Jasta pilots of the Imperial German Air Service throughout the remainder of the war. It was also an aircraft which would go on to serve the Royal Air Force for many years after 1918.

CAPTAIN
David Mary Tidmarsh,
MC, MID, 4/ROYAL IRISH REGIMENT AND 48 SQUADRON, ROYAL FLYING CORPS

The son of Mr and Mrs David Tidmarsh of Lota, Limerick, Ireland. Educated in Ireland and at Stonyhurst (1905-1909). David's brother, John – also educated at Stonyhurst – a Regular Army officer of the West Riding Regiment, attached Royal Air Force, was killed in an aerial collision whilst instructing a pupil in Doncaster on 3 September 1918 (his name is incorrectly spelt, 'Tidmarch', in CWGC records). David was gazetted Second Lieutenant to the 4/Royal Irish Regiment on 23 April 1915. Transferring to the RFC in August 1915, he was, shortly afterwards on 7 October 1915, awarded the Royal Aero Club Certificate (Number 1833). Having completed his further formal training, he was awarded his 'Wings' and posted to 24 Squadron in England before accompanying that unit to France in February 1916. On 2 April 1916, Tidmarsh, with Lieutenant S J Sibley, shared the first victory for the newly arrived Squadron. This was to be the first of seven victories for Tidmarsh, earning him the military aviation distinction, 'ace'. The Official History records the impact of the debutant Squadron, equipped as it was

with the new DH2 which, it was hoped, would at last counter the 'Fokker Scourge', *'On 25 April two officers of the Squadron who were escorting the Fourth Army reconnaissance beat off many attacks and showed that the DH2 could manoeuvre with great success against the Fokker. Five days later, Second Lieutenant Tidmarsh of the same squadron (No.24) left some FE2b's which he was escorting and attacked a Fokker which dived so steeply to avoid him that it crashed on the roof of a building in Bapaume and fell to pieces before the De Havilland pilot had got close enough to fire a shot'* (Leutnant Otto Schmedes of FA32 was his unfortunate victim). Tidmarsh was awarded the Military Cross for this and other examples

of gallantry, *London Gazette* 31 May 1916: '*For conspicuous gallantry and skill when attacking hostile aircraft on several occasions, notably on one occasion when he dived on an enemy machine and drove it down wrecked to the ground*'. Tidmarsh returned to England in October 1916, taking up an instructing post at the School of Air Gunnery. Hopefully refreshed, he returned to France in March 1917, bringing out the new two-seater Bristol Fighter with 48 Squadron. In rapid succession, he got two OOCs and two destroyed between 8 and 11 April but fell to Kurt Wolff later on what had been, until then, his most productive day. Repatriated in December 1918, he finally left the service on 28 October 1919.

SECOND LIEUTENANT
CATOR BARCLAY HOLLAND,
48 SQUADRON, ROYAL FLYING CORPS

Born in 1896, he was the son of Mr and Mrs C B Holland of 7 Holmefield Road, Wimbledon. He was educated at Malvern College (1910-13). Accepted into the RFC in July 1916, he gained his Royal Aero Club Certificate (Number 3626) on 30 August 1916. Despite having his 'ticket', he was sent to observer's school on 28 November 1916 and subsequently posted to 48 Squadron on 18 December. Accompanied the Bristol Fighter-equipped Squadron to France in March 1917. Holland was Tidmarsh's observer in all four of his victories with 48 Squadron. Wounded in the fight with Wolff, he was taken by his captors to the nearest hospital for treatment. Repatriated on 30 December 1918, he left the service on 4 March 1919. Qualified as a chartered accountant with Prideaux, Frere, Brown and Company of 12 Old Square, Lincoln's Inn, London WC 2 in the post-war years. Served with the RAFVR in the Second World War. Died in October 1967 at the age of seventy-one.

VICTORY NO. 10
13 April 1917 RE8 (No. A3225) 59 Squadron 0856

The RE8s of 59 Squadron were still endeavouring to combine their recce and photography duties with the provision of their own supposedly protective cover. But, and it was a big but, whether flying reconnaissance or flying 'shot-gun', an RE8 was still only an RE8, with all of its fundamental limitations as a fighting machine. The 13th of April was to be an exceptionally unlucky day for the Squadron, losing, as they did, a whole formation of six machines to Jasta 11 in a matter of minutes. A 59 Squadron RE8 was the first of four kills in one day for Kurt Wolff.

A successor to the docile BE2 series, the RE8 was a stable enough aeroplane albeit one that tended to catch fire a little too easily, so much so that it soon became known as the 'flying coffin'. Still, despite all of this, it continued to be operated by the RFC and subsequently by the RAF, to the war's end.

On this day 59 Squadron was assigned a photo job to Etaing, 15 kilometres east of Arras – with one aeroplane (A3203) to carry the camera. The formation took off at 0810 and was led by Captain G B Hodgson who had been involved in a fight with Wolff only a week before. They had been promised an additional escort of FE2s of 57 Squadron and Spads of 19 Squadron, but in the Great War, in the absence of air-to-air radio communication between aircraft, keeping and making a rendezvous was a hit and miss affair. On this occasion, it was a 'miss'.

Jasta 11 – together with a Jasta 4 pilot who somehow inveigled himself into the action – dropped onto the luckless REs and in a series of running combats brought the six REs down, all but one falling over areas north of their target, Etaing. Wolff's RE8 fell north of Vitry-en-Artois.

LIEUTENANT
ARTHUR HORACE TANFIELD,
**3/ROYAL WARWICKSHIRE REGIMENT AND
59 SQUADRON, ROYAL FLYING CORPS**

Born on 18 May 1897, he was the son of solicitor Arthur George Tanfield and Mrs Tanfield of 167 Hampstead Road, Handsworth, Birmingham (later 18 York Road, Edgbaston). He was educated at the local prep school before going on to King Edward's School, Birmingham (1908-15). Offering his services as soon as he left school, he was gazetted Second Lieutenant to the 3rd Battalion of the Royal Warwickshire Regiment on 25 September 1915. His application to join the RFC was approved in the summer of 1916. After successfully completing his pilot training, he was appointed a Flying Officer on 8 January 1917 and accompanied 59 Squadron to France in the following month. His remains were never recovered and hence he is commemorated on the Arras Memorial, France. Age 19.

LIEUTENANT
ANDREW ORMEROD,
**ROYAL FIELD ARTILLERY AND
59 SQUADRON, ROYAL FLYING CORPS**

The son of John and Jane Omerod of 328 Colne Road, Burnley, he was born in 1890. A pre-war volunteer in the Royal Horse Artillery (TF), Ormerod (above) was mobilised in August 1914 and sent to Egypt with his unit in the following month. He had risen to the rank of Sergeant Major and was serving in Gallipoli when, on 7 November 1915, he was gazetted Second Lieutenant to the East Lancashire Brigade, Royal Field Artillery. Commemorated on the Arras Memorial, France. Age 27.

VICTORY NO. 11
13 April 1917 FE2b (No. A827) 11 Squadron 1235

This, Wolff's second claim of the day, was one which went down into the British lines and hence was not immediately identified by the Germans. Von Richthofen led Jasta 11 against the formation of 'Fees', which had taken off from their base at Izel-le-Hameau at 1125, bringing one down just below the Scarpe river, south-east of Arras. Wolff then hit a second 'pusher' which went down some 1,000 yards south and west of Bailleul-Sir-Berthoult. Both were downed in the front lines, with Richthofen's crashed

victim seen to be shelled and destroyed. The other FE – Wolff's victory – was noted as 'forced to land' inside Allied territory – map ref 'H28.a'. In fact, the FE was a virtual 'write-off'. The propeller, wing centre section, nose of nacelle, undercarriage and top planes were all badly damaged and the lower wings smashed, but at least the crew were unhurt. What was left of the machine was sent to No.2 AD for 'repair'. Jasta 11 were credited with two victories, one to the master and one to the pupil.

LIEUTENANT
CHARLES ERIC ROBERTSON,
11 SQUADRON, ROYAL FLYING CORPS

The son of Norman and Lilla M Robertson of Walkerton, Ontario, Canada, and husband of Mary Robertson. Eric – he preferred that name – Robertson, a Lieutenant in the Canadian Militia and an instructor at the Curtiss Flying School, Toronto, was living in Milton, Halton, Ontario, when he was accepted for the Royal Flying Corps on 7 December 1915. After crossing the Atlantic, he confirmed his flying prowess by gaining the Royal Aero Club Certificate (Number 3946) on 3 December 1916. At about this time, he met and married Mary, a nursing sister who was working for the American Red Cross at St Katherine's Lodge Hospital. Joined 11 Squadron in France on 28 March 1917. Surviving – virtually unscathed – his confrontation with Kurt Wolff, he was to be killed in action three months later on 12 July 1917 – his BF2b shot down by anti-aircraft fire. At the time he was an Acting Captain and in temporary command of 11 Squadron. Eric's twenty-three-year-old observer on 12 July, Sergeant John Frazier Carr, (Number 65251), from Sunderland, was also killed and they lie together in Vis-en-Artois British Cemetery (Fr421). Eric Robertson was twenty-eight years old.

SECOND LIEUTENANT
HORACE DENOON DUNCAN,
**6/ KING'S ROYAL RIFLE CORPS AND
11 SQUADRON, ROYAL FLYING CORPS**

Born on 3 November 1894, he was the son of Scots-born solicitor, D Duncan and Mrs Duncan of 7 Egerton Road, Kimberley, South Africa. An articled clerk to a firm of chartered accountants, he enlisted in the 1st Kimberley Regiment in 1914 and served for two years in German South West Africa. Embarked at Capetown on 22 April 1916 aboard the ss *Saxon* bound for England – at his own expense! Accepted for officer training, he was gazetted Second Lieutenant into the 6/King's Royal Rifle Corps, then based at Sheerness, on 26 September 1916. A transfer to the RFC followed on 27 February 1917. After completing his observer training, he was posted as a probationary to 11 Squadron in France early in the following April. He survived Kurt Wolff's attack on 13 April only to be severely wounded on 28 June 1917 – fractured skull, compound fractured bones of the face. After a period hospitalised in France, he was transferred to Hampstead Hospital in London and then sent home to South Africa on medical grounds in November 1917.

VICTORY NO. 12
13 April 1917 Nieuport XXIII (No. A6768) 29 Squadron 1630

Victory number three for Wolff this day came during a third sortie in the late afternoon and was another which went down into the British lines. Six aircraft from 29 Squadron had taken off at 1545 on a defensive patrol along the front. Either intentionally or accidentally the six split up. Second Lieutenants Scott-Foxwell and Sadler found themselves flying together at 8,000 feet over Monchy-le-Prieux. They spotted three German aircraft flying west and the pair turned to attack, opening fire

from about 100 yards. Scott-Foxwell fired 200 rounds but was then hit himself, with most of his controls shot away. The Nieuport, uncontrollable, went down to the ground near Monchy, an enemy fighter following him down. No sooner had Scott-Foxwell crunched in than the German proceeded to attempt to shoot him up on the ground, fortunately without success. In the meantime, Scott-Foxwell's erstwhile companion, Ferrebee Sadler – who later identified a red biplane and two green-coloured biplanes amongst his attackers — was frustrated, with his guns jamming after only ten rounds. Sadler deciding that discretion was definitely the better part of valour, scooted for home. Ferrebee Sadler, 9/Durham Light Infantry and 29 Squadron, RFC, from Gateshead, would fall to Leutnant Schäfer of Jasta 11 eight days later on 21 April 1917.

Many years later, Scott-Foxwell would reminisce about this action, describing how, as he and Sadler chased three German machines, he flew around a cloud and came face to face with half a dozen Albatros Scouts who proceeded to shoot him up. Scott-Foxwell carefully noted his crash time as 1620 and although he himself was OK, his machine was wrecked. Shortly after this incident, 29 Squadron's Medical Officer felt that Scott-Foxwell had been badly shaken up by his experiences and sent him back to England for a prolonged rest.

SECOND LIEUTENANT
BASIL SCOTT-FOXWELL,
ROYAL NORTH DEVON HUSSARS YEOMANRY AND 29 SQUADRON, ROYAL FLYING CORPS

Born on 8 November 1895, he was the son of Mr and Mrs Scott-Foxwell of 'Broadlands Cottage', Shepperton, Middlesex. Initially enlisting into the Royal Naval Division in March 1915, he was subsequently gazetted Second Lieutenant to the Royal Devon Hussars Yeomanry on 23 January 1916. He joined his regiment at Holt in Norfolk but soon was laid low with a bad dose of influenza and bronchitis, in consequence of which, he was admitted into the Military Hospital at Hounslow. Discharged fit on 5 June 1916, his application to join the RFC was granted three months later. Following the usual period of training, he was awarded his 'Wings' in January 1917, joining 29 Squadron in France within weeks. Shot down out of control by Wolff, he crashed just behind the British front lines. Apart from being badly shaken, Basil suffered no serious injury. Though he was sent home for 'a spot of recuperative leave', immediately upon his return his CO launched him into a heavy schedule of flying duties. Basil, however, had lost his appetite for flying and it showed — his lack of confidence affected his competence. Hospitalised in France, he was diagnosed as suffering from nervous debility. Inevitably, perhaps, he was formally struck off RFC strength and transferred back to the Royal Devon Hussars. He tried, on a number of occasions, to return to the RFC but after further spells in hospital, including the 4th London General Hospital, Denmark Street, London, he was finally and formally refused. Just as surely a casualty of the Great War as if he had suffered actual physical harm.

VICTORY NO. 13
13 April 1917 Martinsyde G102 (No.A1564) 27 Squadron 1852

Apparently not content with three victories in one day – more than the great majority of fighter pilots would achieve in a whole career – Wolff was again flying in the fading evening light. With ruthless efficiency he attacked and sent down a straggling Martinsyde Elephant, a component of a bomb raid upon Henin-Lietard. The Squadron had taken off at 1805, rendezvoused with other elements from 19, 25 and 66 Squadrons and headed for their target. Having dropped their bombs they were on the homeward leg when Jasta 11 fell upon them. For most of their mission they had enjoyed a covering escort but, because of a shortage of fuel, the Nieuports had left them. There is a suggestion that Richthofen's scouts were seen in the distance but were mistaken for the departing Nieuport escorts!

There was some confusion over the claim which was initially and erroneously noted as 'FE A1564' – clearly though, it was G102 which fell near Rouvray less than an hour after take-off.

Jasta 11 had claimed twelve British aeroplanes shot down on this day, with Wolff accounting for four. Both totals were records for the Staffel – collective and individual. Manfred von Richthofen would, of course, equal Wolff's 'four in a day' before the month was out.

SECOND LIEUTENANT
MICHAEL TOPHAM,
27 SQUADRON, ROYAL FLYING CORPS

The eldest son of Francis David Topham and Mrs Pauline Topham (née Whitley) of 42 Hadlow Road, Tonbridge, Kent. Born in India in 1896 – his father was a manager with the Madras and Southern Mahratta Railway – he was educated at Yardley Court and at Tonbridge School (day boy, 1908-14) where he was a member of the OTC and represented the school in the shooting VIII.

In his last term he gained an open scholarship for science at Downing College, Cambridge but instead of taking up his place, he enlisted in the 19/Royal Fusiliers (2nd Public Schools Battalion) in September 1914. Two of Michael's three brothers also served in the Great War – the fourth brother being too young. Michael was one of the 4,000 original recruits who 'fell in' in Hyde Park one late summer Saturday afternoon before being sent off to Epsom for training. Promoted to Sergeant, he constantly refused a commission before eventually accompanying his battalion to France in November 1915. Already an accomplished marksman, he soon gained a reputation as a sniper, on one occasion famously accounting for a very well known and very troublesome German sniper, nicknamed Ginger Fritz. When, on

another occasion, the Germans turned a searchlight on the Fusiliers' trenches, Michael 'turned it off' with one shot. Badly short of subalterns in 1916, the War Office decided to return the whole of the 19/Royal Fusiliers back to England to be drafted into various officer cadet battalions. An illness forced him to spend some weeks in hospital which delayed his passing out but he was eventually gazetted Second Lieutenant to the General List, destined for the RFC, on 5 August 1916. After training at Oxford and elsewhere, he was awarded his 'Wings' and appointed a Flying Officer on 15 February 1917. Sent to the front in March 1917, he was mainly employed on bombing raids and defensive patrols. On the day he was killed, his formation had, due to adverse weather conditions, become somewhat separated. The solitary and isolated Topham would prove an easy target for the deadly skills of Kurt Wolff. In July 1917, his family received a report from the Red Cross stating that he was shot down and instantly killed on 13 April. The report also clearly identified the number of his machine. Although presumably given a military funeral by the Germans, his grave was subsequently lost and he is commemorated on the Arras Memorial to the Missing, France. Age 21.

V I C T O R Y   N O .   1 4
14 April 1917   Nieuport XVII (No.B1511)   60 Squadron   0920

No doubt keen to emulate the previous day's outstanding achievements, Jasta 11 were up early on the 14th. They certainly got off to a good start. A five-machine patrol (A Flight) of 60 Squadron, led by Captain Alan Binnie MC, had taken off at 0830. They spotted a German two-seater forty-five minutes later and dived to attack. Only one of the A Flight pilots returned to base and we are dependent upon him for some of the detail of the debacle that followed. Jasta 11, led by von Richthofen, saw the Nieuports attacking their two-seater colleague and flew to his aid. Binnie, an Australian, was no novice but he was obviously completely surprised by the unexpected arrival of the Albatros Scouts. Binnie himself was shot down by Lothar von Richthofen, the other three falling to brother Manfred, to Sebastian Festner and to Wolff.

All four came down in the Drocourt-Gavrelle area. Second Lieutenant J H Cock was killed outright, Second Lieutenant L C Chapman, mortally wounded whilst Binnie (who had to have his left arm amputated) and Lieutenant W O Russell were taken prisoner. The sole survivor, Second Lieutenant G C Young, saw the beginning of the encounter but as his gun had jammed, he spun out of the fight. Having cleared his gun some minutes later, he flew around looking for the others. The sky was ominously empty.

The day produced eight victories for Jasta 11, not quite up to the previous day's record but still chillingly effective.

SECOND LIEUTENANT
JOHN HERBERT COCK,
NEW ZEALAND EXPEDITIONARY FORCE AND 60 SQUADRON, ROYAL FLYING CORPS

Wolff, like his mentor Manfred von Richthofen, kept trophies of his triumphs in his room. The Number '7691' (top) is from his 5th victory (an FE2b from 11 Squadron). The lamp shade is A-3338 taken from the 48 Squadron BF2a shot down on 11 April 1917. *(Via Greg VanWyngarden)*

Born on 19 March 1893, he was the son of Joseph Henry and Elizabeth Mary Cock of Nelson, New Zealand. He was educated at Nelson College (1906-10) where he joined the Cadet Force, attaining the rank of Sergeant. Worked as a clerk in his father's business, J H Cock and Company Limited, Merchants, Wanganui. Joined the NZ Territorial Force in 1912 and was commissioned in the same year. When war was declared, he was so anxious to accompany his friends to the big adventure, that despite holding a commission in the TF, he asked to be allowed to join the 3/ Wellington Infantry as a private soldier on 13 August 1914. Sailed with the original NZ contingent to Alexandria on 15 October 1914, serving in Egypt until the assault on the Gallipoli peninsular. Landed on Anzac Beach on 25 April 1915, survived the slaughter on the first day but was wounded four days later – *'gun shot wound left scapula'.* Evacuated with many other wounded to Kaser-el-Aini military hospital, Cairo. From Egypt he was evacuated home to New Zealand on 9 June 1915. His health and fitness restored, he sailed for France on 7 April 1916 and was again wounded in the trenches on 31 May 1916. After treatment in France, he was invalided to the 2nd London General Hospital, Brockenhurst for recuperation. Again restored to health, an application for transfer to the RFC was approved and he reported for training shortly after being gazetted Second Lieutenant on 24 September 1916. Qualified for his Royal Aero Club 'ticket' (Number 4150) on 18 January 1917. His personal courage already proved beyond question, he also showed sufficient aptitude as a pilot to be recommended for the crack 60 Squadron. Buried at Beaumont Cemetery, France (Fr1310). Age 23.

VICTORY NO. 15
14 April 1917   SPAD VII (No.A6746)   19 Squadron   1829

An evening line patrol by 19 Squadron over the area Ballieul-Sir-Berthoult, Vitry, Sains and Bullecourt was engaged in the failing light by Jasta 11. Two Spads were claimed, one by Wolff, the other by Lothar von Richthofen. Wolff, after a hard fight, brought his opponent down east of Ballieul and although his victim fell directly into the battle lines, its destruction was soon confirmed and added to his growing score.

Lothar's opponent – Lieutenant J W Baker – was hit and wounded in the air but nevertheless managed to dive over the lines and get home. Still the claim was upheld and took Lothar von Richthofen's total to seven.

LIEUTENANT
EDWARD WALTER CAPPER,
MONTGOMERYSHIRE YEOMANRY AND 19 SQUADRON, ROYAL FLYING CORPS

Above: St Paul's Parish Church, Maitland, NSW, Australia. Inscribed memorial stones to Edward Capper and to his father flank the entrance.

Right: Von Richthofen, Krefft, Wolff and Otto Brauneck discuss tactics on the château steps in April 1917.

One of the five sons of Mr Harry Hyne Capper and Mrs F P Capper of West Maitland, New South Wales, Australia. The family business – they were crockery retailers – was long established in the area, some forty miles or so outside Sydney. Like his four brothers, Edward was educated at Barker College, Hornsley, NSW (1899-1907). All five Capper boys joined various branches of the armed forces. Edward, an accomplished horseman, journeyed to England to receive a commission in the Montgomeryshire Yeomanry on 5 June 1915. Transfer to the RFC followed in the following year with an appointment to Flying Officer being gazetted in July 1916. Only Harry, of all the Capper brothers, survived the war and it was that lone survivor who, in 1938, formally presented Edward Capper's treasured 18 carat

gold watch to his old school to be held in his memory in perpetuity. The parish church of Maitland – St Paul's – has at each side of its entrance, inscribed memorial stones dedicated to the memory of Harry Hyne Capper Senior (30 years a churchwarden) and to his son, Edward Walter Capper, *'Flight Lieutenant RFC, Killed in Action, Péronne, France, 14 April 1917, aged 27 years'*. Edward's body was never recovered and he is also commemorated on the Arras Memorial to the Missing, France.

VICTORY NO. 16
16 April 1917 Nieuport XVII (No.B1509) 60 Squadron 1030

Sixty Squadron's Nieuport Scouts were again mauled badly by Jasta 11 on this April morning. The British patrol had taken off at 0805 to head for Vitry. The 'clock' on the Allied side of the Western Front had changed again on 15 April, so that German time was an hour later. Jasta 11 were alerted to the intruders by a telephone call and took off to intercept. As soon as contact was

established, a running fight began between Biache and Roeux.

Three Nieuports were shot out of the sky, a fourth – with its pilot mortally wounded – managed to land behind German lines, only for its occupant, Australian Trevor Langwill, to die in captivity the following day. As pointed out in our preceding book (*Under the Guns of the German Aces*), we found difficulty in establishing just who shot down who in this particular action. Such evidence as there was, finally decided us that Second Lieutenant D N Robertson had fallen to Lothar von Richthofen in the front-line area. Festner's claim came down inside German lines, so we concluded that this had to be Second Lieutenant R E Kimbell, who fell near Roeux. Given all of this, logic dictates that Lieutenant John Elliott was Wolff's victim.

The fact that the Germans made only three claims when four RFC machines were lost, might suggest that Langwill had become somehow detached from the dogfight before he landed – his departure largely unnoticed by both sides. His mortal wounds, however, undoubtedly testified to the fact that he had been shot up in combat. From Newcastle, New South Wales,

Langwill was buried by his German captors with due ceremony at Douai.

LIEUTENANT
JOHN MACCREARY ELLIOT,
LORD STRATHCONA'S HORSE AND 60 SQUADRON, ROYAL FLYING CORPS

Born in 1897, he was the son of Dawson Kerr Elliot and Mary Alice Elliot of Winnipeg, Canada. Gazetted Lieutenant to Lord Strathcona's Horse on 15 February 1916. Successfully sought transfer to the RFC and gained his Royal Aero Club 'ticket' (Number 3888) on 27 November 1916. His remains were never found and hence he is commemorated on the Arras Memorial to the Missing, France. Age 19.

VICTORY NO. 17
21 April 1917 BE2e (No.2766) 16 Squadron 1730

This 16 Squadron BE2e took off on a recce sortie at 1510 hours, specifically tasked with locating concentrations of barbed wire protecting the German front-line trenches and strong-points ahead of the British and Canadian advances. Five minutes later, a second BE (2915) of the same Squadron took off, this one crewed by Lieutenant J P C Mitchell and Lieutenant G R Rogers. Over the front, at 1620, German fighters closed in on the observation machines. 2766 was attacked north-east of Vitry, the pilot, Eric Routh, wounded, his machine damaged. Despite his own discomfiture and the damage inflicted upon the BE2e, Routh managed a forced landing at map ref: T.26.a.2.1. Whilst they were still airborne, Mackenzie in the observer's seat, had seen the other BE also attacked and catch fire in the air. As the flaming wreckage dropped, one of the occupants fell, or jumped, out at about 300 feet. Wolff claimed his victim as down north of Willerval, in the front-line area. This BE was seen to land, so presumably cannot be confused with the 'flamer'.

Still the events of this day are not entirely clear cut. The RFC losses started with a 16 Squadron BE damaged by AA fire in the early afternoon. Later on, Jasta 11 accounted for two further 16 Squadron BEs (as described above). As Jasta 11 was despatching the BEs, a 29 Squadron patrol engaged them east of Fresnes with disastrous results – three Nieuports being shot down and their pilots killed. Here again we have that unlikely scenario – five RFC losses (not including the one lost to AA fire) but only four claims by Jasta 11. German fighter pilots, like their British counterparts, were certainly not slow in coming forward with claims for confirmations of combat victories. The tendency amongst aero historians has been to credit one each of the three Nieuports to Wolff, Lothar and Schäfer. Only one of the BEs has received accreditation – and that to Wolff.

As with events on 16 April, the reason for the discrepancy in overall numbers may be found in the fact that the Nieuport flown by Second Lieutenant Alan Bertram Morgan came down some way from the combat area. He is reported as having died the next day. Quite possibly, his body was actually discovered by the Germans on the following day and that date has since become the recorded and accepted one – not an uncommon occurrence.

CAPTAIN
ERIC JOHN DAUBEN ROUTH,
MID, KING'S ROYAL RIFLE CORPS AND 16 SQUADRON, ROYAL FLYING CORPS

The son of Vice-Admiral Henry Peter Routh, MVO, and Ethel Routh of Farringdon, Alton, Hampshire, he was born on 21 January 1895. Educated at Malvern (1909-12) where he was an enthusiastic member of the OTC. Gazetted to 5/KRRC on 29 September 1914. Sent to join a battalion of his regiment at the front, he boarded the ss *St Andrew* on 27 September 1915 but was returned home on the following day suffering from burns to the right forearm and face caused by the explosion of a bomb – presumably a training accident. Admitted to Lady Cooper's Hospital, Hursley Park, Winchester, he would have to wait until the following November before he was pronounced fit. During his sojourn in hospital, Routh applied to transfer to the RFC. On 2 April 1916, he was awarded his Royal Aero Club Certificate (Number 2697) and awarded his 'Wings' and appointed a Flying Officer on 8 July 1916. Wounded in the fight with Wolff, he was returned to England for medical treatment. Promoted to the rank of Major in the RAF by the war's end, he decided to make the service his career. Amongst his many postings in the years between the wars, was a particularly challenging one to Kurdistan. A Wing Commander in the Second World War, he was Mentioned in Despatches for valuable services before retiring finally from the RAF on 10 October 1945.

SECOND LIEUTENANT
ALEXANDER GEORGE RIDDELL MACKENZIE,
ROYAL FIELD ARTILLERY AND 16 SQUADRON, ROYAL FLYING CORPS

Born on 10 September 1888, his father was a hotelier in Nethy Bridge, Inverness-shire, Scotland. Qualifying as a civil engineer, he held a position with a firm in Inverness from 1906 to 1910, before joining a railway construction company in Buenos Aires, Argentina. In 1914, like so many other expatriates in South America, he returned to the UK at his own expense, 'to do his bit'. Enlisting first as Sapper into the Royal Engineers, he was next gazetted Second Lieutenant into the Royal Field Artillery on 22 October 1915. Transferring to the RFC, he was posted for training as an observer to Brooklands in early 1917. Joined 16 Squadron at the front on 17 March 1917. Emerging unscathed from his encounter with Kurt Wolff, he later joined Number 1 Balloon Company to be employed as a 'balloonatic'. By April 1918, he had been promoted Lieutenant and, by now, probably worn out and war weary, was given a job as a Recording/Admin Officer. Posted to the Home Establishment in February 1919, he finally left the service in the following April. Returned, post-war, to Scotland to take over his father's hotel and also managed a farm. Served in the Morayshire Home Guard in the Second World War.

VICTORY NO. 18
21 April 1917 Nieuport XXIII (No.A6755) 29 Squadron 1745

As the action with the BEs ended, so the 29 Squadron Nieuports became embroiled with the Jasta 11 Albatri. Captain E F Elderton had led the six-strong OP away at 1630 and soon afterwards saw German aircraft some way off in the distance, just too far away to engage. The patrol appears to have become split up as the Squadron records include no details of the circumstances of the fight except the rather bald statement that three pilots failed to return. The three lost pilots included the twenty-one-year old Ferrebee Sadler, who had been with Scott-Foxwell in the fight with Wolff on the 13th.

SECOND LIEUTENANT
CECIL VICTOR DE BURGH ROGERS,
29 SQUADRON, ROYAL FLYING CORPS

Born on 24 August 1898, he was the elder son of John Mackarness Rogers and Louisa Victoria Rogers (née Wilmot) of 'Springmead', Bexley, Kent and educated at Forest School, Walthamstow. After leaving school he entered the business world in London, living in 'digs' at Kitsbury Terrace, Berkhampstead. Joined the Inns of Court OTC (Number 6/1/6255) on 16 September 1915 and was gazetted to the RFC via the General List on 21 July 1916 – whilst still only seventeen years old. Having completed his pilot training and been formally awarded his 'Wings', he had been at the front for only a short time before his fatal encounter with Kurt Wolff. Buried in Tilloy Cemetery, France, (Fr581). Age 18.

VICTORY NO. 19
22 April 1917 FE2b (No.A5501) 11 Squadron 1710

The 'pushers' of 11 Squadron had a very bad day on the 22nd. Their attempts to photograph and reconnoitre the Drocourt-Quéant line came to a disastrous conclusion during the mid-afternoon, as they ran into Jasta 11. 11 Squadron lost three 'Fees', and had four others shot-up. Casualties included three aircrew wounded and two others injured. Manfred von Richthofen and Wolff each claimed an FE. Schäfer's claim was incorrectly noted as a 'BE' but, in fact, was clearly the third FE. Wolff's victim came down at Hendecourt, the only one to fall on the German side. Von Richthofen's Fee crashed during a force-landing attempt near Lagnicourt, inside British lines. Schäfer picked up a Fee a little later than the other two, its pilot supporting his wounded observer as he wrestled to land his machine despite having had most of its controls shot away. Having landed successfully, the gallant pilot pulled his wounded observer to safety as their grounded FE2b was blown apart by shell fire.

SERGEANT
JOHN KENNETH HOLLIS,
NUMBER 2479, 11 SQUADRON, ROYAL FLYING CORPS

The son of J and Susan Hollis of 26 Chambercombe Road, Ilfracombe, Devon, he was born in India in March 1892. When the war came he was a motor engineer by trade, living at home with his widowed mother. Enlisted into the RFC (2 AM) at Farnborough on 2 December 1914. Promoted Air Mechanic 1st Class on 1 June 1915 and Corporal on 1 December 1915. Learnt to fly at his own expense, being awarded the Royal Aero Certificate Number 4013 on 28 November 1916. Formal pilot training with the RFC followed and he was appointed a 1st Class Pilot on 26 February 1917. Wounded in four places and taken prisoner after his encounter with Wolff, he would remain in captivity until Boxing Day 1918. Whilst a prisoner in Germany, he wrote a letter to his observer's parents (qv) describing in detail their last day in action and the manner of Tolhurst's death (see below). Continued to serve with the Royal Air Force until 1 December 1922 when he returned to civilian life.

LIEUTENANT
BERNARD JOSEPH TOLHURST,
11/THE DUKE OF WELLINGTON'S REGIMENT (WEST RIDING) AND 11 SQUADRON, ROYAL FLYING CORPS

The elder son of Mr and Mrs Bernard Tolhurst of Ditton Court, Maidstone, Kent. Born in Southend-on-Sea in 1892, he was educated at Beaumont, at Stonyhurst and at Exeter College, Oxford. Played cricket, football and hockey for his school and for his Oxford college. When war broke out he joined the Inns of Court OTC, receiving a commission in the West Riding Regiment on 17 October 1914. Acted as Brigade Bombing Officer for some months in 1915, finally going to France in early 1916. Transferred to the RFC in early 1917, joining 11 Squadron in France shortly before his death. His pilot, Sergeant John Hollis, wrote to Tolhurst's parents from captivity in Germany, *'We left the aerodrome on Sunday afternoon at 3 pm with six other machines to do photographic reconnaissance in the Arras district. At about 3.45 pm we commenced an action with a squadron of German aeroplanes, four in excess of our number. Your son was one of the first to open fire from my machine; after a few minutes fighting, the enemy, with a great burst of fire, put out my two chief controls, thereby rendering my machine somewhat uncontrollable. I myself stopped a bullet in the shoulder, but we continued fighting, your son keeping wonderfully cool. A little later he (your son) was hit, and my engine almost stopped. By this time we were practically at the enemy's mercy, as the engine had been hit and I had only one remaining control which was cut a little*

later. Your son, however, who had control of our machine guns, was still fighting well, despite the fact that he was badly wounded and weak from loss of blood. The fighting still went on as heavily as ever, but I thought we might just manage to reach our own lines, as we were gliding in the right direction. Your son was soon too weak to stand but he continued using one of his guns while on his knees, and did some very effective work. As we neared the ground I saw that we could not reach our lines, and tried to tell Mr Tolhurst, but found he was unconscious. I tried to throw the guns over the side, but was unable to stand, as I had received four wounds altogether. Shortly afterwards we struck the ground, being less than half a mile on the wrong side. We were both thrown out, and I got a crack on the head which knocked me silly. How long I remained so I cannot tell. When I recovered, however, Mr Tolhurst was lying a few yards away from me. We were both between two of the enemy's trenches. We were taken by the Germans into the nearest trench. While we were there your son (who had not been hurt in the fall) recovered consciousness and asked me how I felt. I answered, 'I feel shot all over' and he said 'So do I'. He asked for a drink and I gave him a flask of spirits that I always carried. We were later taken into a dug-out and received medical attention. When the doctor had finished with me I was carried into an adjoining room. The German doctor very shortly came to me and he said, 'Your friend, I am afraid, is going to die; he has been shot three times in the stomach'. He was soon brought in and laid beside me on a stretcher, but was unconscious and a little delirious. He never recovered again,

and died muttering, 'Got un', got un'. Your son died like a hero, and it was really a marvellous piece of work his fighting so well and so long when he was so badly wounded'. He is buried in Vis-en-Artois Cemetery, France (Fr 421). Age 25.

VICTORY NO. 20
22 April 1917 Morane P (No.A6727) 3 Squadron 2005

The Morane crew were operating from the unit's Advanced Landing Ground, having left their base at Laviéville at 1130 that morning. After several forays over the front from the ALG, they were seen at around 1930, flying a last sortie before making their way back to their permanent base. A 3 Naval Squadron pilot was, from a distance, a spectator to the attack. Apparently busy with their camera, they appeared to the navy flier to be completely surprised when Wolff swooped in. The Morane folded and broke up as it fell. Wolff placed his claim over the front line to the west of Havrincourt.

LIEUTENANT
FRANK LESLIE CARTER,
2/EAST SURREY REGIMENT AND
3 SQUADRON, ROYAL FLYING CORPS

The elder son of Mr and Mrs W B Carter of Fort George, Gosport, Hampshire, Frank was educated at Chapel Royal Choir School and at Hurstpierpoint College (1910-14). After leaving school, he embarked on a business career in Manchester but the war intervened and, of course, he joined up, volunteering for the first Public Schools Battalion, Royal Fusiliers. Finding the military life to his liking, he entered Sandhurst with a view to obtaining a regular commission. Following the usual training, he was gazetted Second Lieutenant to the 2/East Surrey Regiment in April 1915, joining his regiment at the front shortly afterwards. Wounded in July 1915, he returned to the UK for hospital treatment. Having had his fill of life in the trenches, he applied for a

transfer to the RFC. He had served at the front only a matter of weeks when he encountered Kurt Wolff. Buried in Hermies Hill Cemetery, France (Fr530). Age 21.

SECOND LIEUTENANT
ALBERT STANLEY MORGAN,
SOUTH AFRICAN INFANTRY AND
3 SQUADRON, ROYAL FLYING CORPS

The son of Albert M and Florence Morgan, originally from Leytonstone, Essex but later of Manor Mount, Forest Hill, Kent, Albert junior was born in 1888. When war came in August 1914, he was living and working as a civil servant in South Africa. Able to drive a car and to ride a motor-cycle, he opted to enlist at Potchefstroon into the South African Royal Engineers, being posted to the 1st Company, Signal Section. Morgan saw service during the rebellion in South Africa and in the German South West African campaign, transferring first into the Pretoria Regiment and then into Enslin's Horse. Accompanying a contingent of South African Infantry to France on 21 April 1916, he served in the trenches until securing a transfer to the RFC. Qualifying as an observer in February 1917, he was – subject to approval by the South African High Commission – offered a commission in the RFC. The complication for Morgan, which the High Commissioner was obliged to point out, was that many employers in South Africa, including the Civil Service, had generously agreed to continue to pay their normal civilian salaries to men who volunteered for active overseas service with the SA forces. By accepting a commission in the RFC, Morgan would, effectively, leave the SA services and lose the relatively substantial salary he was currently enjoying. After due consideration Morgan decided to accept the commission and suffer the financial consequences. The formal notification of the commission came through on 22 April 1917, the very day he was killed in action. Morgan is variously reported in official sources as 'Corporal' or as 'Second Lieutenant'. Effectively – and perhaps, uniquely – he took off as a Corporal and was killed in the air as a Second Lieutenant. Buried in Hermies (British) Cemetery, France (Fr529). Age 29.

VICTORY NO. 21
26 April 1917 BE2g (No.A2806) 5 Squadron 1635

Detailed for an artillery observation sortie for the 57th Siege Battery, this 5 Squadron crew took off at 1500 hours. Little over half an hour later they were pounced upon by Wolff, soon afterwards to fall in flames inside the German lines to the east of Gavrelle.

This was a special day for Kurt Wolff as he received the Knight's Cross of the Royal Hohenzollern House Order with Swords, to add to his Prussian Iron Cross 1st and 2nd Classes. A Bavarian, he would also receive his own state's Military Merit Order, 4th Class, with Swords. He had now passed the 'invisible threshold' of the 20 victories needed to be considered for the ultimate accolade of the Pour le Mérite – but for this he would have to wait a little while longer. At least he had achieved the Hohenzollern House Order, normally a pre-requisite before the award of the Blue Max could be considered.

LIEUTENANT
HUMPHREY BRIAN THOMASSON HOPE,
4/NORTHAMPTONSHIRE REGIMENT AND 5 SQUADRON, ROYAL FLYING CORPS

Born in 1896, he was the son of William Hodgkinson Hope and Berta Hope of 22 Hans Crescent, Sloane Street, London. Commissioned into the Northamptonshires on 23 September 1915. A transfer to the RFC followed in 1916 and he was appointed Flying Officer upon the completion of his pilot training on 15 December of that year. His remains were never recovered and hence he is commemorated on the Arras Memorial to the Missing, France. Age 20.

SECOND LIEUTENANT
LAWSON ELLIS ALLAN,
WESTMORLAND AND CUMBERLAND YEOMANRY AND 5 SQUADRON, ROYAL FLYING CORPS

The youngest son of insurance manager James Allan and Mrs Allan, originally from Chislehurst, Kent, later of 'Mapleholme', Bidston Road, Oxton, Birkenhead, Cheshire. The Allans lost their eldest son, Stanley, a Lieutenant serving with the 7/King's Liverpool Regiment (TF) at Festubert on 15 May 1915. Born on 31 May 1897, Ellis (below), like his eldest brother, was educated at Birkenhead School and at Sedbergh (1910-15), where, as well as enjoying a successful scholastic record, he excelled at athletics and rugby, playing for the XV in his last three years there. A member of the Sedbergh OTC,

he secured a commission in the Westmorland and Cumberland Yeomanry soon after leaving school in 1915. Served in France as his regiment's Signalling Officer from November 1915 before successfully seeking transfer to the RFC in late 1916, returning to France and 5 Squadron as an observer in early 1917. He was due to return home to train as a pilot shortly after the date of his death. In a letter to his parents, Allan's CO told them that he and Hope, his pilot, had been attacked by six hostiles, going on to say, *'Everything points to the fact that both he and his pilot must have been killed at once, as eye-witnesses of the* *fight saw his machine strike the ground completely wrecked on the German side of the lines'.* A fellow officer also wrote, *'On Thursday afternoon last at 3pm he went on a flight to do artillery observation. The 57th Siege Battery, for whom he was observing, rang up later in the afternoon to say the aeroplane ranging had been brought down in the German lines by an enemy machine. His signals stopped at the same time'.* Yet another pilot reported the BE2g, *'on the ground behind the German lines – rather badly crashed'.* Commemorated on the Arras Memorial to the Missing, France. Age 19.

VICTORY NO. 22
27 April 1917 FE2b (No.7698) 11 Squadron 2020

Eleven Squadron, RFC, suffered again at the hands of their eponymically numbered Jasta. This time they lost two machines, one each to Wolff and Lothar von Richthofen. The Fees were on a Line Patrol, having taken off at 1720. Attacked by a number of Jasta 11's Albatri, both of the two defeated FE2bs fell into the front lines. Second Lieutenant Percy Robinson in 7698 later reported that one of Wolff's bullets had gone right through his right thigh, but still he had managed to get the 'pusher' down – albeit to a forced landing. His FE2b crashed into a shell hole 500 yards inside Allied lines near Gavrelle, the impact throwing him clear of the cockpit. He was knocked out for several minutes, but, happily, survived.

SECOND LIEUTENANT
PERCY ROBINSON,
7/MANCHESTER REGIMENT (TF) AND 11 SQUADRON, ROYAL FLYING CORPS

The son of Mr and Mrs Robinson of 403 Convanore Road, Grimsby, he was born in Doncaster, Yorkshire, on 1 November 1893. Educated at Heneage School, Grimsby, he enlisted into the Royal Fusiliers and was sent to France on 31 May 1915. Returned to England to be commissioned in the 7/Manchester Regiment (TF) on 20 November 1915. Accepted into the RFC in the autumn of 1916, he successfully completed his pilot training and was sent out to join 11 Squadron in France on 20 March 1917. Following his encounter with Wolff, he was returned to England as a stretcher case. As well as his physical wounds and injuries, he was suffering badly from insomnia, nightmares and general nervousness. August 1917 found him under-going treatment in Mrs Mulliner's Hospital, Clinton Court, near Rugby, frantically engaged in a running correspondence with RFC HQ, as to why, exactly, he had received no pay since February. Eventually he was able to return to light duties with 38 Training Squadron, Rendcombe, Cirencester, but was still far from well. In February 1918, having obviously lost his appetite for flying, he applied for a transfer back to the infantry. His medical condition was kept under review until the war's end when, at last, he was allowed to return to civilian life.

2AM
H W TILLEY,
NUMBER 45441, 11 SQUADRON ROYAL FLYING CORPS

The extent of the injuries Mr Tilley received in the crash are not known, nor, indeed, are details of his subsequent career in the RFC/RAF.

VICTORY NO. 23
28 April 1917 BE2e (No.A2745) 16 Squadron 1120

The Corps squadrons were again busy over the front lines, and this particular crew were engaged in registering the fall of British artillery. They had taken off at 0940 and had not long been at work when Wolff found them. In his official debriefing after his return from captivity in Germany at the beginning of 1919, John Wischer stated: *'I was on an artillery patrol from Gavrelle, practically up to Lens. I crossed the lines below Gavrelle and had to go further over [the lines] than usual for haze was bad to the east. I had just started on work when three Albatros Scouts attacked. My observer replied and one scout went off, but the other two kept on. I was only at 1,500 feet and after side-slipping etc, I lost height but up to then I had my engine. Then after a few more bursts from the EA and I was side-slipping under his nose, my engine stopped, then all I could do was hope I could reach our lines. At this time I was wounded in the ankle from the air and another bullet hit my heel, fired from the ground in all probability. I glided down, one machine still firing at me, then he left at 200 feet and I landed south-west of Oppy, and as we were attacking that village that day, I did not know whether we were in German hands or our side's. We landed in rather a hot corner and got into a shell hole and my observer and I kept a look out and then saw some Germans coming.'* Wischer's observer, Arthur Baerlein, in his debriefing, was a little more succinct: *'We were attacked by five EA five miles over the lines. Engine eventually hit and put out of action. Forced to land, pilot also hit. BE2e smashed in a shell hole. Lt Wischer taken to Douai hospital.'*

SECOND LIEUTENANT
JOHN VICTOR WISCHER,
**ROYAL GARRISON ARTILLERY AND
16 SQUADRON, ROYAL FLYING CORPS**

Born in Hawthorne, Australia, on 19 March 1896, he was the son of Victor Louis Ferdinand Wischer and Amy Wischer (neé Meeson). He was educated at the Church of England Grammar School, Melbourne, joining the Citizen's Forces (55th Regiment). Shortly after war was declared and finding that no officer under 23 years old could be appointed to the Australian Imperial Forces, he came to England at his own expense, living with his mother's sister, Dora Meeson Coates, at 52 Globe Place, Chelsea, until securing a Special Reserve commission with the Royal Garrison Artillery on 9 June 1915. Served for seven months in France before returning to England to have his tonsils out! Became attached to the Royal Flying Corps on 9 August 1916, being selected for pilot training. Granted his Royal Aero Club Certificate (Number 3792) on 10 November 1916. Shortly afterwards on 27 November, Wischer crashed an Armstrong Whitworth (Number 6223). Thrown out on impact, he damaged his left foot by fracturing his astragalas and also chipped a piece of bone on his heel. Returning to duty on 31 January 1917, he shortly afterwards joined 57 Squadron at the front. Wounded and taken prisoner after his fight with Wolff, he remained in captivity until his repatriation on 6 January 1919. Demobilised in August 1919, he returned to resume his studies in Melbourne.

SECOND LIEUTENANT
ARTHUR ADOLF BAERLEIN,
**ROYAL FIELD ARTILLERY AND
16 SQUADRON, ROYAL FLYING CORPS**

Born on 27 November 1886, the son of Mr and Mrs Baerlein of London. Educated at University College School, Hampstead and at Sedbergh. By the end of 1914, Baerlein had passed all the Bar examinations and qualified as a barrister. He initially enlisted as a private soldier but soon received a commission with the Royal Field Artillery on 30 January 1915. His unit, A Battery, 68th Brigade, Royal Field Artillery — embarked at Avonmouth on 30 June 1915, bound for Alexandria and the Mediterranean Expeditionary Force. Shortly after arriving on 12 July, he was admitted to hospital for several weeks before, on 10 October 1915, accompanying his brigade to Mamoura Camp, Egypt. Within days, the 68th had moved to Salonika whereupon Baerlein was struck down with appendicitis and shipped off to Malta for treatment aboard the hospital ship, *Oxfordshire*. Returning to England in May 1916, his request for transfer to the RFC was granted and after successfully training as an observer, he was sent to France and 16 Squadron shortly before his encounter with Kurt Wolff. At first reported missing, believed killed, his parents were immensely relieved to learn in June 1917, that he had been taken prisoner, albeit wounded. His first prison was Fort Zorndorf where, after three months, he escaped with Captain William Leefe Robinson VC, only to be re-captured two kilometres short of the Swiss border. Imprisoned next at Wessel, he and Captain Robinson made two further attempts at escape before being caught trying to bribe a German guard. The two were court martialled, sentenced to three months close confinement and sent to Clausthaal on 10 May 1918. At Clausthaal, Baerlein was soon at loggerheads with the Senior British Officer, Major General Hurdis Secundus Lalande Ravenshaw, CMG, who had expressly forbidden escape attempts because the chances of success were slight and failures inevitably brought harsh reprisals in their wake. The ruling appalled at least two other senior officers at the camp, who, like Baerlein and Robinson, believed it was their absolute duty to escape — if they could.

Colonel G C Cole-Hamilton CMG, DSO, Royal Irish Rifles and Lieutenant Colonel Lord Farnham, North Irish Horse attached Royal Inniskilling Fusiliers, pointedly asked Ravenshaw to commit his 'no escaping' order to paper. The General refused and, after re-considering his position, withdrew the order. Baerlein and others immediately started a tunnel. However, before that enterprise could come to fruition, another opportunity to escape presented itself. Dressed in civilian clothes, Baerlein and Lieutenant R R Mackintosh, Royal Scots Fusiliers and RFC, managed to smuggle themselves into the orderlies' section of the camp. Despite their initial success, they were soon challenged and exposed by a suspicious orderly. A subsequent Court of Enquiry conducted by the camp's escape committee was halted in its early stages by Major General Ravenshaw. A report later drawn up by Baerlein and Mackintosh clearly inferred that the orderly who had exposed their escape attempt subse-quently confessed that he was acting under the influence of Major General Ravenshaw! The Armistice came shortly afterwards and the matter appears to have been laid to rest. Baerlein was repatriated to England on Christmas Day 1918, able, at last, to resume his career as a barrister. Major General Ravenshaw died in unusual circumstances in June 1920. He had joined an elephant hunt led by Major Pretorius, a famous 'white hunter' who had gained a great reputation for daring scout work in the East African campaign. Pretorius was employed by the Cape Provincial Government to cull the large herds of elephants in the Addo Bush, a dense forest jungle north of Port Elizabeth. Ravenshaw detached himself from the party and was found dead two days later, his rifle still grasped in his hand.

VICTORY NO. 24
28 April 1917 BE2f (No.2557) 5 Squadron 1745

Wolff met another 5 Squadron recce machine in the late afternoon. The BE2f was on a photo job over the front, having taken

off at 1625. They lasted just twenty minutes. With his guns blazing, Wolff dived on the observation machine and forced it down behind the British trenches where it was wrecked in a crash landing west of Gavrelle. Both men scrambled clear, physically unhurt, each counting himself extremely fortunate.

SECOND LIEUTENANT
NORMAN CARTER BUCKTON,
EAST LANCASHIRE REGIMENT AND 5 SQUADRON, ROYAL FLYING CORPS

The son of Percy and Janet Buckton of 'The Poplars', Cleveland Road, Wanstead, Essex, he was born on 11 April 1898. After completing his education at Brentwood Grammar School (1906-15) he unsuccessfully attempted to gain a place at the Royal Military College, Sandhurst. He did, however, eventually succeed in obtaining a commission in the East Lancashire Regiment (*London Gazette* 26 January 1916). An application for a transfer to the RFC approved, he completed his pilot training and was sent to join 5 Squadron in June 1916. His entry into combat flying was delayed by a spell in hospital and it was not until 24 March 1917 that he commenced active service with 5 Squadron. Luckily, he and his observer survived Wolff's onslaught and Buckton continued operational flying. After three months at the front, Buckton was returned to the UK and was appointed to a series of training squadrons as an instructor. After the war Buckton served – with the rank of Captain – at RAF HQ, Cologne, with the Army of the Rhine. Next he was sent to Ireland, that unhappy country being once again in a state of turmoil. Soon Buckton was beset with his own troubles, a Court Martial on 14 July 1921 resulting in a forfeiture of seniority. There was also an apparent involvement in an infamous incident when the wounded John O'Connor – a suspected rebel – *'was murdered in his bed'* by British soldiers. Norman Buckton resigned his commission on 12 September 1921.

SECOND LIEUTENANT
GARTH RICHARD O'SULLIVAN,
ROYAL IRISH RIFLES AND 5 SQUADRON, ROYAL FLYING CORPS

Born in 1897, he was the son of Dr J A and Mrs R O'Sullivan of 56 Pembroke Road, Dublin. Educated at St Vincent's College, Castleknock, he was, soon after leaving school, apprenticed to the Mercantile Marine via the Lord Line. Early in the war, he volunteered for Dublin's version of the nationwide 'Pals' movement, becoming a member of D Company of the 7/Royal Dublin Fusiliers. O'Sullivan and the Dublin 'Pals' landed at Suvla Bay on the Gallipoli Peninsular on 7 August 1915. His Dardanelles experience was short-lived as he – like so many others in that ill-fated campaign – succumbed to dysentery and was invalided home within three weeks of his arrival. After recovering, O'Sullivan (below) was gazetted Second Lieutenant to 6/Royal Irish Rifles on 9 December 1915, before soon afterwards being transferred to the 15th (North Belfast) Battalion of the same regiment. Wounded, he nevertheless survived the terrible slaughter of the Ulster Division on the first day of the Battle of the Somme on 1 July 1916. Recovering his health yet again, he was accepted into the RFC on 3 January 1917, becoming an observer on probation only three weeks later. Sent to 5 Squadron on 3 February 1917, he was 'loaned out' to 16 Squadron on

31 March before returning again to 5 Squadron on 14 April 1917. Formally appointed a Flying Officer (observer) on 8 May 1917, he was by then a seasoned operational flyer and a survivor of a Wolff victory. After a short leave he returned to the front only to suffer an attack of scabies for which he was hospitalised until 23 June 1917. On 14 July 1917 he was again posted to 16 Squadron for a short period before returning to the Home Establishment on 4 August 1917. Sent to France again on 7 February 1918, this time as an instructor on the aerial ranges.

Returning to the UK to train as a pilot, he was given his 'Wings' and sent yet again to 16 Squadron on 9 April. Wounded on 19 August 1918 when he suffered slight concussion, he returned to duty on 14 September. Garth O'Sullivan finally returned to the Home Establishment for the last time on 4 January 1919, having survived not only Gallipoli but also the bloodiest day in the history of the British Army *and* an all-out attack by the German ace, Kurt Wolff – not to mention the day-to-day perils of operational flying over the Western Front. The luck of the Irish?

VICTORY NO. 25
29 April 1917 SPAD VII No.A6681 19 Squadron 1210

The circumstances of this action have been given something of a romantic 'gloss' over the years. The story often presented is that knowing General Trenchard and his influential Adjutant, Maurice Baring, were due to visit 19 Squadron at Vert Galant later that morning, Harvey-Kelly immediately took off upon hearing the news that a red enemy machine was in the vicinity – his intention, presumably, to present the head of MvR to his chief!

Of course, Harvey-Kelly, amongst the most experienced of airmen, would know that Manfred von Richthofen's machine was not, by any means, the only red German aeroplane on the Western Front. He would also know that to take only two relatively 'green' pilots against the might of Jasta 11, would be foolhardy in the extreme. A far more prosaic but much more likely explanation is that H-K was simply on a routine flight when he had the great misfortune to run into the Richthofen squadron.

The fight was short. Manfred and Lothar von Richthofen sent down the two squadron pilots; Wolff despatched Harvey-Kelly to the ground at Sailly-en-Ostrevent. Lunch in the 19 Squadron Mess was a sombre affair. The trio were overdue and the worst was expected. Trenchard and Baring thanked their hosts and took their leave. *'Tell Harvey-Kelly I was very sorry to miss him'*, said the Commander-in-

Chief. Baring commented later that he knew from the tone of Trenchard's voice that he doubted his message would ever be delivered to the intended recipient.

MAJOR
HUBERT DUNSTERVILLE HARVEY-KELLY,
DSO, MID, ROYAL IRISH REGIMENT AND 19 SQUADRON, ROYAL FLYING CORPS

Far right: The Boss in 1916. Major General Hugh Montague Trenchard, CB, DSO, General Officer Commanding the Royal Flying Corps in the Field. ADC to the King.

Born on 9 February 1891, he was the son of Colonel H H Harvey-Kelly, Indian Army, and Mrs Constance Jameson Harvey-Kelly of Barham Lodge, Buckingham. Gazetted Second Lieutenant to the Royal Irish Regiment on 5 October 1910. He developed an interest in aviation and gained one of the earliest Royal Aero Club Certificates (Number 501) on 30 May 1913. Became famous as the first pilot to land in France in the Great War. He led the first three RFC squadrons to join the BEF on 13 August 1914, landing at Amiens at 0820. The Official History credits H-K – albeit helped by two other machines of 2 Squadron – with being the first to bring down an enemy machine in aerial combat on 25 August 1914. Forced to land, the German crew hared away across the fields. H-K and his observer, Lieutenant W H C Mansfield, set down alongside the Taube and continued the pursuit of the German crew on foot. The chase was in vain, the enemy escaped. The aeroplane was stripped for souvenirs – probably the first time in warfare this particular form of looting took place – and set alight. One of 5 Squadron's pilots, Second Lieutenant C W Wilson, later claimed that the credit for the small victory on 25 August should have gone to his

Right: Captain the Honourable Maurice Baring, Trenchard's hugely influential Aide – intellectual, man of letters, sometime war correspondent for the *Morning Post*.

observer, Lieutenant C E C Rabagliati (King's Own Yorkshire Light Infantry and RFC) and his hunting rifle! Wilson's diary entry for 29 August 1914, reads: *'Lunched at hotel in Compiègne, many pilots of the RFC collected. Harvey-Kelly (Lieutenant of 2 Squadron) posing as successful warrior, relating his method of downing Huns and showing small plaque taken from machine downed by Rab and 398* (the Number of their machine). *Stopped him in full career and claimed first Hun for 398. He had landed beside our prey and attended to its burning! H-K handed the plaque gracefully to me, "Your bird, I think"'.* H-K was Mentioned in Despatches and created a Companion of the Distinguished Service Order (*London Gazette* 18 February 1915), *'for services in connection with operations in the field'.* He became a Captain on 23 May 1915 and a squadron commander, Temporary Major, on 30 January 1916. H-K is buried in Brown's Copse Cemetery, Roeux, France (Fr 604). Age 26.

VICTORY NO. 26
29 April 1917 FE2b (No.A5483) 18 Squadron 1700

An 18 Squadron camera-toting machine was being escorted by FEs of its own squadron. The formation had taken off at 1420 to operate over the Fifth Army front. Two FEs were downed, one by Manfred von Richthofen, the other by Wolff. It was the Baron's third kill of the day, Wolff's second. Wolff claimed his victim down south of Pronville, inside British lines. The pilot, under extreme pressure by Wolff and knowing that his observer was wounded, was relieved to get down relatively intact. A third FE was also shot about and the observer wounded – but this one got home safely.

SECOND LIEUTENANT
GEORGE HASTINGS STONE DINSMORE,
74/BATTALION, CANADIAN EXPEDITIONARY FORCE AND 18 SQUADRON, ROYAL FLYING CORPS

Born on 4 July 1893, he was the son of Dr George Hastings John Dinsmore and Mrs Dinsmore of 42 Wilcox Street, Toronto, Canada. After completing his education in Toronto, he entered the service of the Canadian Bank of Commerce on 18 August 1911. In July 1915, he was working in the Inspector's Department at the head office of the bank in Toronto, when he decided to enlist into the 74th Battalion of the Canadian Army. Gazetted Lieutenant to the 48th Regiment (Highlanders of Toronto) on 23 January 1916. Two months later he proceeded overseas to join the 74th Battalion, CEF. By August 1916, he was in command of his battalion's Machine Gun Section with the rank of Temporary Captain. Successfully applying for transfer to the

RFC, he took a reduction in rank when he was gazetted Second Lieutenant, Special Reserve, RFC, in December 1916. Embarked upon his pilot training at Oxford before going on to Edinburgh and Yorkshire. Awarded his 'Wings' and appointed Flying Officer on 8 April 1917, just three weeks before encountering Kurt Wolff. In a letter home, Dinsmore gives his (slightly coloured) version of the encounter with Jasta 11: *'.....our formation was violently attacked by numerous fast enemy scouts. Three of them insisted on thrusting their affections upon me and, though my observer accounted for two, the third brought me down with my observer killed. By the best stroke of luck I managed to reach a very advanced post in the front line, followed thereto by Mr Hun, showing all sorts of hate by showering me with machine-gun bullets. My own escape was marvellous, as my boot and coat were both torn by machine-gun bullets, though I was unhurt. The Hun has the advantage in these scraps, as we go some ten miles into his country looking for trouble, but he rarely returns our visits. Of course, such engagements don't always occur, but we always get heavily shelled by the anti-aircraft guns ('Archies', as they are called), and from these I had several very narrow escapes'.* George Dinsmore survived the war with the rank of Captain, Royal Air Force.

SECOND LIEUTENANT
GEORGE BEAUMONT BATE,
9/LOYAL NORTH LANCASHIRE REGIMENT AND 18 SQUADRON, ROYAL FLYING CORPS

Born on 21 May 1895, he was the son of master brewer George Bate and Millicent Bate of The Rhyddyn, Caergwle, near Wrexham and 51 Colville Gardens, Bayswater, London. Educated at Downside (1909-11), representing the school in the hockey XI. In April 1915, he enlisted into the 19th (Public Schools) Battalion, Royal Fusiliers, accompanying that unit to France in the following November. The Public Schools Battalions were disbanded by the War Office in April 1916, the men sent home to Officer Cadet Battalions. Bate was gazetted Second Lieutenant to the 9th Battalion of the Loyal North Lancashire Regiment on 26 September 1916 and returned to the front for a second winter in the trenches. An application to join the RFC was approved and he returned to England for observer training in March 1917. He was involved in an action on his very first flight over the front on 23 April 1917. He and his pilot, Second Lieutenant E L Zink, were engaged by an enemy aircraft which Bate sent down OOC. In the course of the action, Zink was wounded and Bate's tunic was torn by a machine-gun bullet but they returned safely to base. Six days later Wolff shot Bate through the heart. His commanding officer wrote to his parents: *'It is almost a miracle that the pilot is alive today, as their machine was terribly shot about'.* George Bate was buried initially about 3,000 yards north of Beaumetz-les-Cambrai, north-east of Bapaume but was, post-war, re-interred in Quéant Road British Cemetery, Buissay (Fr646). Age 21.

VICTORY NO. 27
30 April 1917 BE2e (No.2910) 13 Squadron 1735

This final day of Bloody April saw Wolff score his 22nd victory of the month. The 13 Squadron BE crew were on their second sortie of the day, having already flown a mission over Brebières at mid-day. They took off for a photo op at 1508, intending to cover an area of the XVII Corps front but going down to the chillingly efficient Wolff almost an hour and a half later. The BE2e's pilot, Trollope, was very severely wounded in the air, his observer killed outright. Despite this, Trollope managed to bring his machine down inside British lines west of Fresnes, only to have his crippled machine shelled to smithereens by German artillery.

SECOND LIEUTENANT
WILLIAM KENNEDY TROLLOPE,
13 SQUADRON, ROYAL FLYING CORPS

Born in May 1896, he was the younger son of architect John Evelyn Trollope, FRIBA, and Maud Trollope of 'Glenwood', Virginia Water and 28 Craven Street, Strand, London. Educated at St Christopher's, Eastbourne and at Uppingham (1911-14). Commissioned to the RFC (Special Reserve) in May 1916, he was immediately sent for pilot training. Gained the Royal Aero Club Certificate (Number 3689) on 21 July 1916 and his official 'Wings' shortly afterwards. Following a brief leave at home, he was sent to join 13 Squadron in France on 30 August 1916. Engaged mainly on reconnaissance missions, he flew with a number of different observers including Lieutenant G G Coury, a Liverpudlian who had been awarded the Victoria Cross on the Somme whilst serving with the 4/South Lancashire Regiment. Details of his last flight – with Second Lieutenant Augustine Bonner – and his subsequent fate were given in a letter to his parents by the Squadron padre: 'On 30 April 1917 immediately after his last leave, he went out on 'photography'. Flying home in the afternoon, he was attacked by five German planes of the latest and fastest type. His observer was immediately killed and your son badly wounded in many places. He, however, made a marvellous landing from a height of 5,000 feet just inside our lines. The enemy immediately heavily shelled the machine lying helplessly on the ground. Notwithstanding this murderous fire, one of our gallant soldiers left the shelter of the trenches, unstrapped the unconscious officer and brought him to the safety of our lines but was unfortunately severely wounded himself. Lieutenant Trollope successfully underwent a dangerous operation but he died on 3 May'. He is buried in Aubigny Cemetery, France (FR95). He was 21 years old.

SECOND LIEUTENANT
AUGUSTINE BONNER,
SOUTH STAFFORDSHIRE REGIMENT AND
13 SQUADRON, ROYAL FLYING CORPS

Augustine Bonner.

The younger son of the Reverend Henry Bonner, Minister of Hamstead Road Baptist Church, and Margaret Elizabeth Bonner of 31 Radnor Road, Handsworth, Birmingham. Born on 13 January 1897, he was educated at King Edward's School, Birmingham (1907-12). After leaving King Edward's he became an art student at the Birmingham School of Art. As soon as the war came, he enlisted as a private soldier (Number 14/516) into the 14/Battalion, The Royal Warwickshire Regiment – the 1st City of Birmingham Battalion – the Birmingham 'Pals', in fact. Gazetted Second Lieutenant to the 7/South Staffs on 26 February 1915, he was eventually attached to a battalion of the West Riding Regiment in early 1916. Served in France from February 1916, being wounded two months later. After recovering from his wounds, he was sent back to France in September 1916 but very shortly afterwards transferred to the RFC for training. Subsequently appointed a Flying Officer (observer) with effect from 3 April 1917. Wolff's first fusillade almost certainly killed Bonner, leaving his wounded pilot struggling to take the damaged BE2e back to the British lines. Bonner is buried in Feuchy (British) Cemetery, France (Fr1188). Age 20.

Thus ended April 1917. The RFC lost approximately 245 aircraft to enemy action during the month with Jasta 11 – the most effective of the German 'squadrons' – contributing 89 victories to the overall total. Of these, Wolff and Manfred von Richthofen each claimed 22; Karl Schäfer gained 21; Lothar von Richthofen 15 and Sebastian Festner 10. The Jasta pilots had, undoubtedly, proved their new machines, their tactics and their courage. Although the RFC – still flying, in the main, passé aircraft – had suffered a monumental disaster, still they would not accept defeat. Their courage in continuing their unremittingly aggressive offensiveness defies comprehension.

VICTORY NO. 28
1 May 1917 Sopwith Triplane (No.N5474) 8 Naval Squadron 1050

Wolff celebrated May Day by scoring yet two more victories – business as usual! The first was achieved in a loose dogfight with Sopwith Triplanes from 8 Naval Squadron who had been escorting photo-reconnaissance machines. Six Triplanes had taken off at 0840, led by Flight Commander C D Booker. One of the RNAS pilots, Flight Sub-Lieutenant E D Crundall – who, in the forthcoming July, would narrowly escape after becoming von Tutschek's 19th victory – later recounted how, between Douai and Arras, they had engaged five Albatros Scouts. He said that they could not get in close and were forced to shoot at long range. During the course of the action, one of the 8 Naval pilots, Flight Sub-Lieutenant Roach, was lost to sight. As the fight continued, other German machines came up to the now widely scattered group. Another of the Navy men, Don Shields, was forced down just inside the British lines, his leg broken and his shoulder dislocated but at least he had the satisfaction of claiming one EA shot down. Shields pushed himself out of the downed Triplane's cockpit and, as much as his broken leg would allow, scuttled to the safety of a trench as the German artillery shredded his machine (number N5434) to matchwood. Shields had been shot down by Leutnant Kurt von Döring of Jasta 4, his second victory.

FLIGHT SUB-LIEUTENANT
EDMUND DANIEL ROACH,
8 NAVAL SQUADRON, ROYAL NAVAL AIR SERVICE

The son of Patrick Joseph Roach and Ann Roach (née O'Leary) of 86 St Patrick Street,

The grave of Flt Sub-Lieut Edmund Daniel Roach.

Toronto, Ontario, Canada, he was born on 12 January 1892. Having gained an American Aero Certificate (Number 520) on 29 June 1916, he came to the UK and was accepted into the RNAS in the following month. Formal training followed at Redcar, Yorkshire and at Cranwell (where he lost one month's seniority *'for causing a disturbance with other officers at night in the Duty Officer's cabin'*). Posted to Dover on 12 February 1917, he was hospitalised in Chatham ten days later. His social disease having cleared up to the satisfaction of the doctors, he was discharged as fit for active service on 10 March 1917. Despite his various adventures, he had still managed to 'clock up' 47 flying hours by 1 April 1917 and was sent to the front shortly afterwards. Buried at Cabaret-Rouge Cemetery, France (Fr924). Age 25.

VICTORY NO. 29
1 May 1917 FE2b (No. A815) 25 Squadron 1855

The FE squadron had sent out a formation on a bomb raid followed by a Line Patrol to Izel-les-Equerchin at 1650. The intended target was a bomb dump and each machine carried four bombs. The Fees crossed the lines under heavy AA fire but suffered no casualties. Evidence of what happened next is provided by Geoffrey Harding MC, one of the 25 Squadron observers in his debriefing report filed after his return from captivity at the war's end: *'We had just pulled off our bombs and were doing a recce of the German positions when we saw another FE, apparently in difficulties with two German machines on its tail. We turned our attention to these machines and engaged them while the other FE got away. Within a few seconds we were surrounded by eight other planes, making ten in all, headed by a red machine which the Germans told us afterwards was piloted by Captain Baron von Richthofen. We were flying at 7,000 feet at the time and the red machine which was well above and behind us, dived at us and put an explosive bullet in our petrol tank which set us on fire.*

My pilot, although he was getting badly burnt, dived vertically for the ground and made an excellent landing. Both of us got out of the machine safely and were then surrounded by about 2,000 Germans of the 69th Regiment. No Germans approached the machine until it had burnt itself out. My pilot, Lieutenant French, behaved splendidly throughout and it is entirely owing to his presence of mind that we managed to get to earth. My late CO, Lieut. Colonel Cherry, has since told me that the machine we rescued did not belong to 25 Squadron and he thought that it was probably a captured FE2b used by the Germans as a decoy.'

Despite the CO's colourful embroideries, there is no evidence that the Germans ever used any captured aircraft as a 'decoy'. With so many Allied aircraft in the air, there was little reason for them to set up such a deception. Furthermore, any such machine would be in danger not only from German scout planes but also from their own anti-aircraft fire.

The reference to von Richthofen is

Lt G S French.

The son of solicitor Sidney French and Mrs M A French of 8 St Clements Gardens, Thomson Lane, Cambridge. Gazetted Second Lieutenant to the Cambridgeshire Regiment on 5 August 1915, being promoted to Lieutenant on 21 June 1916. Accepted for pilot training, he reported to Oxford on 11 September 1916. Awarded his 'Wings' on 16 March 1917, he was sent out to join 25 Squadron in France nine days later. Wounded and taken prisoner after his encounter with Wolff, he was incarcerated until his repatriation into Dover on 13 December 1918. Left the service and was posted to the Unemployed List on 19 February 1919.

LIEUTENANT
GEOFFREY PARKER HARDING,
MC & BAR, MID, 1/CHESHIRE REGIMENT AND 25 SQUADRON, ROYAL FLYING CORPS

The son of Mr and Mrs Harding of 42 Hardy Street, Blackheath, London SE. Gazetted Second Lieutenant to the 1/Cheshire

interesting. Presumably the German ground troops identified the red machine as belonging to von Richthofen whereas, in fact, the Baron was already on his way back to Germany, leaving Kurt Wolff as acting CO. Such was the power of the legend, however, that anybody flying any sort of red machine was invariably identified as the Red Baron, even after his death.

Harding's pilot, Gerald French, was more succinct in his debriefing report: *'Shot down in flames by EA, slightly burned. Bomb raid.'*

Wolff recorded his victory as coming down south of Bois Bernard. In the same fight Lothar von Richthofen bagged a second FE west of Acheville, forcing it down inside Allied lines near the Arras racecourse and wounding its observer in the process. Was this the FE that 25 Squadron had initially attempted to rescue – the one they assumed had got away?

LIEUTENANT
GERALD SIDNEY FRENCH,
4/CAMBRIDGESHIRE REGIMENT AND 25 SQUADRON, ROYAL FLYING CORPS

Regiment on 17 February 1915 and subsequently promoted to Lieutenant on 3 February 1916. Harding, on the night of 6/7 December 1915, led a raid on the enemy's trenches south of Mametz, which was considered a classic example of the genre. Besides Harding, the raiding party consisted of two other officers (both of whom outranked Harding but agreed to serve under him) and 50 men. Harding led the raid with great panache, killing a number of the enemy and bringing back a prisoner for interrogation. The Cheshire's casualties were one man seriously wounded (he subsequently died) and seven others slightly wounded. Harding was awarded the first ever Military Cross won by the 1/Cheshires and three of the men were given DCMs. The citation for the Military Cross (*London Gazette* 22 January 1916), reads: *'On the night of 6/7 December 1915 in France, he led a bombing attack on the German trenches with great coolness and determination, although the mud rendered the advance almost impossible. He showed great personal bravery and himself threw bombs when the bombers were in difficulties. Several Germans were accounted for and one prisoner taken'*. Transferring to the RFC, he was ordered to report for training on 14 February 1917. Awarded his 'Wing', he was ordered to France and 25 Squadron on 30 April 1917. On his very first day he had the misfortune to be shot down and taken prisoner. Harding was, unexceptionally, a reluctant prisoner, but what was quite exceptional was that he actually succeeded in escaping and getting himself all the way back home to England – arriving on 22 October 1917! Following a lengthy period of leave, Harding returned to the RFC in February 1918, this time to train as a pilot. He did not again serve overseas, leaving the service finally on 19 September 1919. His bravery and ingenuity in effecting his escape were recognised by the award of a Bar to his Military Cross, the announcement of which appeared in the 'Escapers's Gazette' – the *London Gazette* of 16 December 1919.

Geoffrey Harding in 1915 (fourth left, back row) wearing the ribbon of his first MC and pictured with fellow officers of the 1/Cheshires in the area of the Somme.

Staffelführer

Kurt Wolff was awarded the Order Pour le Mérite on 4 May and immediately went on leave. Two days later he was appointed as Commanding Officer (Staffelführer) of Jasta 29, eventually arriving to take up his command on 10 May. Jasta 29 was based at Junéville, on the 1st Army Front. The Staffel had been formed at the end of 1916 and had been operating on the French front opposite Reims, since mid-February, so far, in sharp contrast to what Wolff had been used to, achieving only two victories. Wolff's predecessor, Leutnant Ludwig Fritz Dornheim had fallen in combat to a French Nieuport Scout on 29 April, hence the vacancy. Dornheim had claimed two victories with Jasta 5 before taking over at Jasta 29.

VICTORY NO. 30
13 May 1917 Spad (No.N1377) Escadrille N.37 1155

Wolff soon increased Jasta 29's 'output' by fifty per cent when he downed a French Spad over Beine on the German side of the lines.

SERGENT
FERNAND ALBERT GARRIGOU

Born on 19 February 1891 in Sidi-bel-Abbes, the home and garrison town of the French Foreign Legion. Awarded the French Aeronautical Certificate/Pilot's Brevet Number 2736 on 20 January 1916. His claims included the confirmed 'kill' of an Aviatik two-seater (shared with Sgt de Geuser) on 29 July 1916; an EA over Mesnil-Brunter on 25 September 1916 – rated as a 'probable'; and a balloon at Equancourt – damaged – on 27 September 1916. His efforts were Cited in Orders on 24 August 1916. Wounded in combat on 1 October 1916. Last seen in combat with three German aircraft on 13 May 1917.

VICTORY NO. 31
27 June 1917 Nieuport XXIII (No.A6718) 60 Squadron 2030

On 22 June, Jasta 29 moved its base to Mons-en-Pevelle on the 6th Army Front, now in opposition to the British. Five days later Wolff and his men encountered a 60 Squadron evening patrol near Douai.

Returning from prison camp in December 1918, 60 Squadron's David Murray offered an account of his last combat. Four Nieuports had engaged 11 Albatros Scouts, Murray bringing up the rear. Murray, whose Lewis gun soon jammed, found himself 'ambushed' by eight Albatri, helpless and surrounded. His Nieuport's propeller was smashed, then his engine cut out. By this time he had been wounded in two places, first in the left leg and then in the right arm. There was nothing for it but to make as rapid a forced landing as soon as he possibly could.

LIEUTENANT
DAVID CHARLES GRAEME MURRAY,
ROYAL ENGINEERS (CITY OF EDINBURGH, TF) AND 60 SQUADRON, ROYAL FLYING CORPS

Born on 14 July 1897, he was the son of Charles D Murray, KC, and Mrs Murray of 62 Great King Street, Edinburgh. Educated at the Edinburgh Academy. He enlisted as a Sapper in the REs in 1914 and was subsequently gazetted Second Lieutenant to his local Territorial Force unit of the Royal Engineers on 7 April 1915. Accepted for pilot training with the RFC on 30 November 1916, he qualified in January 1917 but served in the UK until 26 May

1917, until he was sent to join 60 Squadron at the front. Initially reported 'missing', his family were relieved to learn that he had been taken prisoner, albeit wounded. Exchanged into neutral Switzerland on 27 December 1917 as a consequence of his wounds, he was eventually repatriated on 9 December 1918. Finally left the service on 6 February 1919.

Kurt Wolff was now ordered to return to Jasta 11 – this time as CO. His friend and former comrade, Karl Allmenröder, had fallen in combat on this very same day. Wolff lost no time in taking up his new command, arriving back at Harlebecke on the following day. In the meantime, Werner Voss, then with Jasta 5, was appointed to the command of Jasta 29 in succession to Wolff.

VICTORY NO. 32
6 July 1917   RE8 (No.A4313)   4 Squadron   2120

This two-seater crew took off on an artillery observer sortie over the 2nd Army Front at 1710 hours. Under the combined attack of five German scouts, they were seen by observers on the ground to fall in flames near Zillebeke close to the front-line trenches. Wolff, it was, who claimed the *coup de grâce*.

LIEUTENANT
JOHN YATES TAYLOR,
4/EAST LANCASHIRE REGIMENT AND
4 SQUADRON, ROYAL FLYING CORPS

Born on 3 July 1896, he was the son of J W and Mrs Taylor of 39 Eldon Road, Blackburn. He was educated at Wigan Grammar School and at Chester Training College where he was studying to become a teacher as war came. Joined the Inns of Court OTC (Number

4/5/4720) on 9 July 1915 and was gazetted Second Lieutenant to the East Lancashire Regiment on 21 November 1915. Served with his regiment in Egypt before returning to England and transferring to the RFC. Reporting first to Reading on 8 September 1916, his pilot training progressed in the usual manner until he was confirmed as a Flying Officer 18 May 1917. He was able to attend his elder brother's wedding in May 1917 before departing for Flanders and 4 Squadron in early June. He was killed in the air exactly one month after he had arrived at the front and just three days after his 21st birthday. His CO wrote to his parents, *'Apparently their petrol tank was hit, as the machine descended in flames and landed, just on our side of our trenches, a total wreck. The bodies were recovered, and have been buried near the machine'.* Taylor had narrowly escaped death a week or so before he met his nemesis, Kurt Wolff. In a letter home, he described how he had heard a, *'Pop, pop, pop'* and saw three Hun machines above his tail. They were single-seater scouts painted in gaudy colours, *'......they each dived on us in turn, firing their machine guns. My observer fired about 100 rounds into them, with what results we do not know, as they cleared off. We had tons of bullet holes in our planes, one tyre burst, the main spar of the body was shot through, and half my elevator controls were shot away. However, with luck, we managed to land with just crushing the under-carriage'.* Buried in Hooge Crater Cemetery, Belgium (Bel112). Age 21.

LIEUTENANT
GEORGE MUTCH,
DSO, 11/GORDON HIGHLANDERS AND
4 SQUADRON, ROYAL FLYING CORPS

The son of cabinet maker, Alexander Sim Mutch and Jessie Cruickshank Mutch of 1 Albert Place, Aberdeen, he was born on 30 October 1892. After completing his education in Aberdeen, he secured a position with the Post Office – initially as a sorting clerk but progressing to become a telegraphist. Volunteered (Number 1281) in 1912 for the 1st Highland Field Ambulance (TF) RAMC, rising to the rank of Sergeant. Mobilised with the Territorial Force as soon as the war came in August 1914, he decided to transfer to the Regular Army. A posting to the Royal Engineers in his trade as a telegraphist followed on 9 April 1915. However, with his soldierly qualities manifestly apparent, his orders were changed and he was appointed to a commission, being gazetted to the 11th (Reserve) Battalion of the Gordon Highlanders on 29 April 1915. Mutch was soon sent to join the 1st Battalion of his regiment in France and, in February 1917, took part in a brilliantly successful raid on the enemy's trenches during a swirling snow-storm. Eleven Germans were killed and twenty-one prisoners and a machine gun were triumphantly brought back to the British lines. Mutch played a prominent part in the raid, so much so that he was awarded an immediate gallantry Distinguished Service Order, *London Gazette* 12 March 1917, page 2476: *'For conspicuous gallantry and devotion to duty during a raid on the enemy's trenches. He rallied his men and led them forward under heavy fire. Later, with a few men, he rushed an enemy post from the flank and captured the garrison. He was a magnificent example to his men, and to him was largely due the success of the raid'.* 'Gallantry' DSOs to subalterns are rare – ranking only marginally below the award of a VC. Soon after the announcement of the DSO, Mutch transferred to the RFC for training as an observer. He had been at the front for only a matter of days when he was killed. Commemorated on the Railway Dugouts, Zillebeke (Special Memorial), (Bel 127). Age 24.

VICTORY NO. 33
7 July 1917 Sopwith Triplane (No.N6309) 1 Naval Squadron 1100

Six aircraft from 1 Naval Squadron took off at 0850, to provide escort cover for RFC photo-recce aircraft over Dadizeele. Over the front they engaged 15 German fighters, one of which was claimed shot down by Flight Sub-Lieutenant Anthony. Three of the Naval pilots failed to get home – Flight Commander C A Eyre, and Flight Sub-Lieutenants D W Ramsey and K H Millward. The others landed back at their airfield at 10.20.

Cyril Eyre was an experienced flight commander with six victories. It is understood that he was downed by Leutnant

Niederhoff, whilst Wolff got Millward, who fell near Comines.

The Germans claimed four Triplanes this morning, two by Jasta 11 pilots, Wolff and Alfred Niederhoff, one by Leutnant Richard Kruger of Jasta 4, the other by Vizefeldwebel Friedrich Altemeier of Jasta 24. The bulk of the action was by JGI aircraft – Jasta 4 and 11, but Altemeier's claim is around the same time and location. His and the two Jasta 11 claims were independently noted as down inside German lines, unlike the Jasta 4 claim, which was not.

FLIGHT SUB-LIEUTENANT
KENNETH H MILLWARD,
1 NAVAL SQUADRON, ROYAL NAVAL AIR SERVICE

Born in England on 25 September 1895, he was in New Zealand when the war broke out in August 1914. Returning to England at his own expense, he volunteered for the RNAS on 14 May 1916, training at Crystal Palace, Redcar, Cranwell and Dover. With a mere 37 flying hours under his belt, he was sent to join 1 Naval Squadron in early 1917. Millward's relatively brief combat career was not without incident. On 7 May 1917 he engaged two hostile machines, bringing one down out of control. Four days later, he and another pilot engaged no less than six enemy aircraft – again he sent one down out of control. Millward, obviously on a roll, repeated the feat on the following day. Unfortunately, his next serious confrontation on 7 July, ended disastrously. Buried in Pont-du-Hem Cemetery, France (Fr 705). Age 21.

Wounded in Action – 11 July 1917

As if in revenge for the 7 July action, Wolff fell to the guns of 1 Naval just four days later. The Triplanes had flown out on patrol at 07.55 that morning and soon encountered six German fighters. The German machines all began to beat a hasty retreat, diving away. Two of the Tripes tore after them. One was engaged indecisively by Flight Sub-Lieutenant H V Rowley (N5476), his targeted Albatros diving away steeply. The Triplanes began landing back at base between 0910-15, Rowley and Flight Lieutenant Everitt, the belligerent duo who had chased after the enemy scouts, landing later at 10 o'clock.

Wolff had been hit in the left hand during the action which had been fought east of Ypres. The extent to which his machine was damaged is not recorded. His wound was very painful as well as being extremely limiting – flying with one hand was difficult. He tried to make a force-landing near Courtrai, but ran onto some railway lines. The impact of the collision ripped off his undercarriage and turned his machine over, the back of the Albatros coming up hard against a metal fence. The top of the fence was only a few inches from where Wolff's head came to rest. Wounded and badly bruised, Kurt Wolff was taken to hospital. Herbert Victor Rowley was a nineteen-year-old from Crich, Derbyshire. He had joined the RNAS in April 1916 (Royal Aero Club Certificate 3569, 24 August 1916) and after training, arrived at 1 Naval in February 1917. Up to the engagement of 11 July, he had achieved just one victory – on 29 April – and, indeed, he made no claim for his actions of 11 July. He was not to know that his efforts brought to an end the main fighting career of one of Germany's top aces. Rowley would, in fact, end the war with nine official victories – after Triplanes, he graduated onto Camels. He would also achieve Air Rank in World War Two.

In Wolff's absence, Jasta 11 was taken over by Leutnant Willi Reinhard, destined to command JGI after Manfred von Richthofen's

Wolff's Albatros DIII (2099/17) on the Courtrai railway line. Wolff failed – by just a few hundred yards – to make his home field. The crash ripped off his undercarriage before the Albatros turned turtle.

death in April 1918. Wolff impatiently returned to Jasta 11 on at least one occasion before he regained his fitness, his hand and arm bandaged and in a sling. He finally took back his command on 11 September.

After a wounding or the trauma of being shot down – or both – many fighter pilots are never quite the same again and Wolff was no exception. Following a successful string of victories, an enforced and prolonged absence will often cause a fighter pilot to lose his 'edge' and until he regains it – if ever – he will be particularly vulnerable. As if to prove the point, the seemingly peerless Wolff would last just four days after his return to combat.

JGI had a new aeroplane. Anthony Fokker's new machine, the Fokker FI Triplane (or V 4), later more familiarly known as the Fokker DrI, had arrived at

Markebecke (near Courtrai) in August 1917. The first two carried serial numbers 102/17 and 103/17, and were allocated for the use of Manfred von Richthofen, Kurt Wolff and Voss, now commander of Jasta 10. Voss first flew 103/17 on 28 August and on 1 September, von Richthofen downed a RE8 in 102/17 for his 60th victory. When this new Fokker first appeared, it is suspected that some Allied airmen, assuming it to be a Naval Triplane, allowed it to approach them without taking any evasive or defensive action until it was too late.

Voss gained several victories in his Triplane in early September (as detailed in our book, *Under the Guns of the German Aces*). Wolff, now operational once again, took the opportunity to fly the new type for the first time.

Shot Down

Ironically it was to be another Naval pilot that overcame Wolff, this time from 10 Naval Squadron, now equipped with the comparatively new Sopwith Camel. Three Camels took off to fly an Offensive Patrol on the afternoon of 15 September 1917 and by 1630 were near Moorslede. The pilots were Flight Sub-Lieutenants N M MacGregor (B3833), W C Johnston (B3912) and R E Carroll (N6354).

The Naval trio encountered a formation of Albatros Scouts with one Triplane in their midst. The Camels, flying at 10,000 feet, were attacked from above by five Albatros

Flight Sub-Lieutenant H V Rowley of 1 Naval Squadron whose fire may have wounded Wolff in the left hand – a wound which resulted in his subsequent crash onto the Courtrai rail line on 11 July 1917. However, it must be said that 32 Squadron also registered a claim at the same time on this day.

machines and, they incorrectly reported later, four *[sic]* Triplanes. A fight ensued. MacGregor manoeuvred himself into an advantageous position almost on top of the Triplane and, from only 25 yards, opened fire. He watched his tracers ripping into the enemy machine but then had to turn and zoom away to avoid a collision. Looking back and down he saw the Triplane going down in a vertical dive, seemingly out of control.

Norman Miers MacGregor, Wolff's almost unwitting conqueror – he only claimed an OOC – came from London and was 21 years of age (born 29 May 1896). He joined the RNAS is 1916 and after service with 6 Naval – with whom he gained four victories – went on to 10 Naval in September 1917. Wolff was MacGregor's first victory with his new squadron. By the end of the year he would raise his score to seven and be awarded the Distinguished Service Cross.

Wolff could not arrest his earthwards plunge and crashed north of Wervicq at 1730 hours German time, the wreck bursting into flames. His body was recovered and laid in state at St Joseph's Church in Courtrai where a memorial service was held three days later. Oberleutnant Kurt Wolff's remains were soon afterwards taken to his home town of Memel for burial. Age 22.

'With his friendly nature and his quiet modesty, he was one of the dearest and best of comrades to us all. He will live on for all time in the history of the Geschwader as a model of soldierly virtue, as an example that is given only by the very finest.'

BIBLIOGRAPHY

An Aviators Field Book — Oswald Boelcke; National Military Publishing Co, 1917.

Knight of Germany — Prof. Johannes Werner; John Hamilton,1933.

An Airman's Wife — Aimee Bond; H Jenkins Ltd, 1918.

Fighter Pilot — William MacLanachan; G Routledge & Son, Ltd, 1936.

Escape Fever — G P Harding; John Hamilton, 1932.

Fighter Pilot on the Western Front — E D Crundall, Wm Kimber, 1975.

I Chose the Sky — L H Rochford; Wm Kimber, 1977.

Mannock VC (Diary) — Ed. F Oughton; N Spearman, 1966.

Bloody April — Alan Morris; Jarrolds, 1967.

The Sky Their Battlefield — Trever Henshaw; Grub Street, 1995.

Under the Guns of the Red Baron — N Franks, H Giblin, N McCrery; Grub Street, 1995.

Under the Guns of the German Aces — N Franks & H Giblin, Grub Street, 1997.

The French Air Service War Chronology — F W Bailey & C Cony; Grub Street 2001.

Cross & Cockade and *Over the Front* — Societies – various journals.

INDEX